Twin Ambitions

Twin Ambitions
An Autobiography

Alec Bedser
with Alex Bannister

Stanley Paul
London Melbourne Auckland Johannesburg

Stanley Paul & Co. Ltd

An imprint of Century Hutchinson Ltd

Brookmount House, 62–65 Chandos Place, Covent Garden, London WC2N 4NW

Century Hutchinson (Australia) Pty Ltd
16–22 Church Street, Hawthorn, Victoria 3122

Century Hutchinson (NZ) Ltd
32–34 View Road, PO Box 40–186, Glenfield, Auckland 10

Century Hutchinson (SA) Pty Ltd
PO Box 337, Bergvlei 2012, South Africa

First Published 1986

Set in Linotron Sabon by Input Typesetting Ltd London SW19 8DR
Printed and bound in Great Britain

British Library Cataloguing in Publication Data

Bedser, Alec
Twin Ambitions: an autobiography.
1. Bedser, Alec   2. Cricket Players—
England—Biography
I. Title   II. Bannister, Alec
796.35'8'0924   GV915.B/

ISBN 09 163880 1

Contents

Photographic
Acknowledgement

For permission to reproduce copyright photographs in this book, the author and publishers would like to thank Central Press, Sport & General Press Agency, The Press Association, *Daily Express* and Patrick Eagar.

Preface

There was never any doubt in the minds of my twin brother Eric and me that we wanted to be cricketers. Given the choice of owning a gold mine or playing for Surrey, there would not have been a moment's hesitation. Cricket was our life blood. Nor, for me, was there any doubt about my ambition, once my playing career had ended, to serve the game which has always meant so much to me. Trite though it may sound, I genuinely wanted to give something back to a game which had enriched Eric and me with so many wonderful experiences, not only at home but in Australia, which I regard as my second home, and South Africa. I happily admit to being a complete and incurable cricket addict, and I am never more content than when I am in the company of those who have fallen under its spell.

I have had two major strokes of luck. First, to be born with a talent that took me to the top. Second, to find a place as a Test selector in 1962, only two years after I bowled my last ball for Surrey. When I began my new career I had no idea that I would still be a selector in 1985, after twenty-three consecutive years including a record thirteen years as chairman. Since 1962 there have been good times and not so good times, powerful sides and not so powerful sides, but the fascination of selecting never diminishes.

I have also witnessed at first hand the sweeping changes that have overtaken the ancient game, both at county and at national level. Sadly, the amateur has gone – inevitable, but still a great loss – overseas stars have too often dominated the county scene, making the task of choosing the national side more difficult, the jet age has led to a glut of Test matches and rushed tours, politics has forced South Africa into isolation, and limited-over competitions have been successfully introduced. Sponsorship is now a telling factor in the game's financial stability. The Packer revolution, linked to commercial television in Australia, not only split cricket asunder but produced a new breed of cash-conscious stars and a small army of agents and middle men.

Not all the changes in recent years have been to the long-term benefit of cricket. Indeed, in the sixties there were so many experiments with playing conditions and the like that perhaps the most sensible suggestion came from Surrey – to call a halt to all reforms for three years while the County Championship regained its breath. Surrey had a point.

Not the least interesting change has been in the reporting of cricket. Since Test matches and important cup ties are now instantly relayed on television, the newspapers have been obliged to look behind the scenes for stories with a greater emphasis on personalities. And, with cricket needing all the publicity it can get in society's more leisured days, the game and the media have come closer together. In general this has benefited cricket, and, as chairman of the selectors, much of my work involved close contact with writers and broadcasters. I always tried to be honest and helpful and found the majority of reporters to be fair both in praise and in criticism.

In writing this book I am grateful for the cooperation of Alex Bannister, who, as a former *Daily Mail* writer, needs no introduction to readers wherever cricket is played. We have been friends and touring companions for over forty years. I also wish to acknowledge the debt I owe to *Wisden Cricketers' Almanack*, not only for facts but to refresh the memory of events which are slipping into history. If *Wisden* is the indispensable reference book, *The Cricketer International* has also been invaluable, and my thanks go to the respective editors, John Woodcock and Christopher Martin-Jenkins.

True autobiographies, a wit has said, need to be disgraceful, otherwise they are not to be trusted. The last of my aims in this book is to be disgraceful; rather, as I look back on my playing career, nothing would be better if I could go through it all again, from Surrey Club and Ground onwards. I hope readers will enjoy sharing some of my experiences, tolerate my opinions, and remember that at all times I have a passion for cricket and cricketers, for I firmly believe the game to be one of the better inventions of mankind.

Woking, 1985

1

A Tram to the Oval

Picture, if you will, two soberly clad youths, identical in every detail, intently watching from the Thames Embankment the prewar trams clanking over Westminster Bridge, and you have the beginnings of my (our) story. Almost half a century later I smile at the thought of my twin brother Eric and me using up our lunchtime in a solicitor's office to gaze at passing trams, for no other reason than they were heading in the direction of Kennington and The Oval cricket ground. Every short lunchbreak we were drawn to the same spot to dream dreams as inevitably as the compulsive gambler to the roulette wheel.

During those odd little rituals it would have been an unpardonable fantasy to have visualized us as Freemen of the City of London, which, among other privileges, entitles us to be hanged by the neck with a flaxen cord. In my darker moments as a Test selector it was a consoling thought. We also remember our first visit to London on a choir outing from Woking and our fear at being lost amid the crowds.

I suppose the trams served as a symbol of our most cherished aspiration – to play cricket for Surrey – and our fascination with them was a subconscious expression of our passion for the game. We had the often silent conspiracy of twins, and deep down we both knew we were unlikely to be able to resist the call of cricket.

As boys we played soccer as full backs for Woking Boys and Surrey Boys and had visions of wearing the red shirt of Arsenal. But our football aspirations paled beside the dreams of batting and bowling at The Oval, inspired after a visit to see Surrey v. Middlesex organized by the vicar of All Saints Woodham Church, the Rev. R.T. Jourdain. He also took us to Lord's in 1932 to see our first Test match – an historical occasion because it was India's

13

first official Test. (The second Test I ever saw was the first one I played in, at Lord's against the Indians in 1946.) The Rev. Jourdain was such a cricket enthusiast that he provided bats and balls and organized matches with other choir teams. The games were played on a glorious ground in the Woodham Hall estate. On one side were giant rhododendrons, with lovingly tended lawns and rose gardens on the other. In the background stood the stately big house. In such surroundings it was natural for a love of cricket and the countryside to be implanted in our minds. It was an idyllic environment.

Visits to The Oval and Lord's were a novel experience for two boys from the country. Our terraced house bordered Horsell Common, which was a blaze of colour in the summer, and a short step from the great sandpit where the Martians landed in H. G. Wells's *The War of the Worlds*.

We always walked the 1½ miles to school – at Monument Hill Central School – arriving as early as possible for an hour's cricket on the rough common nearby. After school we would have another session. Eric won a prize of 1s (5p) for making the top score for the Woodham Church choir team, a welcome addition to the 7s 6d (35p) a quarter we received as choirboys. As we had no pocket money, any extras were gladly accepted and without a thought of endangering our amateur status.

At one time Woodham Cricket Club ground was so sadly neglected that it looked like an untended hayfield. We organized a squad of four or five boys, who exhibited varying degrees of enthusiasm, to try to preserve the wicket. Water from a canal 300 or so yards away was carried in leaky tins, entailing an excessive number of journeys and much faith. Eventually enough water was spread on the ground to justify the use of an old roller, yet another heavy demand on youthful energy and optimism, but I guarantee that no Test strip was ever given more loving care. By a miracle it became flat enough to use, and used it was.

Joking apart, I am sure the constant exercise made us both strong and durable, and we took it as a compliment when in the 1950s, a colt was named Bedser Twin at Sandy Carlos-Clarke's training stables at Lambourn, so named, it was said, for its staying power. The Surrey dressing-room members suggested that a more apt name would have been Bookie's Friend.

14

At fourteen and a half we entered a solicitor's office in Lincoln's Inn Fields. We caught the 8.05 a.m. commuter train from Woking, returned home at 7.30 p.m., and went straight to evening school until 10 p.m. to study book-keeping and shorthand, which served me well in my later business career and as manager of England teams in Australia. On Saturday mornings we worked until 1.30 p.m. and left the office feeling like released prisoners. Once outside we tore to a cricket ground, eating sandwiches on the way.

Presumably in the course of time Eric and I would have become competent enough solicitor's clerks, catching the 8.05 from Woking and resignedly settling for a life of routine, but I do not think the Lord intended to cast us in that role. A warning sign from above might have been my gaffe of putting two letters in the wrong envelopes. A highly confidential financial statement must have made interesting reading to its surprised recipient. The memory of that awful mistake still brings a hot flush of embarrassment, but, like a dropped catch, it was all too easily done.

Like those of many boys, our imaginations were fired by our heroes. We worshipped the incomparable Jack Hobbs, a man of intense modesty and humility, Wally Hammond, who was to be my first Test captain, and the other prewar Titans. Hammond made a deep impression on Eric and me when he played against the village team at Chobham and was seen wearing his England touring blazer. To our eyes no emperor in all his finery could have been a more inspiring sight. When, years later, I was handed my England cap and blazer, I thought of my father – bless him – scraping together enough cash to offer us either a couple of days at the seaside or a bat. Never was a decision made with greater speed.

Jack Hobbs and the dashing England captain, Percy Chapman, were once guests at a Woking Cricket Club dinner. Chapman was told that the young Bedser twins had even bigger hands than he did. He was loath to believe it possible, and we were duly summoned and comparisons made. In fact, we had the bigger hands, and Chapman proceeded to take an orange from the table and test our catching ability, but we were too overcome in the presence of the great man to do ourselves justice.

The discovery that even the gods of the cricket fields had human foibles like the rest of us came as something of a surprise. On

15

another occasion we were at The Oval and watched a little dressing-room attendant struggle to the gates with Frank Woolley's considerable baggage. He was rewarded with two pennies of the old coinage and stood in shocked amazement until that splendid Surrey all-rounder, Jack Parker, put it right with two half-crowns from his own pocket. Woolley, we learned, was not a lavish spender.

When we were seventeen, Allan Peach, the ex-Surrey all-rounder, opened his cricket school at Woking, to our great delight. He became almost a second father to us, and during weekends we were his willing helpers. Arriving long before the doors were opened, we would bowl almost nonstop from 10 a.m. to 6 p.m., and relished every minute. One of Allan's assistants was Harry Baldwin, who became a first-class umpire, and, by coincidence, was standing at Lord's in my first Test.

It was at that time that Eric and I made a crucial decision by the toss of a coin. Looking back, it emerges as one of the most fateful things we ever did. We thought we would have a better chance of making a county side if we had different bowling styles. We were both medium-fast with identical run-ups. The loser of the toss, it was decided, would change to off breaks, and that was why I continued to bowl medium-fast and Eric developed off spin. Allan Peach thought that Eric would make a good off-spinner.

There was a lot of deliberation before we finally made the plunge to become full-time cricketers, for in the prewar depression security was the main objective. My parents did not want us to follow Dad's lot as a bricklayer. Many is the time he worked in drenching rain, for if he did not work there was nothing coming into the house. To be laid off in bad weather was a serious blow to the family – no work, no pay.

Nevertheless, I am eternally grateful that we gave up our safe job in the solicitor's office and joined the Surrey staff in April 1938. I still remember the diffidence Eric and I shared on that day. We were both impressionable and, by today's standards, painfully innocent and starry-eyed. We positively oozed eagerness and a desire to please. We were too awed to sit down in case we took a senior player's seat – and they were all senior – or got in the way, and we spoke only when we were spoken to. We revered the famous players and were slightly scared of the officials. If the future had been revealed before my eyes on the unforgettable morning of my initiation as a pro I would have scoffed in utter disbelief.

It was not as if we were complete strangers. Allan Peach was the Surrey coach and it was he who was responsible for our joining the club. He had shown us the dressing rooms and pavilion, and there were never friendlier characters than Alf Gover, Bob Gregory, Eddie Watts, Tom Barling, Stan Squires and Jack Parker, who formed the backbone of the side. In those days the seniors, at least at The Oval, took the juniors under their wing to teach the golden rules to be observed both on and off the field and they exercised a kindly but firm authority. The older Surrey pros had an almost paternal influence.

At that time there were two separate sets of staff at Surrey – the ground staff, who worked on the ground itself, and the professional playing staff. No one could sign as a professional until he was seventeen. Arthur McIntyre, later to become wicketkeeper for England, started on the ground staff and graduated to the playing staff.

So many sweeping changes have been made that it is impossible to compare the lot of today's young pros – or should I say cricketers? – with my day. When I went to The Oval amateurs and pros had different quarters. There was even a class structure within the pro ranks with the capped (the senior players) and the uncapped occupying different parts of the dressing room. The juniors were required to change in a dressing room downstairs, and unless we were invited to do so, we were not allowed to sit with the others.

Herbert Strudwick, the great wicketkeeper, once told me that when he joined the Surrey staff in 1898 he strayed into the forbidden area used by the senior pros. Tom Hayward, one of cricket's greatest classical batsmen, immediately demanded to know who he was. When told his name, Hayward replied, 'You have the advantage of me. Your place is downstairs.'

Capped men were very jealous of their status and came down like a ton of bricks on a junior trying to get above his station. Pads and boots had to be blancoed to a spotless white, and blazers worn in the dining room at lunch and tea and in the pavilion. You were told, 'If you're not a cricketer yet, at least you can look like one.' Discipline was accepted as a necessary part of the system, and, as far as I was concerned, I was too happy to be doing the job I

17

liked best, and too busy, to care about privileges, equal rights and possible unfairness. I was proud to be part of Surrey; the feeling that everything was done for the good of Surrey remained with me, and I certainly did not feel inferior or rebellious. I never lost a wink of sleep because I was expected to walk round the pavilion and not through the Long Room. The amateur-pro situation gave rise to more misgivings outside the game than inside, largely because the system was misunderstood. Maybe my county was lucky with its amateurs and capped players. I have heard some old pros complain bitterly that they were the victim of high-handed attitudes and some of the old-time pros could be most unhelpful to younger players – but not at The Oval.

It was tough at times but, looking back, always fair. There are no shortcuts to the top, that is if the intention is to stay there. The normal prewar working day for young players, if we were not playing in a match, was to have two-hour net sessions in the morning and afternoon, followed by two more hours' bowling to members in the evening. The ground-staff bowlers quickly got to know the levels of generosity displayed by individual members. Some would tip a shilling, others 6d. There wasn't much of a rush to bowl to the 6d end. Six hours of bowling a day not only made for accuracy – and, without it, swing, spin, pace changes, the lot is a futile exercise – but developed the essential back, shoulder and leg muscles. In the winter we trained with Kingstonian and Fulham football clubs and did labouring work; without that kind of training I am sure I could never have carried the workload that came my way at home and abroad. Bowling is hard work, so it is essential to get strong as well as fit. Our legs were already strong from the amount of walking we did as boys; there was no question of travelling everywhere by car. Even further back, Tom Richardson, one of the fastest bowlers of all time and a man of Herculean strength, was said to be in the habit of walking to The Oval from Mitcham carrying his cricket bag.

In our first two years as professionals we played for the Young Players of Surrey, Surrey Club and Ground and the Surrey Second XI in the Minor Counties. I made my first-class debut for Surrey in 1939 in the fixtures with Oxford and Cambridge universities, but failed to take a wicket in either game.

It did not take me long to learn the truth of cricket's oldest axiom, that attack is the best form of defence, and that there is no better way for an individual or a team to play than with controlled aggression. In 1938 the late Percy Fender, still regarded as the most astute of county captains, occasionally led Surrey's Club and Ground side. I was given a fascinating insight into his methods, and he had as great an influence on me and my approach to the game as did the incomparable Don Bradman in later years. Both believed in carrying the fight to the opposition, to probe for and exploit any weakness, and once on top to stay there. Both Fender and Bradman in their different ways were an inspiration to play with and against. At The Oval the players' chat often centred on Fender. Even Douglas Jardine, accepted by the public at large as one of England's great cricket generals, suffered by comparison.

In one Club and Ground fixture a very good Epsom club side were dismissed cheaply before lunch. During the interval I overheard the other amateur member on our side ask Fender what he intended to do.

'Are we going to bat on and then let them get some runs?' he inquired.

'No,' was the emphatic reply. 'We'll get enough runs to declare and then we'll bowl them out again.'

At the time I felt the skipper was asking a lot, but one of his strengths was never to let slip a psychological advantage. His tactic paid off and Surrey went on to win.

Greatly daring — for he was not that kind of man in his heyday — Eric and I confused Fender when he was captaining another Club and Ground match. He usually told us apart by the brass toecap on my right boot — the standard type used by pace bowlers. On that occasion Eric, unknown to Fender, also wore a toecap. He was told to open the bowling but I did so instead and the skipper did not notice.

There had been a time when I doubt if we would have been foolhardy enough to risk incurring the displeasure of a captain as famous for his discipline as he was for his tactical genius. Frank Chester told me that when he was an umpire the first thing he did on receiving his list of matches for the season was to see how many times he was with Surrey. Fender's knowledge of the laws and conditions of play was so great that Chester was in constant fear of making a mistake. And according to one of the more printable stories handed down in the Surrey dressing room, when Alf Gover, having his second slip catch of the morning put down, exclaimed, 'Is there no justice, no God?', Fender reproved him with 'Gover, you're dropped for two matches for offending the deity.'

Oddly, in his thirteen Tests, Fender never captained England, nor did he ever win the championship for Surrey. Groundsman 'Bosser' Martin's shirtfront pitches at The Oval were heavily loaded against bowlers, making it difficult to finish a match, and Fender's lot was to be overindulged with batsmen and on short rations with bowlers. But his guile enabled him to conjure up wickets for himself and others and make victories out of nothing.

No one went through the motions with Surrey. Inevitably we had our off days and bad matches, and to 'gee' each other up we could be unmerciful critics on the field. We seemed to be lucky with injuries, but we were pretty fit and strong and most of us were used to soldiering on. Being on a match-money basis meant that everyone played if he could. The other factor, at least in our early days, was the tremendous competition for places even in the Second XI. You felt that if you did not play someone else would take your place and it would be difficult to get back in. Everyone in the team was paid the same match money irrespective of who he was. As we were all in the same financial boat, there was no envy on grounds of money.

When I first joined Surrey I was paid £2 a week in the summer, plus match money, which did not amount to much at that stage. For Young Players of Surrey, the lowest rung on the ladder, the payment was 5s (25p), rising to 25s for Club and Ground, and £4 (home) and £6 (away) for Surrey Second XI in the Minor Counties Championship. A county cap received a basic salary of £400. During away matches we paid for our accommodation, which meant we did not go for five-star hotels. Senior players sometimes stayed with opponents on a home-and-away basis to save cash. Extra engagements were welcomed, and Surrey members occasionally arranged games on Sundays and paid the players a fee – usually 25s which to us in those days was a lot of money.

By prewar standards the returns were not all that bad, but winters were the problem. Our first retainer was £1 each a week, and job-hunting was difficult. There were few openings for those seeking all-the-year-round employment, let alone young cricketers on a seasonal basis. I found would-be employers very suspicious of the qualifications of a cricket pro, which was understandable. Eventually the only work Eric and I could find in our first winter was at The Oval itself, where the banking at the Vauxhall end had to be moved to bring in the boundary by several yards. Eric and I, together with Arthur McIntyre and Geoff Whittaker, shovelled the earth and took it by wheelbarrow to the new position. We were hard at it for several weeks. To get to The Oval in time we left Woking at 6.30 a.m. In February we thankfully took up coaching jobs at an indoor cricket school at Kingston, run by Andy Kempton, a great friend of Jack Hobbs, who later made a name for himself by discovering Tony Lock and Jim Laker. If nothing else, we were supremely fit by the time we reported at The Oval in mid-April.

Having been brought up to be thrifty I decided not to touch my £1 retaining money but to live on what I could earn. As a result after thirty weeks I had a little nest egg in Post Office savings. Our minds were set on becoming proficient cricketers and no sacrifice was too large to achieve that end. However, we had hardly got under way as professionals than the Second World War intervened.

2

War Stops Play

Like others of our generation, Hitler's war took a large slice out of our playing careers. At the time Eric and I were only in our second year as professional cricketers and we felt as though our world had fallen apart. Millions of others, of course, were in the same boat, but a sportsman's life is fleeting and passes all too quickly. Whether we returned was in the lap of the gods, and, if we did, it was possible that we would be too old or simply not good enough to be first-class cricketers.

Yet in an odd, roundabout way, I, as a bowler depending much on physical strength, probably benefited from those long years of enforced absence from the game. Doctors have since told me that ligaments continue to grow until the mid-twenties and are subject to stress, and there can be little doubt that I would have bowled many overs between 1939 and 1946 had the war not intervened. Instead, I returned to cricket at the age of twenty-seven physically hardened and mentally far more mature. In every respect I was better equipped to meet the challenge of top-class cricket in the postwar years.

Eric and I first received our call-up papers in June 1939 when the war clouds were still gathering. We knew that university students were allowed to defer their call-up in order to finish their courses, and decided that if that applied to students why not to professional cricketers as well. We managed to get a deferment until the end of the season and were instructed to report for training with the Royal Artillery in the September. For some reason our enlistment with the RA was cancelled, so instead we immediately volunteered for the RAF as our father had served with both the RFC and the RAF in the First World War. When we went to sign on the recruiting sergeant, taking one look at our size, suggested we should join the Guards instead.

Two weeks after being inducted into the RAF we again received papers for the Royal Artillery, but by then it was too late. In fact, being in the RAF meant that we avoided the fate of many of our schoolmates who enlisted in the same Artillery unit and were later taken prisoner in Dunkirk.

Our stint in the RAF Security Wing was often lightened by the inability of superior officers to tell us apart. Occasionally only one of us would attend pay parade, going up twice in the line, and we never once aroused suspicion. At Halton camp we devised a scheme to share our guard duty. Two hours on guard was too long, in our opinion, so we decided to do one hour each. Unfortunately, one night Eric forgot to take the key for the arms cupboard with him when he relieved me, and by mischance was asked to produce it by a warrant officer. I had the key but it was Eric who was in the guardroom. We could not explain that away, and the warrant officer realized what we had been doing. Luckily he took it as a joke and our years of crime remained officially undetected.

Our being identical twins led to some curious encounters. When we were in France in 1940, an elderly man suddenly knelt at our feet as if paying homage and a curious crowd gathered. Embarrassed, we did not know what we were expected to do until someone explained that a local superstition held that seeing identical twins was a lucky event.

We were soon to be grateful that another sighting of twins saved us from years in a POW camp. When the Germans broke through in the spring of 1940 we stood by a roadside with hundreds of others waiting for a miracle. The miracle of the moment would have been four wheels and enough petrol to reach a Channel port. We had all but given up when a van stopped and a cheerful voice shouted, 'I can't leave you behind.' The driver turned out to be a Surrey member from Wimbledon. He took us halfway to the coast before the engine died with a last apologetic cough. By the greatest of good fortune we managed a tow and eventually reached the coast, where we spent an anxious and uncomfortable day and night clustered under the cliffs before we were rescued, borne across the Channel to Dover and on to Halton Camp.

In 1943 we sailed from Greenock on the Clyde on a Dutch ship, one of a large convoy, to Algiers, and twenty-five of us, all over six feet and with full kit, bumped our way 500 miles to Tunis in a cattle truck. I'll never forget that journey, which lasted seven days, for there was no water for a wash, and we scrounged hot water from the driver to brew tea. It was so uncomfortable and utterly crazy that we spent most of the time laughing.

Our final destination was Naples, and on the day we chose to visit the ruins of Pompeii Vesuvius erupted belching red-hot lava and sending a wall of flaming earth sliding down its slopes. Villages disappeared in its wake and some ash descended on Bari, 160 miles away on the east coast.

At Caserta we visited the grave of Captain Hedley Verity, the famous Yorkshire and England bowler, who died from wounds received leading an infantry attack in a corn field in Sicily. I revisited the hallowed place when MCC stopped at Naples on the voyage to Australia in 1954, and skipper Len Hutton put a Yorkshire tie around the headstone.

As the Germans fell back we moved up to the north of Italy. At Perugia Eric fell ill with jaundice and became a patient in the military hospital. One morning, when I went to visit him, I was seized by a very stern ward sister in a corridor. In outrage she ordered me back to bed 'this instance'. Then, stepping back to take a second look at me, she exclaimed, 'Good heavens, he's lost his colour!' I told her she was talking to the wrong Bedser, but she was only persuaded of her mistake when she followed me to Eric's bedside, and saw him in the full glory of his rich jaundice yellow.

Towards the end of the war we were obliged to consider whether virtually seven years lost to cricket was too vast a gap to make good. The prospects in the RAF were not unattractive if we held our ranks – Eric as warrant officer and myself as flight sergeant. In 1943 we had both been promoted to warrant officer, but rather than be parted – which this would have meant – we decided that only one of us should accept the promotion. Once again we settled our future by the toss of a coin. Eric won, and we shared the extra pay. We finally decided to leave the RAF. The pull of cricket was too strong.

When we returned to Surrey after the war The Oval was in a shambles. The ground had been requisitioned as a POW camp for German parachutists at the beginning of the war, and when the threat of an invasion diminished it was used as an AA gun site, then as a barrage balloon and searchlight base, and finally as an assault course. Nobody who saw the mess was prepared to bet that first-class cricket would be played there the following season. But Surrey was fortunate to have backroom staff like Bert Lock, the head groundsman. With a team of boys and pensioners, he began the great clear-up in October 1945. Once the initial debris had been cleared, the concrete posts dug up and carted away and the holes filled in, scythes and sickles eventually uncovered the area once used by Jack Hobbs, Andy Sandham and Co. as the square. Bert Lock set his own levels, organized transport and laid 45,000 turves brought from Hoo marshes in Kent. Starting at 8 a.m. and working until they could no longer see the pitch, he and his make-shift staff somehow got the ground into playable shape. The practice nets had been gnawed by rats. Bert sat in the east stand, often in freezing winds, repairing the nets to have them ready for the new season in early April 1946. I have always thought of him as an unsung hero.

Great sides are always built to last and one of Surrey's major strengths, both before and after the war, was its pool of quality reserves and backup staff. The same was true of Yorkshire – at least until the war. Somehow the true Yorkshire spirit was never regained, despite their titles in the sixties. Surrey's nucleus was formed from Young Surrey players and, in the postwar years, Ken Barrington, Micky Stewart, Tom Clark from Bedfordshire, and Peter Loader started their careers. Peter May was at Charterhouse, earmarked for greatness even as a schoolboy. Another stroke of luck was the billeting at Catford of a former bank clerk named Jim Laker who was seeing out the last days of his army service. That he should join the local club whose president, Andrew Kempton, also captained Surrey Second XI made it seem he was ordained to play for Surrey. Before the war Jim was a young no. 4 bat for Saltaire in the Bradford League, and Yorkshire, apparently unaware that he had developed off spin on matting wickets in Cairo during the war, did not oppose his registration. Years later Sir Len Hutton, recognizing him to be the best off-spinner in the country, sounded Jim out in the hope that he might return, but by then Laker was a Surrey man. In his army days the Test leg-break bowler Peter Smith had done his utmost to persuade Jim to go to

Essex. By coincidence he finished his career with Essex, but it was a remarkable bonus for Surrey that he arrived at The Oval.

Andrew Sandham, Jack Hobbs's famous partner, was the Surrey coach and Herbert Strudwick, one of England's finest wicketkeepers, was scorer. They represented a treasure house of wisdom and knowledge. Mr Sandham (as he was properly addressed) went straight to the core of every technical problem and his dry humour was pungent. He was almost inevitably in Jack Hobbs's shadow although their partnership produced sixty-six stands of 100 or more, and he scored 107 first-class centuries. One day at The Oval Hobbs was out in the first over and Sandham went on to complete a double century. As he left the ground his eye caught an evening paper poster: 'Hobbs fails'.

Sandham played in only fourteen Test Matches and scored 325 and 50 in the last Test against the West Indies in 1930, but never played for England again. How many caps would he have won today?

Struddy's memories would emerge in the most unexpected places. On one occasion Eric was driving him to Blackheath and, as the car climbed the steep hill leading to the heath, he began to recall his first ever visit to the Blackheath ground. 'Tom Richardson, Bill Lockwood and Ernie Hayes were in the team,' he said. 'We all wore boaters and watch chains spread across our waistcoats. Halfway up the hill we had to get out and help push the carriage as the hill was too much for the horses.' The pages of history would unroll as Struddy slipped in names like Dr W. G. Grace, Wilfred Rhodes, whom he found the most difficult of all bowlers to take with his uncanny flight and variation, C. B. Fry and Struddy's close friend Sir Jack Hobbs.

Standing close to Struddy one morning while a discussion was going on as to whether the opposition should be put in to bat, I heard him say, 'The Doctor used to work on the theory that you took what the gods offered, and never to concede first innings unless you were more than sure you could bowl them out cheaply.' I have often thought of those sage words when captains have gambled with the odds no better than evens.

Struddy had the endearing gift of being able to laugh at himself; one of his favourite anecdotes concerned an amateur underarm bowler named T. J. Moloney, who figured in a number of Surrey trial matches just after the First World War. Jack Hobbs jokingly went down the pitch only to be stumped, an act which Struddy was to regret for Moloney was promoted to the county team. Much of Moloney's bowling was down the leg side, which meant the wicketkeeper was in constant danger from decapitation from swinging bats.

Came the Whitsun Bank Holiday match against Nottinghamshire and a packed Trent Bridge roared with laughter when Moloney went on to bowl. After his opening ball a voice roared, 'Keep him on, Fender, I'm going home to fetch my old woman. She hasn't had a good laugh for a long time.' The mood changed when three of the home batsmen were caught on the boundary.

Then Moloney bowled so wide that the batsman swung round and a full-blooded hit went straight into Struddy's stomach. 'Much to my surprise I caught it – purely in self-defence,' he said. 'But that was the last straw for me, and after the match I told the captain, "If Moloney plays I won't." And that was the last we saw of Moloney.'

On another occasion Struddy assured the Surrey dressing room that he knew how to play G. H. Simpson-Hayward, the famous lob bowler from Worcestershire. He went on, 'I told everyone that as I had kept to him on tour with MCC in South Africa that I could detect which way the ball would turn. Of course, that was a fatal thing to say for when I went in I was out lbw to his first ball – a full-pitcher at that. It took me a long time to live that one down.'

We would listen fascinated. There was the occasion in 1911 just after he had been chosen to tour Australia, in the series to be dominated by the bowling of Frank Foster and Sydney Barnes. On the way to Lord's with the Surrey bowler Bill Lockwood the horse drawing the hansom cab stumbled and fell going over Vauxhall Bridge. Their two cricket bags fell off the cab, but it was anything but an ill omen as Lockwood took 9 wickets during the day. 'Matey,' declared Lockwood, 'I'm sure to go with you to Australia.' But he didn't.

In the first outing for the Players against the Gentlemen Struddy was worried that he might not be able to spot Albert Trott's well-disguised faster ball. Struddy asked him to give a signal as a warning, but Trott, an Australian who played both for his native country and England, refused, adding, 'You'll find it soon enough.' When Trott produced it the ball shaved a bail and ended on the surprised wicketkeeper's toe, causing him quite a lot of pain. As he hopped around Trott called down the pitch, 'You found it all right, then?'

W. G. Grace was more understanding after he had bowled Struddy for his second duck for Surrey against the old London County team at the Crystal Palace. 'Why didn't you tell me you wanted one off the mark, youngster? I would have given you one,' he said in his high-pitched voice. The departing batsman, however, was not all that unhappy as the FA Cup Final was being played on that April afternoon also at the Crystal Palace between Sheffield United and Southampton. He was able to watch the second half, and on the Monday he again saw one of the players, C. B. Fry, who, switching to cricket with a versatility impossible today, scored 82 for London County at The Oval.

Struddy always said that he never saw a better wicketkeeper than Godfrey Evans – although there were perhaps half a dozen his equal – and he was envious of the better protection later generations enjoyed. The old wicketkeepers devised their own makeshift protection. Fred Stedman, one of Surrey's keepers, used to put a copy of the old South Western Railway timetable under his shirt. After one thump on his chest he turned to the slips and through gritted teeth groaned, 'I shall have to catch a later train tonight, that one knocked off the 7.30.'

One of Struddy's golden rules for bowlers was to attack the off stump of a good batsman, a precept which I adopted faithfully throughout my career. It is a bowling principle which still holds good; there is a tendency today to bowl too much at middle and leg.

Not the least contribution to the team spirit in those triumphant Surrey years came from our irrepressible physiotherapist Sandy Tait, the Cockney son of a Spurs footballer. Sandy had also been stagehand at several music halls and he enlivened many a train journey with his anecdotes and his party piece on the 'bones'. Batsman Stan Squires, who sadly died ·of a rare blood disease in 1950, was a dab hand on the ukelele and accompanied many a sing-song. Stan's theme song began: 'They tell me the Oval's a terrible place. The organization's a flaming disgrace.' Then there was the one: 'Life's a ball to hit or miss.' The second line referring to the quality of the bowling was made to rhyme and can be left to the imagination.

It was with the connivance of Jack Hobbs, who umpired, that Eric and I played a prank on the immortal left-hander Frank Woolley when he turned out for Old England against Surrey for the Surrey Centenary Fund in 1946. We arranged that I would bowl the first three balls of an over and that Eric, fielding at mid-off, would come on halfway through and complete the over with off breaks. To our surprise, no one noticed, either on or off the field, and Woolley was heard to comment that he was fascinated by the change in pace and style by one bowler in the course of an over.

The occasion was graced by the presence of the late King George VI, and when the lined-up teams were presented, His Majesty stopped in front of Eric and me. After a long scrutiny he remarked, 'I think I could pick you out another time.' It transpired that the King had been shown our photographs before leaving the pavilion. He had studied them long and hard; when he came face to face with us it was, believe me, somewhat disconcerting to be stared at by one's monarch. A month later, during my first Test, at Lord's against India, the King moved along the line of England players, stopped in front of me and asked, 'Where is your brother?' I replied that he was playing for Surrey against Oxford University at Guildford. The King smiled and said, 'I hope he is well.' I could scarcely credit that he should have remembered us.

When I arrived at Lord's for my maiden Test, having travelled from Woking to Waterloo by train, taken a tube to Baker Street and then humped my big leather cricket bag on a bus to the ground, I had only eleven first-class matches and 46 wickets behind me. My biggest occasion until then had been the Test trial at Lord's where I had picked up the wickets of Len Hutton and Wally Hammond.

Lord's was packed and, luckily for me, I was in the thick of the action right away. Eric, down in Guildford, spent all his free time listening to my progress on the radio in the house of the groundsman, Jack Patterson. I was able to bowl from the nursery end, my favourite end at Lord's as I could make the ball go away with the slope and also swing in against it to the batsman. My first victim was Vijay Merchant, caught on the leg side by Paul Gibb standing up. I finished with 7 for 49 in 29.1 overs and 11 wickets in all, and England won by 10 wickets. I also scored 30 runs in a stand of 70 with Joe Hardstaff, who hit 205 with such elegance that I was grateful not to have been bowling to him. Joe, a member of the distinguished Nottinghamshire cricketing family, told me that I had booked my passage to Australia – until that moment I had honestly never given the prospect a thought – and handed me his England cap with the words, 'Take this home and give it to your mother.' Although Joe never wore a cap – and I cannot picture him in a helmet – it was a generous thing to have done as players were awarded only the one cap. I still have it at home.

The Second Test against India was played at Old Trafford. I had pulled some rib muscles in my previous game and was in some discomfort. Not wishing to miss the Test, I went to see Bill Tucker, an orthopaedic surgeon, who gave me an injection so that I could play. He warned me that I would be in some pain, but it would go off with exercise. This treatment worked very well – I took another 11 wickets at Old Trafford. Perhaps it was fortunate that the last Test at The Oval was cut short by rain. As one of the older players remarked, if I had taken another 11 wickets I would have been obliged to retire at the height of my fame.

At that time food was still rationed. During our stay in Manchester breakfast at the team's hotel consisted of one small sausage, half a fried tomato, one rasher of bacon, toast and a single pat of butter. When I got to the ground I used to scrounge cheese rolls from the caterers, and one of my abiding memories is touring Manchester's back streets in search of fish and chips.

On the last day of the Second Test – Tests at that time lasted three days only – England were in the field for the whole of the last day, held up by India's last pair, S. W. Sohoni and D. D. Hindlekar (whom we knew as 'Handlebars'). Stumps were drawn at 6.30, which meant I missed the train back to London. I had to wait to midnight for the next and it was chock full of servicemen. Doug Wright of Kent and I had an uncomfortable journey standing in the corridor all the way to London where we arrived at 5 a.m. Surrey was due to play Glamorgan later that day, so I snatched a few hours' sleep on the massage table at The Oval before play started at 11.30.

I had been raised in dressing rooms ringing with the praises of Wally Hammond and he was my idol, but sadly I was disillusioned by that first Test series under his captaincy, and again in Australia the following winter. I found him to be below my ideal as a captain. I was still inexperienced and would have appreciated some words of advice and encouragement from the great man on the first big occasion of my cricketing life. Instead, Hammond gave me the briefest of welcomes and left me to myself and my thoughts. Fortunately I changed beside Doug Wright, who had played for England before the war, and he proved a good friend. Yet the only real advice came from Bill Bowes fielding at mid-on. And no one was more qualified to help than Bill, one of cricket's deepest students and thinkers. He was the first of seventeen new-ball partners for England, which in itself must be something of a record.

Hammond rarely discussed field placings and tactics with me, and between matches in Australia the team saw little of him. At least I escaped the type of verbal chastisement he gave Denis Compton in his first Test against Australia at Trent Bridge in 1938. Having scored a brilliant century Denis went for a celebratory 6 and was caught at deep square leg. When he returned to the dressing toom Hammond was waiting for him, and instead of congratulations there was a telling-off although England had a big total on the board. 'You don't do that against Australia. Never, never do it again,' Compton was told in no uncertain terms. No doubt Hammond was right, but there are ways of reprimanding a young player and as a result Compton never warmed to his captain. Few penetrated Wally's thick layer of reserve, but, again, he came into the game when the young player was often left to himself. Leslie Ames once told me that it was three years before his presence was really noted in the Kent dressing room!

When I bowled to Hammond in the nets I realized what a batsman he must have been in his prime. He was an instant judge of length, had a flawless technique, and arms and wrists of steel. He drove with equal power off either front or back foot. After one session at Melbourne I mentioned his qualities to the late Jack Ryder, who had been watching. Jack was captain of Australia in 1928–29 series when Hammond made an aggregate 905 runs with successive scores of 251 at Sydney, 200 and 32 at Melbourne, and 119 not out and 177 at Adelaide. 'I had to have two extra-cover fieldsmen on the fence and he still hit the ball to the pickets,' said Jack. 'How that man could hit a cricket ball!'

I was never naive enough to believe that the best players automatically make the best captains, but I was surprised that a master like Hammond could be as tactically orthodox as he was. I never knew whether he thought I was bowling well or badly. I might add that did not affect how I approached my task. Field placing is an art which needs experience, and in this respect alone I could have benefited from his knowledge. Fortunately I learned pretty quickly by trial and error as I went along and I did not need to be told by the captain or anyone else when I did not come up to scratch. Those were the days when a prized wicket would get a 'Well-bowled'. We could get along without back slapping, hugging and the rest of today's displays of enthusiasm. Even the fall of the biggest rabbit of a tail ender now becomes the subject of celebration and, to judge from comments and letters that come my way, the sight is repugnant to many spectators and television viewers.

There was always a distance between Hammond and his players, and even when he visited England after settling in Durban on his retirement there was still a reluctance to unbend. For the sake of old times and as a gesture of my personal admiration for one of the truly great players I went to Heathrow to greet him. When he saw me there was a polite 'Hello. How are you?' and he was gone. Yet he could be kind and thoughtful. In 1946, while I was touring Australia, Eric came out as well; he was worried that his presence might be an embarrassment to the England team. Hammond anticipated his fears and assured me he would be welcomed as one of the party. I have often wondered whether the impression of aloofness he often gave was due to a basic shyness. I think at heart he was a very shy and private person.

It hardly needs to be said that neither Hammond nor his successor Norman Yardley had a price against Bradman's overwhelmingly superior team. The most astute and determined captain cannot hope for more than limited success when he is out-gunned in all departments.

3

The Other Half

In Australia Eric is known as the Other Half, and when a big stand developed during Walter Hammond's series in 1946–47, it did not take long for the barrackers to tell me, 'You'll never get 'em out. Send for Eric.' England could have done far worse; in later years as a Test selector I have often yearned for an off-spinner of Eric's calibre. If the temptation is to dismiss this opinion as prejudiced, let me say I have not been alone.

Years later the journalist Clif Cary reported a conversation between old Test cricketers in Melbourne. They said that it was a pity Eric changed to off spin. Cary continued, 'A Bedser at each end with the new ball would have given our chaps a headache or two.' At which suggestion Lindsay Hassett murmured, 'Heaven forbid.' Ian Craig added that Australia should also be thankful that Jim Laker played for Surrey and restricted Eric's chances because Eric was a very high-class bowler too. To be mentioned in the same breath as Jim was a great compliment.

There were no fewer than nine pace bowlers among the thirty-four professionals on the Surrey staff when we joined. Eric might well have made it in his original style, and we could have opened with the new ball at opposite ends. As it was, I have no doubt that, had he not been destined to compete with the genius of Laker, Eric's reputation would have been far higher. He had to be content with being a capable all-rounder, getting most of his bowling chances when Jim was away playing for England or when the batting conditions were good.

Yet Eric was good enough to take part in the 1950 Test trial on the famous 'sticky' at Bradford when Laker took 8 wickets for 2 (one being a single to Eric when Jim kindly bowled a full toss to get him off the mark). It might have been a different story if

33

England, and not the Rest, had batted when the pitch was at its worst.

Cricket fate has not been kind to Eric. In 1956 he was deprived of the double of 1000 runs and 100 wickets by the weather, but skipper Stuart Surridge acknowledged that Surrey might not have retained the County Championship without him.

Possibly he could have furthered his career if he had gone to another county as a first-choice off-spinner and high-order batsman, but he was a Surrey man through and through, and his heart would not have been with any other side. More importantly, it would have separated us, and such a thought never entered our heads. We followed the same path, and that was that. Also, in those days a two-year qualification period was necessary if one wished to change counties – this in turn affected entitlement to a benefit.

Eric, who is my senior by ten minutes, never begrudged his role in our partnership. Since we have shared most things for as long as we can remember, we naturally shared the satisfaction of my wickets for England.

Like many twins, we dressed the same, and when we were at school we invariably made the same mistakes and obtained the same marks. Teachers, believing we might be exchanging answers, moved us to opposite sides of the classroom. The result was the same: we still tended to use the same phrases in an essay and make the same mistakes in arithmetic. Even now one of us can start a letter and the other finish it.

Identity confusions became part of our lives and we began to get used to curious eyes and jokes about identical twins. We accepted it as adding to the fun of life. On one occasion, when we were playing for Woking Cricket Club, Eric was accused of attempting to bat twice when I walked to the crease. The visiting team and their umpire refused to believe there were two of us until Eric was brought from the pavilion and we stood side by side. An enterprising local journalist sent the story to the national papers, and we were so scared by the subsequent notoriety that we stayed at home until the publicity had died down.

Almost all our friends have been caught out. In our first match after the war for Surrey against MCC at Lord's, I took 6 wickets for 14, and Denis Compton came into the dressing room, thumped Eric on the back and said, 'Well bowled, Alec.'

Later in 1946, thanks to the generosity of Alfred Cope, a football pools promoter who donated £500, Eric was able to join me in Australia. At that time he had not met Don Bradman and, as he walked into the foyer of the Windsor Hotel, Don called out, 'Hello, Alec. How are you?' Wally Hammond explained to him, 'You haven't met this fellow before – he's Eric.' Don was astonished.

In Sydney I went for a haircut. Later that day Eric visited the same barber, who looked at him in blank amazement. 'Cripes, mate,' he gasped, 'it hasn't taken long for your hair to grow again.'

'No,' replied Eric. 'I guess it must be the hair oil you use.'

The barber stood there with a puzzled face, but Eric did not let on.

Field Marshal Montgomery – like King George VI – was quite certain that he knew which of us was which when we played for Surrey against Old England at The Oval in 1946. He studied our faces for what seemed to be an interminable time and announced, 'I can tell them apart.' We would have dearly loved to put him to the test.

We never attempted to confuse umpires or scorers in County Championship matches, but there were two muddles not of our making. At Northampton I was told to go into bat before Eric for a tactical reason, and it so happened we were soon at the crease together. Unfortunately in the scorer's box Herbert Strudwick, whom we dearly loved and would never wittingly have caused anxiety, had not been advised of the change in the batting order and my runs went to Eric and his to me. The correct scores should have been: Bedser, A.V., c. Greenwood b. Merritt 25; Bedser, E.A., b. Partridge 10. Heaven knows what might have happened if we had been involved in one of those hideous mix-ups when both batsmen run up and down the wicket together and both sets of bails are on the ground. Umpire Frank Chester once told me he was involved in such a muddle and was as confused as the rest. The next morning one of the classy newspapers carried a description of the incident and added: 'Fortunately Chester was able to bring his authority to bear with a decision which was satisfactory to all.' 'All I did,' laughed Frank, 'was to run in from square leg shouting,

"We'd better toss for it." One of the batsmen, a tailender, volunteered to go to save arguments.'

The other Bedser identity muddle was in 1952 playing for Surrey against Lancashire at Old Trafford when Stuart Surridge took me in with him to try to hold out for the last few minutes of the day. Normally Eric opened and, again, the scorers were not told. Unfortunately I was caught and bowled by Roy Tattersall who, understandably, was credited with Eric's wicket. The only Lancashire fielder not to be deceived was Cyril Washbrook, one of my close friends on tour in Australia, New Zealand and South Africa. Otherwise Eric might have been charged the next morning with attempting to bat twice in the same innings.

We agreed to act as guinea pigs during an investigation on identical twins conducted by a Birmingham doctor. We were put through a series of scientific tests and were found to have the same eight blood classifications, the same weight down to an ounce, the same height, and our teeth are the same shape. Inexplicably, Eric, sitting in the stand, lost the same amount of weight as I did bowling in the heat of Adelaide one day.

Being in the public eye, we had to play along with the jokes and accept the publicity. We were the first 'victims' in the popular BBC panel game 'What's My Line?', and in another television show we were separated to put our thought processes to the test. We were asked half a dozen questions and gave almost the same answers. Eric was then shown three cricket bats and asked to select the one I would choose. He was right. The sequel was a deluge of letters claiming the programme had been rigged after a rehearsal, but that was not the case. So far as the bat was concerned, I thought that there was a reasonably simple explanation: we had shared bats in our youth, and what would suit Eric would suit me.

When I went on tour to South Africa in 1948–49, Eric was fortunate enough to get sufficient work to meet his expenses so that he could go as well. Outward bound aboard the *Durban Castle* I travelled first class with the team – the four amateurs and the manager, Brigadier Mike Green, sat at a separate table in the dining room – and Eric was tourist class. The fact that there were two Bedsers aboard was evidently not known to one lady notorious for her intake of pink gins. Sitting at her adopted place at a bar, she happened to turn round and see two Bedsers instead of the usual single figure. She gave a horrified stare and left saying, 'Oh, my gawd.' The barman complained that we had scared away his best customer.

I always remember South Africa for its genuine hospitality, the vision of the sun rising above Table Mountain as our ship slipped into the bay, the awesome power of Victoria Falls and the fascination of hippopotami and crocodiles in the Zambesi, and, strange to relate, another set of twins named Alec and Eric Bedser from Kei Road.

Our connection with the other Bedsers began when we were motoring between Port Elizabeth and East London, and stopped at Kingwilliamstown for a brief rest and a much needed wash and brush-up. While waiting for a pot of tea to arrive I idly glanced at a local newspaper, and by chance my eyes rested on the 'Births, Marriages and Deaths' column. To my surprise I saw the name of Bedser, not a common name, and the announcement of the birth of twins to Mr and Mrs Sid Bedser, of Kei Road, near Kingwilliamstown. Apparently there was a move locally to name the boys Alec and Eric. The parents did not object, and we were invited to become godparents. The christening was arranged for the following Sunday. As we set off we were followed by a veritable cavalcade of newshawks who were fascinated by an unusual human story.

Kei Road proved to be a small, isolated community, reached by long, winding, dusty roads through parched land. The church was small and corrugated, and the two babies looked exactly alike. Originally Alec was handed to me, and Eric to Eric, but so many photographs were taken and the babies exchanged several times that in the end we had no idea which was which. No doubt Mother knew Alec was holding Alec (or Eric) and Eric was holding Eric (or Alec), but our side of the Bedser family remained totally bemused. The babies were so tiny that we could have held them in the palms of our hands. The ceremony ended with the organist telling me that he had supported Kent all his life and his happiest days were when they beat Surrey.

Sadly, there is an unhappy ending to the story as Alec was killed in a car crash. The last we saw of them was when two strapping young men called on us in London. Alec's death must have been an unbearable loss for his brother.

As twins Eric and I have shared most things as a matter of course. When I first made England's team Eric was frequently asked what he thought about my success, the suggestion being that he might be slightly envious. He simply did not understand the implication. We have always worked together in complete harmony and many is the time I have thought it unfair that the fruits of our joint endeavours should have sometimes fallen to me alone. It would have been intolerable if Eric had shown the slightest hint of resentment or reminded me that so much had hinged on the flip of a coin. Eric, and not I, might well have received the OBE and later the CBE. But we agreed that the first award was not due to the Other Blighter's Efforts, as I had bowled 15,346·4 overs in first-class cricket. Just how many balls I actually bowled would make an interesting calculation, starting from school to club, and through the various tiers of matches for Surrey, second-class fixtures, benefits, nets and so on.

My CBE in 1982 was a step up – the OBE insignia had to be returned – and on my second visit to Buckingham Palace I found myself lining up by a familiar face, a fire officer who had been next to me when we both had received our OBEs in 1964. Now he, too, was a CBE.

I owe much to my Other Half, and if it is deemed that I served the game, then cricket also is in his debt.

4

Tests and Tours

So many Tests are being played throughout the cricket world that I fear the coinage is being debased; there is a danger of saturation and apathy on the part of the public. Simple facts supplied by the noted statistician Bill Frindall point to the problem of quantity displacing quality. When the 1000th Test was begun in Hyderabad in November 1984, between Pakistan and New Zealand, the second 500 Tests had been played in only twenty-four years as against the first 500 in over eighty-three years. The last 100 took less than four years, and a record twenty-eight Tests were played in 1983–84. Clearly, with the West Indies, India, New Zealand, Pakistan and now Sri Lanka joining the international ranks – the grand days of the triumvirate of England, Australia and South Africa have long been overtaken by the march of time – the number of Tests has inevitably increased.

It makes nonsense of the record books. Sunil Gavaskar, as an example, made as many appearances for India in five years as Donald Bradman made for Australia in twenty. There are many such illustrations, and perhaps the time will come when *Wisden* will carry two sets of records embracing the old and the new eras, for performances can no longer be compared.

In a recent summer one leading newspaper did not even mention the arrival of the Australians in England. At one time such an omission would have been unthinkable. Indeed, leading correspondents used to be sent to Mediterranean ports to meet the liner carrying the Australians and send daily stories from the ship, such was the interest. There used to be a full-scale press conference at Tilbury. Much the same occurred in Australia, with correspondents from the eastern states converging on Fremantle and often being obliged to clamber up the side of the ship by precarious rope ladders.

On one tour George Duckworth, the team's scorer, baggage master and general confidant, pointed out a journalist to the gathered players with the warning, 'Don't say a word to him. He'll crucify you.' A few hours later in Perth George opened an evening paper and was amazed to read a syndicated piece from the very journalist quoting George to the effect that England had sent the wrong team. It took him some time to live that one down.

Dr W. G. Grace's 1873 team left Southampton on 23 October and did not arrive in Melbourne until 13 December; half the players were so storm-tossed and debilitated by sickness that it took them weeks to recover. How those unfortunate sufferers must have dreaded the return voyage the following May. On my three playing visits to Australia the sea voyage took four idyllic weeks, a time not unprofitably spent as a real team spirit was forged. There was also a stop-over one-day game at Colombo, in which, on the 1950–51 tour, I played although I had suffered a slight leg strain. Skipper Freddie Brown decreed that I should not bowl, but after a while the crowd set up a chant, 'We want Bedser, we want Bedser.' Brown came up and suggested that I might just turn my arm over. I was immediately hit to the boundary, and the chant went up again, but this time with the words, 'Take Bedser off, take Bedser off.'

Now the journey from Heathrow is measured in hours, not days, and boredom and jet lag are the main hazards. International cricketers use the airways with almost the same frequency as England county players drive up and down the motorways. Tours are no longer five – or six-month affairs with a sensible acclimatization period and a build-up to the first Test, but concentrated, functional visits, the ultimate in instant cricket. Yet I have been surprised to read that tours should be cut even further to consist of only Tests, one-day internationals and a modicum of other fixtures. Such a programme would be wrong for cricket as it would not enable players to adapt to new conditions. Sir Frank Worrell once told me that it took him some time to readjust to the difference in the light and the pace of pitches when he returned to his native Caribbean while he was studying at Manchester University.

In Australia the conditions are such that at least two weeks should be allowed for net practice at the start of a tour to give players a fair chance of finding their feet, especially as it takes two or three days to overcome jet lag. As a broadcaster and journalist in Australia in 1951–52 I saw the powerful West Indies, who had comfortably won in England, become victims of an odd itinerary. They went into the First Test after only two two-day games, at Newcastle and Townsville (Queensland), and one first-class fixture in which they were roundly beaten by Queensland. They not only lost the First Test and the series, which was unofficially regarded as deciding the championship of the world, by an emphatic margin, but were exposed as vulnerable to fast bowling. Afterwards, to add to his indignities, the skipper, John Goddard, got into hot water with his Board for blaming the itinerary for many of his side's misfortunes. As a neutral observer I thought that John had a strong point.

In 1946–47 we remained in Perth, the first staging post, for three and a half weeks (partly due to the shipping situation) – almost a third of the time allowed for a complete tour in the eighties. Perth had a concrete-like pitch which was so hard that Doug Wright landed slap on his back bowling his first ball. The hard, black soil, sporting very little grass, was slippery to those unused to it, and studs, which served their purpose at home, were useless. I was advised to have special boots made, with soft toecaps and running spikes fitted to the soles. On the hard pitches my toe was constantly being jammed against the end of the boot until the blood oozed through. I came to understand what severe punishment the old fast bowlers had taken in Australia.

From Perth we took two days in a train without air-conditioning to cross the 1700 miles of the Nullarbor Plain to Adelaide. If a window was opened for a little air the compartment immediately filled with dust. At one point the track is arrow-straight for 300 miles, roughly the distance from London to Penzance. I am sorry for the modern tourists who see more of the inside of jet planes, airports and hotels than the real Australia. From the train I watched an emu matching the train's 40 m.p.h. and kangaroo hopping alongside. Yet a life-time grazier from South Australia assured me that the only wild kangaroo he had seen were two that were stunned by his car on a lonely stretch of outback country road. At one stop an old Aborigine came up to the train and accepted a bottle of beer, biting off the metal stopper with his teeth and downing the contents in one gulp.

A story is told of a rancher and his native stockmen in the outback listening by the campfire one night to a crackling radio broadcast describing Stan McCabe's innings of 232 in faraway Nottingham in 1938. The only light came from the fire and the stars above, and one of the Aborigines said, 'If he can play like this in the dark, how many runs would he score in the light?'

There was a memorable stop at Kalgoorlie to change tracks; the whole town seemed to have turned out in spontaneous greeting, bearing practical gifts of trays of cold beer. Alas, such moments of true Aussie hospitality are less possible these days, more's the pity.

MCC also had a date at Port Pirie, which, at the time, could have been used as an authentic setting for a western. The rail track ran down the main street and the train drew up almost outside the main door of the hotel. We expected to hear a tinkling piano in the background and see a cowboy come hurtling through the swing doors. Up-country matches meant a lot to the local players and officials, but now, with shorter tours, there is less chance of such traditional fixtures.

The only air trip we had on my first tour was by flying boat from Sydney to New Zealand, although we flew home, again by flying boat, with overnight stops at Darwin, Singapore, Calcutta, Karachi, Bahrain, Cairo and Augusta (Sicily). My knowledge of geography was vastly improved. I wonder what on earth would happen if a new Bradman or Hutton had an aversion to flying.

For the eight-month tour of Australia and New Zealand I received basic pay of £550, and Wally Hammond awarded me a full bonus of £263. Income tax on those sums came to £216 18s and £118 7s respectively. At the time of writing a three to four month tour of Australia is worth some £10,000 or so, with bonus and prize money as well. As it was, I would have gladly gone to Australia for nothing and swum all the way. Rationing was still in force, but we were given extra clothing coupons by MCC to help in buying our kit. My expenses were as follows:

	£	S	D
Cabin trunk	30	0	0
Dinner suit	20	0	0
Evening shoes	3	16	4
3 evening shirts	3	15	0
3 pairs flannels (white)	11	8	0
6 shirts (white)	18	13	0
1 pair cricket boots	8	0	0
3 bats	9	0	0
2 suitcases	10	0	0
	£114	12	4

I doubt that £114 would buy a quarter of those items these days.

I returned to England in 1947 an immeasurably better bowler. Facing Donald Bradman, Arthur Morris, Sidney Barnes (even to get the ball past his barn-door bat was an achievement), Lindsay Hassett and Co. on shirtfront pitches was tantamount to a university course in cricket. Eleven wickets in my Test debut at Lord's and 11 more in my second Test at Manchester, highly satisfactory though they were, did not make me an international bowler, and I stood in respectful awe of Bradman. When I first bowled against him my main hope was not to be hit to the boundary too often.

There will never be a batsman to match him. The more I bowled to him the more I learned, not the least being to concentrate as I had never concentrated before and, as my experience increased, to pay meticulous attention to my field placings. It had been drummed into me hard enough by Allan Peach and my older Surrey colleagues that I had to bowl straight and to a full length. If I strayed from length or line I was deservedly punished. Seeing some of today's short-pitched stuff at fast medium pace, I shudder to think what Don and the others would have done to it.

A turning point in my career was to bowl Don for a duck in the Fourth Test at Adelaide with a ball which he generously described as the finest ever bowled to him. It started on the line of the off stump, swung late to hit the pitch on or about the leg stump, and came back to hit the middle and off stumps. My stock was boosted sky high and I gained considerable confidence. I had discovered my so-called leg-cutter, in which I actually spun the ball, during

43

the Bradman-Barnes record fifth-wicket partnership of 405 in the Second Test at Sydney. I was bowling to Barnes, who knew all about my in-swing. To tempt him into error, I tried to make the ball go straight through without deviation. Allan Peach had taught me how to stop the new ball swinging by holding it across the seam in a leg-break grip. To my surprise, and that of Barnes, the ball went away from leg to off after pitching. Barnes's first reaction was to study the pitch with suspicion, and when he found it to be totally without blemish, he stared at me in disbelief and called out, 'What the hell's going on?' From that moment I knew I could spin the ball at a good speed, a considerable addition to my armoury.

At Adelaide I almost bowled Bradman with the first ball of his second innings when he played forward, missed, and the ball shaved the off stump. Another centimetre, and I would have had the greatest batsman of all time for a pair. I was too elated by getting him once in the Test to feel greedy. To put our duels into perspective, Bradman scored 187 in the First Test at Brisbane, 234 at Sydney, and averaged 97.14, while my 16 wickets cost 54.75 each from 246.3 eight-ball overs. Australia had totals of 645, 659, 536 and 487, and frankly, England's elderly side – only Godfrey Evans, Denis Compton, Jack Ikin and myself were under thirty – never had a realistic chance, particularly as the pitches were so perfect for batting.

Luck always plays a part in cricket; strangely, it seems to follow the stronger side, and it certainly followed Australia in 1946–47. There was controversy over a chance offered by Bradman early in his comeback innings in the First Test. I was at short leg, a perfect position to judge, and I thought that an edge to Jack Ikin off Bill Voce was a straightforward, legitimate catch. However, the decision went against England. I have often thought since that Don's reprieve was the best thing for cricket in the long term. He had been far from well and if he had failed he could easily have retired and not come to England in 1948. His presence on that 1948 Australia tour was an important factor in restimulating the game and reawakening public interest after the barren years of war. Also, had he been given out and called it a day, I would not have had so many legendary duels with him.

Immediately Australia were out Brisbane had one of its raging tropical storms. In less than an hour the ground was flooded, in some parts to a depth of two feet. The stumps, covers and sight-screens were floating and hailstones the size of golf balls dented the roofs of cars in adjoining streets. The match seemed a certain write off, but, incredibly, play began at noon the following day. I set the scene to pay my little tribute to the genius of Walter Hammond.

Within an over or two I understood why the Australians were so adamant in their belief that wickets should be covered (although a cover would have been useless on this occasion), and later why the light of reverence shone in the eyes of contemporaries who saw Hammond in his prime. He scored just 32, which is nothing on paper, but I count it as one of the greatest innings it has been my privilege to witness. Many a highly praised double century would not bear comparison in a straight test of sheer quality and tech-nique. Here were Keith Miller (7 for 60), Ray Lindwall and the left-armed Ernie Toshack, difficult enough in favourable conditions, bowling on a perversion of a pitch resembling thick glue. When the ball pitched its flight was hopelessly unpredictable. Some kicked almost perpendicularly, while the half-volley was apt to fly over the unfortunate batsman's head as he went half forward. It was rather like expecting century breaks from Steve Davis on a bumpy snooker table.

Incredibly Hammond found a method not only to survive but to make the occasional scoring stroke, executed with a power and fluency which made the players gasp. He would wait for the overpitched delivery to drive. To the short-pitched he would stand aside and ignore it, making no effort to make contact with the bat. In theory this might suggest a simple technique available to all; in fact it required an uncanny judgement of length, and Hammond's judgement was so exact that he scarcely collected a bruise. In contrast Bill Edrich, obliged to employ all the guts for which he was justly famed, was pummelled as if he had been in a boxing ring as a loser for ninety minutes, and returned with a mass of black and blue bruises. Edrich would never pretend to aspire to Hammond's class, but as a fighter he bowed to no man.

In the wake of England's defeat on that tour Hammond's leader-ship was criticized. One objection was that he travelled separately from the rest of the party. So far as I was concerned that was relatively unimportant and would not have been noticed if the results had been reversed – it might even have been commended! Maybe it was a mistake for Hammond to have returned to cricket after the war, and it has even been suggested that as he had seen it all before he was bored, but the fact was Australia were at least two classes better and Hammond helped to get Test cricket going again. Personally I was grateful for that one glimpse of the vintage Hammond on an impossible Brisbane wicket, as well as his 200 in the first match in Perth.

Whenever it is claimed that Gary Sobers stands as the undisputed all-rounder of all time I mentally protest that Hammond should be so easily forgotten. He, too, was not only a great batsman and slip fielder, but a fine bowler who could open with the new ball at a lively pace and on occasions turn to leg breaks. A superb athlete, he was of a breed who can excel at any ball game. Remember also that Hammond was one of the greatest players on wet and turning pitches – something the modern player does not have to contend with.

I prepared for Don Bradman's 1948 Australians by working in a nursery at Woking. For four months Eric and I dug up trees on a piecework rate. We must have dug up quite a lot for, once again, we were able to save our winter pay from Surrey. It is amusing to reflect that I did not go with Gubby Allen's side to the West Indies in 1947–48 because I wanted to rest after a gruelling eighteen months in which I had bowled 3000 overs. Without my improved technique and fitness, and particularly control, I could never have ventured to put into operation the plan which led to three of Bradman's six dismissals by me in successive innings, five for England and one for Surrey.

My strategy was based on the knowledge that he knew I could make the ball move from leg to off from the turf with my leg-cutter, and that I could also bowl a late in-swinger. I also knew that Don liked to get off the mark with a single which was often pushed to the on side. I used two forward short legs, with Len Hutton, a dependable catcher, at backward short leg. To this field I bowled a full-length ball either on or just outside the off stump. The batsman had to play at the ball, an essential requisite. If the delivery was accurate Bradman would be thus induced to play forward and, with luck, he might finish in a half-cock position when the ball swung in to him late. The natural direction of any snick would be backward to short leg, and there it landed on three occasions, to be caught by Hutton.

The sequence started in the fifth and final Test of the 1946–47 series at Sydney, and continued at The Oval in May 1948, when, playing for Surrey, I bowled Don for 146. In the First Test at Trent Bridge he was caught twice in my leg trap by Hutton for 138 and 0, and in the Second Test at Lord's he again went to a Hutton catch in the identical position for 38 after surviving a very difficult chance there at 13. In the second innings Bill Edrich made an acrobatic one-handed catch when the Don was at 89.

Whether the master would have fallen to this ploy in his heyday has been the subject of a lot of discussion. I did not believe that I had found a chink in his armour. On the other hand, so far as I knew it had never been tried before. At the time I was surprised by so many reports that the ball was pitched on the leg stump. Had it been there, Don would have been able to leave many balls alone and to control his stroke better. I always found it was inviting disaster not to bowl to Australians on the off stump to a full length as most were exceptionally strong on the leg side. Bradman's speed of thought and movement, his confidence, his superb use of the crease and placement of his strokes were a revelation and an education to me. Contrary to what has sometimes been claimed, I found his bat in defence was always dead straight. Frankly, I was delighted if I saw an opponent play across the line of the ball, as this is a guaranteed recipe for failure against bowling of any real quality.

Such was Bradman's influence as captain and batsman that I played in fourteen Tests at home and away before I was on a winning side. That was against Australia at Melbourne in 1951. Also broken was Australia's record of twenty-six postwar Tests without defeat. England's previous win had been at The Oval in 1938 when Hutton made his record score of 364. Along with Hammond and Joe Hardstaff, Len was often heard to say how fortunate the Aussies were to find in Ray Lindwall and Keith Miller two match-winning fast bowlers as heirs to Bill O'Reilly and Clarrie Grimmett. English euphoria was so overwhelming after the Melbourne win that Len commented, 'I'm glad that everyone forgets we lost four Tests.'

England should never have lost that series by 4–1. Australia, without Bradman and Barnes, were team building and were far from unbeatable. Maybe it is out of place for a veteran Test selector to question the composition of the team, but I think that the emphasis on youth for the 1950–51 tour was an unwarranted gamble. At the time there were no fewer than eleven selectors – five from MCC, four nominees from the counties and two county captains – and two months before the team was due to leave the captaincy was not settled. Norman Yardley and George Mann could not spare the time from business. Providentially Freddie Brown scored a swashbuckling century for the Gentlemen against the Players and, according to legend, accepted the captaincy while still under the shower.

Brown's previous tour to Australia had been in 1932–33 with Douglas Jardine when Brown was twenty-one. Of that party only he and Bill Voce (twenty-three) were under twenty-six, and Brown did not play in a Test. Maurice Tate and Herbert Sutcliffe were thirty-seven, Jardine, the Nawab of Pataudi and Maurice Leyland were thirty-two and Gubby Allen, Eddie Paynter and Tom Mitchell thirty. Hammond was only one year younger. Yet in 1950–51 Brown's full complement of nineteen – Roy Tattersall and Brian Statham were sent as reinforcements – included seven players under twenty-six while Statham was only twenty and Brian Close nineteen. Back home the ground was rife with experience including Bill Edrich, Jack Robertson, Jack Ikin, Dennis Brookes, Tom Dollery, George Emmett and Les Jackson, who, with his slightly round-arm action in the style of Jeff Thomson (though not with his speed), was highly regarded in county circles. Jim Laker still had to wait two tours before he went to Australia and the commonly held theory that off-spinners were a waste of time in Australia abandoned. Even after he had taken 8 for 2 in the Test trial at Bradford in 1950 Laker was chosen only once in the season's series with the West Indies, although he took 166 wickets at 13.52 during the season.

The lesson to be learned from 1950–51 was not to be overconcerned with age. However, no selection committee, large or small, could have foreseen Denis Compton, then at the start of his knee injury problem, having such a wretched series that his top score would be 27, or that Australia should be so favoured in the First Test at Brisbane. The toss proved decisive and Australia, dismissed for 228 on a good pitch, did not deserve overnight rain which turned the match into a tragicomedy, with England declaring at 68 for 7 and Australia at 32 for 7. Len Hutton, acknowledged as the supreme wet-wicket batsman since Jack Hobbs and Herbert Sutcliffe, was held back until no. 6 in the hope of better conditions and Arthur McIntyre, who was capable of giving him support was run out in the second innings by wicketkeeper Don Tallon, who ran at least 10 yards to collect a wild throw and broke the wicket throwing with his gloved hand. Hutton made a marvellous 62 on an improved pitch before running out of partners.

In the four years since 1946–47 I had acquired better weapons with which to attack my great friend Arthur Morris. The development of my leg-cutter gave him problems. The leg-cutter to a left-hander saw the ball coming in to him, while the normal in-swinger was a late out-swinger to him. My ability to move the ball either way caused Arthur to stray out of position on occasions, because he would move over to his off side. When the ball cut back he was likely to be leg before, because in order to try to get behind the swinging ball he sometimes moved too far to the off side and was so out of position. Again, if the ball moved off the pitch there was a short leg at an angle of 45 degrees – as with Bradman in 1948 – to take a snick. Arthur could not be certain from my action what I intended to bowl, and as I sometimes surprised myself the batsman was hardly likely to guess correctly.

Bowlers are not always so well rewarded. At Melbourne in 1951 I began to despair of finding Neil Harvey's bat edge because the movement of the ball was so late. An odd sort of stalemate developed. Herbert Strudwick recalled a similar incident at Sydney in 1924. Struddy was keeping to Maurice Tate, with whom I was compared, and Bill Ponsford, a mammoth scorer, could not lay a bat on the first sixteen balls he received. After playing and missing, he turned to Strudwick and remarked, 'I've never played against such bowling in my life.' Struddy replied, 'You could have been out sixteen times.' Then 'Horseshoe' Collins took Tate and handled him until the bowler's first spell was completed. Both Collins and Ponsford scored centuries, but Maurice ended with 6 wickets.

In 1950 I had a constant pain in the bottom of my back. Nothing would budge it. I was saved by a chance remark in a bar at Lismore, NSW, the following winter, made to a fellow named Laurie Thew about my complaint. He said, 'Oh, I know the chap for you. He's studied back injuries in America and lives just out of Lismore.' The upshot was a cure by manipulation.

I had caught flu in the early part of the tour and was unwell until just before the first Test at Brisbane. Fortunately, I collected a few wickets against Queensland, which was just as well as I heard afterwards that I was on the point of being dropped for the Test. Had that been my lot I would not have enjoyed a great series of 30 wickets at 16 apiece, including 10 at Melbourne, and gone on to have been the first to take 100 wickets against Australia since 1914. That is the record I count above all else.

After the Brisbane Test Tom Goodman, a much respected Sydney journalist, came up to me and said, 'You're a cunning old so and so. You've been holding yourself back for the Test so you wouldn't get tired.' Little did he know.

Although *Wisden* proclaimed that Hutton, Evans and I were the champions of the 1950–51 rubber, I was dismayed at losing once again. It was by an unhappy quirk of fate that, when triumph duly came four years later and we won the Ashes in Australia, I celebrated in the dressing room and not on the field. *C'est la guerre!*

Naturally I had hoped to crown my battles with the old enemy with a contribution of wickets for Len Hutton's defence of the Ashes. At home I had reached a peak with 39 wickets in the 1953 Test series and thought I still had the ammunition to make my presence felt. Looking back, it is strange to see how the odds were stacked against me, as if the Fates were in conspiracy. As soon as I arrived in Australia in 1954 I went down with shingles, a complaint I do not recommend catching. The only Test of the five I managed to appear in was the unmitigated disaster of Brisbane. I returned in unseemly haste – I wanted to play and Hutton wanted me – but the plain fact was that I was not fit enough. None of the doctors were able to forecast how long it would take for me to recover my strength, and instead of going off for a holiday I resumed in early November against an Australian XI at Sydney and against Queensland on the eve of the First Test. With hindsight I realize I should not have played for three months.

In the Test itself everything went spectacularly wrong from the moment that Godfrey Evans withdrew at breakfast time on the first morning with sunstroke. Hutton, who can never be accused of anything but single-mindedness, proceeded with his plan to concede first innings if he won the toss and to field an all-pace attack. Len got it wrong because he overlooked the fact that before the Queensland game, where the ball had swung in the humid air and the pitch was an emerald green, rain had freshened the surface in the previous week. But there had been no rain in the week before the Test itself. The ground had dried out, without overhead clouds the humidity was low, and there was no movement either through the air or off the pitch. In short, it was a perfect batting wicket and although both Len and his deputy Peter May had achieved impressive results by putting the opposition in to bat in earlier fixtures, there was nothing but extravagant hope to justify the gamble. I had a gut feeling of trouble with a capital T ahead, which was unhappily reinforced when Arthur Morris was missed at the wicket off me in the third over. England could not have caught a cold on that fatal day. I lost count of the number of dropped catches but the figures men said twelve possible chances were missed, of which seven were off my bowling according to the eminent critic, the late Ray Robinson. Amid the deplorable exhibition Denis Compton ran into the boundary pickets and broke a bone in his left hand and was able to make only token visits to the crease at no. 11.

When England get it wrong they are apt to do it in a lavish manner, and Hutton's grand design was in tatters. Australia declared at 601 for 8 and won by an innings and 154 runs. I was one of four bowlers to concede a century of runs; Frank Tyson was the most expensive with 1 for 160 off 29 overs. At that point any odds would have been offered on England taking the series and Frank becoming the man to destroy Australia or, to be strictly accurate, the spear-head of the assault. The odds against must have lengthened after the first day of the Second Test in Sydney when England were out for 154 in their first innings and we were advised to go home as the series would be a flop. Cricket can dig deep pits for the pundits, and at Sydney few took account of the fact that, starting in 1952, Australia's policy was to leave more grass on pitches to encourage bowlers. The averages for the period show the benefits reaped by fast-medium bowlers – I never use the term 'seam' as it is such a loose description covering several forms of bowling. Sydney had had rain for a month and the Test wicket was protected by flat tarpaulins. The result was a piebald strip of green and brown patches and, as the groundsman had not been able to spend as much time in preparation as he would have liked, there was quite a mat of grass on the surface. It was heaven-sent for pace for when the ball hit the green patches it flew and when striking the brown it kept low. The bounce was thus inconsistent, and after one quick glance I could see it was a good wicket to bowl on. However, that was not to be.

I was happy for Len Hutton, Frank Tyson and England that it came right in the end. The 'Typhoon' justified Hutton's confidence in him with 10 wickets. Peter May made a superlative century. Neil Harvey, the other champion, was 92 not out when England won by 38 runs. Only a genius could make runs in these conditions, but then May and Harvey belonged to the elite. Colin Cowdrey was to score a wondrous century in the Third Test at Melbourne on an even more treacherous pitch in only his third match for England and set himself awesome standards for the rest of his distinguished career.

The magical transformation of Tyson after the Brisbane disaster has become part of the folklore of cricket, and has been attributed by some to shortening his run-up. Len Hutton in his book *Fifty Years of Cricket** writes that Tyson speeded up after being felled by a bumper from Ray Lindwall in the Sydney Test. Alf Gover, a noted coach since his playing days ended, helped Frank by suggesting he cut down that wasteful long run without sacrificing speed. Frank was an apt and intelligent pupil, but I do not think Frank's shorter run alone made the difference between failure at Brisbane and sizzling success in a matter of a couple of weeks. Success does not come so easily. The less romantic fact was that the conditions at Sydney were utterly different, favouring the bowlers, and England's catching passed from the ridiculous to the sublime. Nevertheless, Frank took full advantage of the conditions and all credit to him for doing so. He bowled at a frightening pace.

Australia's pitches have progressivly declined since 1946–47. Melbourne in 1954–55 was the worst I had seen until Brisbane, 1979. I was hoping I would play at Melbourne when Hutton asked Denis Compton and me to join him in his pitch inspection before the start of the Third Test. I assumed wrongly that the attack had

*Stanley Paul, 1984.

been restructured for me to play, but when the team sheet was pinned up in the dressing room my name was crossed out. Len had said nothing to me in advance of his intentions. I wish he had. He has since told me and has written in his book that he agonized over the decision and if he could have the chance of a 'replay' he would act differently and at least put me in the picture. I honour Len for being so frank, and equally I sympathize and understand that the pressures on him were enormous; they did not disappear until the Ashes were safely won at Adelaide.

The final stages were almost too much for him and when England came off the field at Adelaide needing 94 to win after Australia's second innings he turned to Denis Compton and said, 'I don't feel like going in again. Will you go in first?' When Denis began to get ready he saw Len buckling his pads and was told, 'I'll be going in first.'

The atmosphere in England's dressing room as Keith Miller turned on some of his special magic and dismissed Hutton, Bill Edrich and Colin Cowdrey for 12 was beyond description. What poor Len endured I cannot imagine. He slunk away, to re-emerge in his moment of triumph like a man who has been reprieved from the gallows.

For long Hutton had shouldered the brunt of England's batting, and he had for ever on his shoulder the spectre of the small but influential few who did not accept the change to a professional captain. Len was very conscious of his position, perhaps excessively so, and by nature and upbringing he is both sensitive and cautious. As a captain he was a long-term strategist and, as such, his success rate was impressive. He deserves to be highly rated among international captains. His stern Yorkshire grounding under the likes of George Hirst, Wilfred Rhodes, Herbert Sutcliffe, Bill Bowes and others made him a realist. Len would wait and strike when the time seemed right. Of course, he had the luck to inherit some outstanding players, the richest vein of talent England have had since the war, but it should always be remembered that he was England's premier technician despite his arm injury. He never lacked a quiet courage, and took the brunt of Ray Lindwall and Keith Miller's attack at the summit of its power with enormous courage and skill. No one was on the receiving end of more bouncers and I never heard him complain.

Apart from the progress of Tyson, the marvellous back-up provided by Brian Statham, and the emergence of Colin Cowdrey and Peter May, Len's luck was with the pitches, and he must have had a moment of satisfaction at Melbourne when a full-length ball from Tyson almost took Keith Miller's cap off. The next, of shorter length, shot along the ground. It was here at Melbourne that the pitch had been watered over the weekend in an endeavour to seal the many large cracks that had appeared. In fact the watering improved the pitch for a while and we were batting.

As nothing hinged on the final Test at Sydney and it was obviously my last chance to play in a Test match in Australia, I half hoped I might be included as a farewell gesture. I was by then fully recovered from the untimely attack of shingles and bowling well, but the thought did not occur to the tour committee. In any case, it would have been a watery farewell as New South Wales was half drowned and the Test was ruined by rain.

To have had my last tour blighted by illness was the biggest disappointment of my career, and Jack Fingleton, the wisest and best of Australian cricket writers, summed it up for me in his book *Masters of Cricket*. 'Bedser in better health than at Brisbane would have appreciated the Sydney pitch for the Second Test. It had been covered from storms and was a "green top". Bill Bowes, a staunch Hutton man, wrote that Bedser would have been in his element in Sydney. Melbourne was also a bowler's pitch from the start.' Yes, I would dearly have liked to have played my part in England's triumph but the important fact, which transcended all, was the final victory.

One of the perks of Test cricket in Australia was the cherished contact Eric and I had with the late Sir Robert Menzies, Prime Minister of Australia and visionary world statesman. Sir Robert's passion for cricket was unsurpassed, and although he was only an average club player he could speak on equal terms with the best on tactics, pitches, player and team ratings, and the rest. The lives of the leading players fascinated him, and he told us that his door was always open to us both. If we went to Canberra, the federal capital, there would be a note awaiting our arrival inviting us to call on him. There was a feeling of meeting not a figure of international renown but a warm friend. No matter how pressing affairs of state, Sir Robert would find time for a chat, sometimes over a meal or a cup of tea. Not long before he died, Eric and I spent two hours with him in his impressive library in Melbourne. Sadly, he was confined to a wheelchair, but when we arrived we found two ice-cold Fosters already poured.

Keith Dunstan, the well-known Australian writer, paid a visit to Sir Robert when he was Prime Minister and described his room, which was like a headmaster's study.

The pictures are different from those my headmaster had.

On one wall there is a photograph of Keith Miller leaning back into a superb late cut. On the opposite wall there is Alec Bedser at the finish of his bowling action, hand almost touching the turf by his left ankle.

There is a great assortment of photographs taken at Prime Ministers' conferences, all looking rather like school teams.

Then there is an actual photograph of a school team, Grenville College Cricket Premiers, 1909. There is a young chap sitting down in front – R. G. Menzies (scorer).

There are some good paintings, including an exquisite Tom Roberts.

Sir Robert was noted for his steadfast loyalty to the Crown – in fact he wanted Australia's new currency to be called royals rather than dollars – and his library walls contained several signed photographs of him with the Queen. During the Melbourne Centenary Test in 1977 it was a touching sight to see them, Sir Robert in his invalid chair, in animated conversation.

At the end of my Australian season as a journalist and broadcaster in 1958–59 I was surprised and delighted to receive this letter from the Prime Minister's office in Canberra:

My dear Alec,

I have written to both the ABC and BBC expressing my warm appreciation of your really splendid comments during the Test matches. I know that you have felt a little modest about them yourself, but many of my friends who are, like myself, cricket enthusiasts have volunteered the same opinion as I hold myself, which is that, for a shrewd and illuminating comment on the actual play, your remarks were quite outstanding.

Thank you very much for the pleasure you gave to so many of us.

With kindest regards.
Yours sincerely.
R. G. Menzies.

Apparently the BBC were not very interested and soon I became a

Test selector, and that put an end to any further thoughts of broadcasting and journalism. Some hold the view that it is wrong to bar ex-players from taking part in administration or Test and touring selection because of writing and broadcasting commitments. Many fine, experienced cricket brains are accordingly not available, but I do not believe it is possible to serve two masters. Sooner or later a conflict of interests is bound to arise; it is up to the individual to decide the path he treads.

Throughout my visits to Australia I have always been treated with great friendliness, consideration and courtesy by all connected with Australian cricket administration and enjoyed some wonderful hospitality for which I am for ever grateful. The same can be said of the MCC, which controlled Test Cricket both home and away in my playing days. The various administrators, secretaries and staff could not have been more considerate and courteous to me throughout my whole career. For example, when I was not selected for the Second Test against New Zealand in 1949, the consideration and courtesy shown to me by the captain, George Mann, and the chairman and the other selectors served as an example to me, and when it came my turn to pass on unwelcome news I always tried to contact the player before the team was made public.

I did not tour the West Indies, India or Pakistan. Pakistan came into the international fold late in my career, and teams sent to India in my time were largely composed of young batsmen on the way up and bowlers on the threshold of the Test side. I might well have gone if the war had not interfered from 1940 to 1946. I was fortunate, however, to go to South Africa in 1948–49 before the politicians took over and sacrificed cricket to further their aims. To those who toured in better times the situation is intolerable. Left to the cricketers of the world the present political impasse would, I am sure, be solved in five minutes flat. But the realistic fact is that politicians on both sides of the fence have the game in handcuffs. It scarcely needs me to express on cricket's behalf the feelings of general disgust when Bangladesh cancelled an England 'B' tour when the players were assembled at Heathrow. Zimbabwe followed suit. Who lost out by these peevish actions? Only the public and the cricketers of Bangladesh and Zimbabwe.

Cricket can only hope for and work towards a solution. One way to prepare for the future would be for a multiracial side, under the aegis of the International Cricket Conference, to make a good-will tour of South Africa. That might be a starting point at least.

One place I shall never forget in South Africa is Durban. In December 1948 I was the non-striker when the First Test was won by a leg bye off the thigh of Cliff Gladwin off the last ball. Until Australia and the West Indies tied at Brisbane in 1960 it was the closest result in a Test. When the last eight-ball over began at Durban in semi-darkness and drizzle, England needed 8 to win with 2 wickets left. There could have been any one of four results, a win to either side, a draw or a tie.

I do not know whether it was better to be in the action, dreadful though the responsibility was, or watching – that is, among those who could bear to watch. Before I went in you could almost touch and smell the tension. On such occasions there is an ominous silence in the dressing room, but once in the middle I was able to concentrate and discipline myself to keep a cool head. Fortunately for England, Cliff Gladwin, bluff, good-humoured and a no-nonsense man from the mining area of Chesterfield, could not have been better in a crisis. I think he actually enjoyed it. As he went in, in a situation which tugged at the stomach, he grinned at the South African skipper, Dudley Nourse. 'What have you got to grin about?' he was asked.

'Coometh the hour, coometh the man,' replied Cliff in broadest Derbyshire – a classic remark which has deservedly become part of cricketing history.

Lindsay Tuckett, a splendid bowler of brisk pace, bowled the fatal over. I took strike and, believe me, it was just about possible to see the ball in the murk. I swished, missed, and we stole a leg bye. Cliff then cheerfully hit a 4 over Eric Rowan's head on the midwicket boundary. If Rowan had been on the boundary edge and not wrongly positioned a few yards inside, he would have had a possible catch. The third ball produced another leg bye, and I managed a single off the sixth. I noticed Bill Wade, the wicket-keeper, was standing back, so I called up Cliff and told him we could make a single if the ball went straight through to the keeper. 'If you miss it, run like mad because I'll already be on my way,' I said. 'Right,' replied Cliff, but when he missed the ball he forgot to run in the excitement and had to scream the scream of the demented to stop me in my tracks. As I scrambled back I realized Wade was in such a state that he could not pick up the ball. He kicked it to the nearest fielder. Also Dudley Nourse had not put a fielder close enough to the bat to stop a single if the ball was blocked or came off Gladwin's body. With Wade standing back the chance of his getting to the stumps in time to take a return could be reasonably ruled out. When the last ball came there was the encouraging thought that England could not lose, but we still had to win, and with a pounding heart I heard Tuckett's footsteps coming nearer and nearer. As the ball was delivered I found myself charging forward yelling, 'Run, run.' I ran as I had never run before or since, and almost before I knew what had happened I was under a pile of fielders – like being at the bottom of a collapsed rugby scrum. For an agonizing moment I did not know whether I had made it. All around me was pandemonium, but as I disentangled myself at ground level I caught sight of Cliff triumphantly waving his bat in the air and the expressionless faces of the fielders. I then saw the stumps at my end were still upright with the bails on, and I knew the most precious run in my career as a batsman had been completed. I am not sure whether relief or exhilaration was the stronger emotion, but I was quite certain that one ordeal of that nature was enough for a lifetime in the game.

Cynics wisecracked that Wade had been weighed and found wanting, but only those who were in the middle knew how impossible the light was, and it is easy to imagine what would have been said if he had stood up to the wicket and conceded byes. As events turned out, it was not only a Test-match-winning run but a series-winning run, for after three draws South Africa might have won the Fifth Test but for a magnificent century by George Mann on a turning pitch. One of the first cables to be opened was from Walter Robins with the words: 'Now I believe in fairies.'

George, one of cricket's good golfers, has since been a valued administrator and leans heavily towards modesty. One story he tells against himself was when he altered the batting order in a Middlesex home match and went in before Denis Compton. 'For a few fleeting moments,' he says, 'I knew what it was like to be Denis Compton. I was greeted with a huge roar, which quickly turned to groans when the crowd realized it was not Denis. And audible groans echo strangely around Lord's!' George was far from being an unattractive batsman himself and could drive with immense power.

One of the memories I relish from the South African tour was the partnership of Cliff Gladwin and Roley Jenkins, who became great cronies. Roley was one of those marvellous characters who, alas, seem to have disappeared from the county scene. As he bowled his leg breaks for Worcestershire he rarely failed to add some spicy comments. To one reverend gentleman from Scotland batting uncomfortably against his leg spin Jenkins observed, 'With your luck you should become Archbishop of Canterbury.' Never lost for conversation Roley, so named for his sailor-like gait, squelched a condescending official who spoilt a compliment on an article Jenkins had written on leg-break bowling by asking, 'Did you write it yourself?'

'Yes,' was the unabashed reply. 'Did you read it yourself?'

After the happy ending at Durban another attempted run deprived me of every bowler's ambition to figure in a Test batting record. In 1948 at Old Trafford Denis Compton and I had scored 121 for the eighth wicket and were only 3 short of England's record for that wicket against Australia set up by Patsy Hendren and Harold Larwood at Brisbane in 1928–29. As I write in 1985 it still stands. As *Wisden* said, I was going well and capable of staying with Denis, who ended with a brilliant 148 not out.

Denis, always an erratic running partner, drove a ball straight to Bradman in the covers and rushed down the pitch, leaving me well stranded. 'You so and so. Why do you have to go and do that?' I said. Denis's judgement of a run was extraordinary considering his genius as a batsman. He even ran his brother Leslie out in his benefit match. Geoff Boycott is another top batsman with a reputation as an erratic runner. As Keith Miller once observed, 'He's got every other aspect of his game so organized and thought out that I cannot understand why he doesn't master the elementary rules of running.'

5

Stuart Surridge's Crystal Ball

Shortly before he started his first season as Surrey's captain in 1952, Stuart Surridge made this entry in his diary: 'Surrey will be champions for the next five years.' Typically, there were no ifs or buts, no get-out clauses about weather, injuries, Test calls, sheer bad luck and all the other imponderables which can turn the wisest cricket prophet into a fool. Stuart was dead right. He was captain for five years and won the championship five times. When Peter May succeeded him with myself as vice-captain the winning streak continued for two more years, a unique contribution to the history of county cricket. Like Jim Laker's 19 wickets for England against Australia in 1956, it is a record likely to survive for the rest of time, especially now that counties have four competitions each season. It was a wonderful privilege for Eric and me to have been members of those great sides, surely the best of all time in domestic competitions.

Stuart was always a bold fellow, bursting with optimism (has there ever been a really successful pessimistic captain?) and never departing from his philosophy of attack all the time, whether batting, bowling or fielding. Eric and I had known him since we were sixteen and played with him, Arthur McIntyre, Bernie Constable and Geoff Whittaker under Allan Peach for Young Players of Surrey. All of us graduated to the Championship side. As a wicketkeeper McIntyre was in Godfrey Evans's class and unlucky not to play more times for England. When Stuart was made captain of Surrey it was like one of the family moving up.

Although Stuart inherited a powerful side which had been joint champions with Lancashire only two seasons before, it still took a lot of faith for him to promise himself such lasting success. Surrey began their winning run in 1952 with 256 points, the highest since

1946, and in 1955 gained 284 points, passing the previous best of 260 by Yorkshire in 1939 when Yorkshire were rated as strong as they have ever been. With Peter May as captain, Surrey did even better in 1957 with 312 points, 94 more than Northamptonshire, the runners-up; Surrey went into first place on 11 June, and by 16 August were champions. Successes in those heady years were usually by comprehensive margins and proof that Stuart's belief in aggressive cricket paid dividends was provided emphatically in 1955 when twenty-three of the twenty-eight matches were won. The other five were lost after Surrey had twice been ahead on first innings. Not a single Championship match was drawn.

For all the talent available to him I am convinced that the right attitudes, so enthusiastically nourished by Surridge, were a major contribution to the sustained success of his sides. If it is said that he had virtually England's attack of Jim Laker, Tony Lock and myself, and later Peter Loader, it can be argued it was all the more meritorious to win with key bowlers so often absent on Test duty.

Surridge was one of the last of the splendid breed of amateurs who led from the front; a touch of the swashbuckler, positive, candid and never asking a player to do anything he would not do himself. One of his first objectives was to make Surrey the best fielding side in the country and, before long, catches bordering on the impossible were taken. The background of gasholders, flats and a high pavilion sometimes leads to errors of judgement when taking a skier. The ball is easily lost, so Stuart had his players practising taking high catches for hours on end. Close to the wicket Surrey were unsurpassed, and the poor batsmen were intimidated by the proximity of the fielders – helmets and shinguards were not used then. One of Surrey's reserves, not familiar with Stuart's methods, jibbed when he was told to move closer to the bat. 'Let's face it, I'm a coward,' he joked. 'Right! Out of the way,' replied Stuart, striding up to take the position himself. The captain's normal position was within a few yards of the wicket on the leg side and he was often moving forward as he took catches. Tony Lock was also stationed behind on the leg side, and it was a familiar sight to see half the field clustered around the bat as Stuart pressed home an advantage. The psychological pressure made all but the strong-nerved batsmen wilt. It was a joy to bowl with so many daring experts able to take the half chance.

Inspiring as the leadership was, nothing would have been possible without Arthur McIntyre's wicketkeeping. I always liked my
wicketkeeper to stand up, and I owed a lot to Arthur's wonderful
attitude and skill. The wicketkeeper sets the fielding standards of
every side and Jack Hobbs always said he should be the first to be
selected. One of cricket's most exciting sights is of good bowling
being backed by catching of a high order. A factor sometimes
overlooked is that, if bowlers are able to induce mistakes and
catches result, then catching standards automatically rise because
a chance is expected off every ball. The sense of anticipation is so
sharpened that concentration becomes second nature. Conversely,
a team without an attack able to create many chances tends to
relax and go through the motions of concentration. I often thought
this to be the difference between Surrey's approach and that of
other teams. Surrey's fielding became legendary and I have not
seen the same standard maintained over a long period by any other
side. Success breeds success, and Surrey were able to generate and
sustain an atmosphere and a sense of pressure which were hard to
combat. In many matches during those remarkable years we often
sensed that opponents were halfway to defeat before a ball was
bowled. Surrey floated on an irresistible tide.

While there was class in abundance, Surrey had the considerable
extra bonus of players with a strong competitive instinct – those
with a will to do well. That spirit was illustrated by Tony Lock.
Like the rest of the side, Tony was thirsty for success. As an
example I quote from *The Surrey Story* by the late Gordon Ross.*

In a match at Bristol, Gloucestershire made 136 to which Surrey replied
with 339, the first seven batsmen all making over 30. Dennis Cox opened
the bowling for Surrey and from a crisply played stroke by George Emmett
the unfortunate Lock was struck on the head and obliged to retire. Surridge
subsequently took Cox off and replaced him with Eric Bedser, who turned
the first ball he bowled the proverbial mile. This heartening sight did not
escape the notice of the injured Lock and, determined not to miss out on
life's golden opportunities, he was soon staggering down the pavilion steps
back on to the battle area. He promptly took 6 wickets for 15 in 24 balls,
the best bowling of his career to date. They don't make spinners' wickets
for Lock to look at from a far distant pavilion.

*Stanley Paul, 1957.

(Sadly, Gordon Ross died suddenly at Lord's on the opening Saturday of the 1985 season. He was a good friend of Surrey.)

Eric, I might add, had 7 wickets in the match, which Surrey won by an innings and 115 runs, despite the absence of Peter May, Jim Laker and me who were playing for England at Headingley in the Test in which India lost their first 4 second-innings wickets to Freddie Trueman (3 wickets) and me without a run on the board.

I lay claim to have been instrumental in changing Stuart's thinking in one important direction in fielding. For generations it had been accepted that the less agile seniors and the bowlers should be close to the wicket to spare them long chases after the ball. In Australia in 1946–47 Wally Hammond gave me specific orders not to run to the boundary. 'I don't want my bowlers to waste their energies doing that,' he told me. To me, as a bowler, it seemed far more logical to take the half chance near the wicket than to save a run here and there, and the half chance was likely to be taken by the younger and more agile members of the team. I put this view to Stuart, and accordingly Ken Barrington, Tony Lock, Micky Stewart and Surridge himself moved into the close catching positions, with devastating results. Not only were they brave, magnificent specialists, but they were also athletic, with sharp reflexes. Some runs might have been conceded in the outfield, but never enough to worry about, while Surrey's close catching became supreme and feared by every opposition.

I had the contrasting experiences of having to slog away in Australia in 1946–47 with little hope of taking wickets and the spur of anticipating a wicket with almost every ball for Surrey when county sides were being routed. In 1955, when Laker, Lock, Loader and myself shared 422 wickets in the Championship alone, Surrey held 383 catches – some straightforward, some roughly described as half chances and some bordering on the miraculous. In his first season as captain Surridge held fifty-eight catches and took fifty-six in 1955, while Micky Stewart took seventy-seven in 1957, and Barrington, who was not originally a slip specialist, and Lock had sixty-four each.

Surridge's relationship with his team was ideal, something special. One immense advantage was that he was not a stranger and we regarded him as one of us. There was no uneasy period which inevitably follows the coming of a stranger to a dressing room. One of the privileges of friendship is a free exchange of views, and we could always tell him honestly what we thought of his plans, and, in turn, he could be equally honest with us. There was no rancour, although there was no shortage of plain talking. The higher the standard expected, the harder it is to maintain – a truism in cricket as in life – but anything said in the heat of battle was forgotten on leaving the field. We would not have dreamed of being on the same candid terms with Stuart's predecessors, but Stuart earned our respect because he was fearless and was prepared to listen. Sometimes he took our advice, sometimes he did not, but there was no doubt that he owed some of his success to having an attentive ear even though he was his own man. The wonder was that he seemed as fresh and as vigorous in his fifth year as he had been in his first. On the face of it some of his gambles were outrageous, and he could not have contemplated making them without an unbounded faith in himself and his team.

In return for loyalty and proficiency, he offered excitement and results, and if a plan misfired he would blame only himself. He took total responsibility. I admit there were occasions when I thought he had gone dotty, and others when I thought he must be infallible. Out of the blue he would announce, 'I think we'd better get 'em in.' The rest of us might shiver with apprehension and think the skipper had flipped at last. A classic example was at The Oval in 1954 when Lock (5 for 2) and Laker (2 for 5) put Worcestershire out for 25. Surrey were 92 for 3, with May and Barrington, two of the finest batsmen in the world, going well in fast-improving conditions. To the incredulity of the entire team Stuart suddenly closed Surrey's innings. If ever there was an eccentric declaration this seemed to be it, even allowing for the fact that the skipper was undoubtedly at his happiest when he was leading the charge on the field. Worcestershire, however, were dismissed by the two spinners and me for 40, leaving Surrey winners, in just over five hours of cricket, by an innings and 27 runs without having reached 100 runs in their own innings. And the rest of county cricket was left to ponder on that fact, particularly the teams due to play Surrey.

Warwickshire were beaten in a day with totals of 45 and 52; my aggregate was 12 for 35, including 8 for 18 in the first innings

The photographer said he wanted an action study. So I ran up and bowled, and I have always rated this as an excellent example of my follow-through. I am a great believer in getting the basic techniques right

Left: Family portraits: on mother's knee. She assures us Eric is left. Often she alone could tell us apart

Top: As soon as we were able to walk we were playing with a ball. Eric already has a bowler's grip

Below: Our late father, Arthur, at the Woking home we built ourselves in 1953. I went straight from helping England to win the Ashes to do labouring work with Eric. Father master-minded the project

Above: The day we shall never forget – we report at The Oval as apprentice professionals and are sent to the nets. I am bowling watched by Eric

Above: Allan Peach, a Surrey stalwart, and our mentor. After recommending us to Surrey he was a major influence in our early careers. We owe him a considerable debt

Below: Sergeants Eric, left, and myself, in the uniform of the RAF during war service which took us to France, the Middle East and Italy

Above: My first tour of Australia in 1946-47 was magic, even if it was hard work on the field. Laurie Fishlock, my Surrey team mate, makes friends with an Aborigine lady

Below: With Tony Lock, Jim Laker and Peter May after selection for England. Surrey had so many Test calls during the record-breaking seven years of the championship that the in-depth strength of the playing staff became a telling factor in our success

Above: Peter May, my Surrey and England colleague – and later a Test co-selector – and I were on opposite sides on this occasion. Peter was playing for the Gentlemen at Lord's in 1961 and I was playing for the Players. Godfrey Evans is wicketkeeper

Below: Sir Don Bradman, the greatest of all batsmen, was a devastating cutter. Here he makes a late cut in a Test at Lord's. The stand-in wicketkeeper is Eddie Paynter, the little Lancashire batsman, with Wally Hammond at slip

Top: One of our great fortunes was to become friends of Sir Robert Menzies, the Australian Prime Minister, who always managed to persuade his fellow statesmen to hold the Commonwealth Prime Ministers' Conference during a Lord's Test match. Eric *(left)* with Lady Harrison, wife of the Australian High Commissioner in London at the time

Bottom: Her Majesty The Queen at The Oval, 1955, when Surrey played the South Africans. Stuart Surridge does the introduction with Peter May to my right and Arthur McIntyre. On this occasion the Queen was spared the problem of trying to separate the identity of the Bedser twins, as we were allotted different places in the line-up

Salad days for Surrey. Padding up for the new season in
1956 when the county title was won for the fifth year running is
Peter May, with the dynamic captain Stuart Surridge. May succeeded
Surridge and I was appointed vice-captain to him

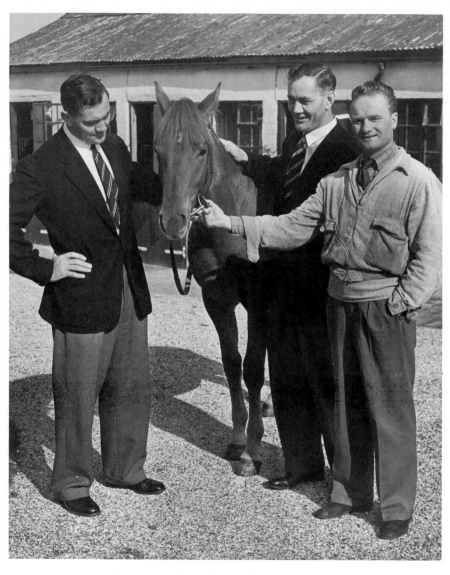

Eric *(centre)* and I make friends with a racehorse named
Bedser Twin, trained by Sandy Carlos Clarke. The Surrey players
renamed it Bookie's Friend!

to equal my best figures in first-class cricket. Such days compensate for the times when it seemed to be written in advance there were to be no spoils.

Another inspiration of Surridge floored Northamptonshire – so often a thorn in our flesh – in 1954. Batting first on a blameless pitch Northamptonshire made only 179. Surrey's reply was strong. May made 169, David Fletcher 55, and Raman Subba Row was 66, seemingly on his way to a century. The orthodox tactic was to hammer home Surrey's advantage with a huge total, but Stuart's instinct was to intensify his attack. Once again he surprised the dressing room with the words, 'I'm going to declare and give 'em an hour's batting tonight. We'll get six wickets by the close.'

Logically, Stuart had no right to expect more than 2 wickets if all went well, as Northamptonshire had Dennis Brookes, for whom I had much respect, Jock Livingston, the Australian left-hander, Norman Oldfield and Brian Reynolds in a strong batting line-up. Yet Stuart's instinct was right. He and I shared the new ball and grabbed 6 wickets for 22. The next morning Surrey completed an innings victory with Stuart finishing with 6 for 39.

In 1955 at The Oval Leicestershire were put into bat. Lock and I dismissed them for 56, and again Stuart closed the innings at 159 for 5 at a time when Eric was hitting the bowling all over the ground. The declaration was so far from the textbook that Charles Palmer, the Leicestershire captain, thought his side had been let off the hook. The next day Surrey cantered to victory.

Of course, Surridge had the players to make nonsense of all preconceived notions but how brilliantly he used his resources. He was a master of psychological warfare and, at times, seemed to be guided by an uncanny intuition to know precisely when to strike. His sheer audacity and confidence were enough to throw the opposition off balance, and he was shrewd enough to understand that county cricketers are apt to react nervously if a successful captain steps outside the normal tactical lines.

Surridge must have been one of the last great amateur captains, but, sadly, he never captained the Gentlemen against the Players at Lord's. I must confess I miss the traditional fixture, which died a death generations ago. The departure of the genuine amateur was a considerable loss to the game. The amateur captain had an independence from his county committee which the professional captain does not enjoy. The professional captain is all too often beholden to a committee who may or may not have the wisdom of experience. But with the changed social order the chances of finding a true amateur have disappeared. The sham amateur was undesirable, a pretence which the public did not accept, and at the time the new breed of amateur without private means cast understandably envious eyes in the direction of the growing tax-free benefits. There was no long-term advantage to being a subsidized amateur. But a lot of flair and fun disappeared with captains like Surridge who were not answerable to anyone but themselves and their team.

Many objective critics thought Stuart would be an impossible act to follow – five years, five titles under a highly individualist and totally extrovert captain. His successor, Peter May, it was argued, had little of the dashing style and adventurous outlook which had swept Surrey along. But Peter's shrewdness was often underrated, and he too could be strong if not in such a spectacular way. He anticipated many of the snags, one of which was his absence for half the season playing for England. He recommended me as vice-captain, a totally new departure for the club. Surrey had never officially appointed a professional captain or vice-captain before, but the club was quick to realize that if the captain was to be away regularly the appointment of a vice-captain was necessary. Also, it was imperative for captain and vice-captain to share the same views to avoid upsets and regrets when one took over from the other.

I took much pride in my selection and at the end of my first season as vice-captain in 1958 May was quoted in *Wisden* as follows:

Alec has been splendid in every direction. He remains splendidly keen and has bowled as well as ever. He and I have run the show, including team selection. As an example I quote the case of Barrington. When Surridge retired we started the season minus a slip fielder. We decided to try Barrington, and it was important for the side to be a success. He settled down immediately and took well over fifty catches. Apart from Alec, I do not single out any individuals because we remain essentially a team. Our success is based very much on the fact that we all play for Surrey and not for ourselves.

The last sentence tells, in a nutshell, all that needs to be said about Surrey's seven years as champions. It is sound, old-fashioned common sense.

What we would have collected in prize money by today's standards over the seven years would be interesting to work out, but although we missed out on the cash there were many compensations. I always remember taking Boris Karloff, the star of Hollywood horror films, onto the balcony outside the England dressing room on the Saturday of the Lord's Test with Australia in 1953. The sun shone from a cloudless sky on a packed ground. Not a blade of grass was out of place and there was a hum of expectation in the air. The perfect picture. Gazing around, he turned to me and said sincerely, 'This is like dying and going to heaven.' I once introduced Boris Karloff to Charlie Oakes, the attractive Sussex batsman, before a game at Hove. 'I don't know what to say to you,' said Charlie. 'You ruined my childhood watching your creepy films so that I couldn't sleep at night.'

During those years it was very hard to find a permanent place in the Championship side, and I was interested to hear some former England players who were discussing the current Test team's problems advance the opinion that some of the Surrey reserves of the fifties would now be candidates. Dennis Cox was an able all-rounder, and Laurie Johnson, obliged to move to Northamptonshire for first-team cricket, was one of the country's leading wicketkeepers.

A familiar charge at the time was that the pitches were doctored to help Surrey's bowlers. While it is true they helped to obtain finishes at The Oval they were prepared in accordance with MCC's edict of natural wickets. The aim of the official instruction was to get results, and the theory that Surrey always won because of their pitches was disproved by the fact that the attack was equally successful on away grounds. In fact wickets were taken at a lower cost away from The Oval, where between 1919 and 1939 drawn and high-scoring matches were commonplace. I find it hard to credit that it is possible to prepare a pitch to satisfy the contrasting styles of Lock and Laker on the one hand and Loader and myself on the other, and I often wondered why, if it was so easy for Surrey bowlers, the opposition so seldom made use of the conditions, particularly as it was often said that Surrey's batting was moderate and the weakest department of the team. In truth, the batting attitude faithfully reflected Surrey's positive tactical approach.

While there were four Test bowlers, who had the support of superlative fielding, the batting seldom failed to reach the skipper's directives, and I hardly think players of the calibre of May, Barrington, Clark, Constable, Fletcher, Stewart, Eric Bedser and Raman Subba Row – John Edrich was to arrive in 1958 – could fairly be said to be lacking in quality. Criticism of the batting overlooked the team's overall strategy which required sufficient runs to be able to attack the opposition. Batsmen were obliged to get on with it or, if they could not, to make way for someone else. In early 1952 Fletcher and Eric had opening stands of 162, 205, 94 and 178 – scores which would provoke much comment in these days. Surridge would never have won 101 out of 170 games and lost only twenty-seven – over a period when seven players were on call for England – without batsmen willing to take risks and not be obsessed by averages. If there was a glimmer of a chance of a result Surridge seized it, and he could never have been as dominant as he was if the batting had been inferior.

One example springs to mind. When, in 1956, Surrey were the first county to beat a touring Australian side since Hampshire in 1912, attention was inevitably focused on Laker's incredible performance of taking all 10 wickets in an innings for the second time in the season. But in the excitement Constable's century was almost overlooked. Yet without his invaluable contribution Surrey might not have won a famous victory, for all Laker's brilliance.

Sadly time has taken its toll and Ken Barrington and Tom Clark, who were as much a part of Surrey as the chocolate-coloured cap, are no longer with us. Two more honest and sincere men never lived and it was impossible not to like them. When they finished playing both wanted to give something back to the game. Ken became a touring manager and a Test selector, and Tom worked behind the scenes for Bedfordshire.

From his early days at The Oval until what proved unhappily to be his last selection meeting to finalize the England party for the West Indies in 1981, Ken and I were confidants and good pals. We shared the same dressing rooms as players; he was my right-hand man in Australia in 1979–80, and from 1975 until his death from a heart attack in Barbados he was a selector, playing his full part conscientiously and with sound judgement. He was wrapped up in every job he undertook in cricket, and a fine servant of the game was lost in his prime. It would be idiotic to suggest we were always in complete agreement over every issue or on how we saw players when we were choosing Test teams and touring parties – selection, after all, is largely a matter of pooled ideas and compromise – but we were as one in a dream of a powerful England, how we wanted cricket to be played, and its universal welfare.

Ken shared my worries about the numbers of overseas players and its effect on England's overall standard, over rates and the scenes which besmirched cricket's good name. From the strength of his 6806 runs and twenty centuries in Test matches he could not understand why basic batting techniques were ignored. If one thing irked him it was a player's delusion that he had nothing more to learn once he had appeared for England. He never forgot his own faltering start for England when he was prematurely hailed as a champion and was selected in the face of Surridge's opinion that he was not yet ready. After two Tests Barrington went back to county cricket for four years before he had another chance. He provided the classic example of the need for a thorough apprenticeship before promotion is considered. He always said he was grateful to be able to return to Surrey and to be able to continue to learn without the glare of publicity and too much being expected of him too soon. Nevertheless, the experience coloured his outlook and he concentrated on becoming a run-accumulator and 'percentage' batsman. In so doing he sacrificed much of his natural gifts of stroke play, and to counteract the rash of in-swing bowling he adopted a two-eyed stance which all but eliminated his off drive and made him over-reliant on the cut – he was a truly brilliant cutter – the hook, the pull and the on drive. Few have been stronger on the leg side, and he was essentially a back-foot player. All the best batsmen have been masters on the back foot.

Ken might have been frugal and overdefensive at times, but it is important to remember that pitches in his period favoured bowlers; I have seen some deliberately pitch well outside the leg stump to him for over after over. And then he would be blamed for slow scoring. He had an unanswerable reply to any critic – a century against every Test-playing country, and a Test century on every Test match ground in England. If he had adopted different methods

69

he might have ended with fewer runs and played more attractively. Perhaps, who can tell? I talked with him on this very theme at a dinner just before he left for his ill-fated journey to the West Indies, and he agreed that if he could start all over again he might favour a different approach. But many's the time as a selector that I wished for a player of half his ability and determination around whom England's batting could be built. He retired two years before he planned to do so after a mild thrombosis suffered during a double-wicket tournament in Melbourne. His second and fatal heart attack in Barbados during a tour of the West Indies in which he was assistant manager might well have been hastened by the accumulating problems of his job. He loathed any departure from the real spirit of cricket for, at heart, he was very much a conventional idealist. The Packer war and the attitude of some of the players deeply upset him, and, being a friend of all men, he was aghast that South Africa should be outlawed from the international cricket community. Politics were too devious for his uncomplicated honest nature and philosophy.

I doubt whether any manager has quite enjoyed the success he had in India where his popularity was unbelievable, partly because he was naturally friendly and outgoing and greatly enjoyed a laugh. He was also a first-class mimic and could take off his contemporaries down to the last gesture. Cricket was the love of his life after his family, and after that came golf and fast cars. One of his ambitions was to drive to The Oval in a Rolls. One morning he arrived in a borrowed Rolls determined to park in his usual spot, but, alas, he couldn't get through the Hobbs Gates!

At the end the one comfort was that his wife, Ann, was with him and he had been doing the work he liked best – helping England and the new generation of players.

How thrilled he would have been with Ian Botham and England's triumphs in 1981 for he had quickly seen Ian's potential, describing him in his early days as 'another Keith Miller'. At the time many sound judges thought Ken had gone overboard in his praise. I am sure he looked down with pride at the memorial service at Southwark Cathedral attended by representatives from all walks of life, including Sir Alec Douglas Home and Sir Hector Munro, then Minister for Sport. Ken was not only a great cricketer but an

70

honest-to-goodness, upright man who always acted honourably in his all too short life.

Tom Clark came from Luton with a reputation to maintain as a free stroke-making batsman and such was his high ability that his reputation was never lost. He comfortably made the transition from Minor Counties to first-class level and came very close to the England side. Before I became a selector I was told it was a straight choice for one match between Brian Close and Tom, and Close got the vote on the strength of his extra experience. I would have been glad of Tom's name before me in recent years! Tom was a handsome, good-looking batsman always looking for runs and steeped in the game. We used to call him 'Wisden' because of his encyclopedic knowledge of facts and figures. As the years rolled by he suffered much pain from an arthritic hip; it was the measure of the man that he never complained.

The major honours passed him by, but far worse players have won an England cap. He accepted his lot with a patient grin and with all the philosophy of a modest and model cricketer. They never came any better than Tom.

6

The House that the Bedsers Built

Nineteen fifty-three was a momentous year for me in many ways. At the end of the season the *Playfair Cricket Annual* recorded: 'A. V. Bedser had a fine record-breaking summer. The present total of 221 wickets is a record for Test cricket; he has bowled the most balls in Test cricket and his thirty-nine wickets against Australia last summer was a record for the series.' Not only did England regain the Ashes after nineteen years, but Surrey retained the County Championship. In all I bowled 1253 overs and took 162 wickets that season.

In itself the 1000–plus over work rate was par for the course at that time, but I had been bowling intensively for several years and Surrey thought it high time I had a free winter. Accordingly, I did not go with Len Hutton's side to the West Indies. Later I learned that Len had hoped to nurse me through the tour and play me only in essential matches. But, so far as I was concerned, that plan would not have worked. When on tour I always liked to be completely involved; I am not one to lie on a beach. Even so, at the end of the season I was repeatedly asked if I would put my feet up or sun myself in Spain. But Eric and I had other plans. As soon as the season ended we became general labourers, mixing concrete, humping bricks, digging trenches for gas, electricity and water, and doing other odd jobs. We were helping to build our new family home.

For thirty-five years we had lived in a modest terraced cottage on the fringe of Horsell Common. At first we rented it, for 12s (60p) a week and later bought it outright, but we had long outgrown the accommodation. We found a site nearby and, with the help of a young assistant in the architect's office of Woking Council, my father drew up the plans. Having been a bricklayer he was able to supervise the project, and the specialist jobs like wiring, tiling and carpentry were done by ex-schoolfriends on a contract basis. Work actually started in August, while I was helping England regain the Ashes, and we were able to move in the following March with the satisfied feeling of having accomplished something worthwhile by our own efforts. Of course, without my father's professional skill it would not have been possible, and the house stands today as a fitting memorial to a fine, upright man, a craftsman of the old school, who was liked and respected by all who knew him.

At the start of the 1953 season there were hopes that at long last Australia might be beaten and the Ashes recovered. It would be going too far to suggest the side had broken up in the post-Bradman period, but they were in the throes of rebuilding, although they still had a formidable backbone in the new captain Lindsay Hassett, Arthur Morris, Neil Harvey, Keith Miller, Ray Lindwall – still good enough to collect 26 wickets in the series – and Bill Johnston. Unfortunately Johnston was handicapped by injury, which greatly weakened Australia's attack. I was not unhappy that the great opening partnership of Morris and Sid Barnes had broken up. I always thought Barnes did not have quite the recognition he deserved. He was certainly one of the best opening batsmen I ever faced, particularly on the pitches of Australia in 1946–47, and one of the most difficult to get out.

All five Tests were gripping and England had to fight desperately to take the series only in the final match at the Oval. England needed team effort, and fought from first to last. Hutton, the skipper, had hoped that Trueman and I would form his opening attack, but Trueman was doing his National Service. In *Fifty Years of Cricket* Hutton writes:

If Trueman had been playing regularly for Yorkshire and therefore for England, he would have been invaluable. Without him I had to use Bedser to the best possible advantage, including keeping him reasonably fresh for the arrival of the new ball. A Bedser-Trueman partnership throughout the five matches would have been ideal, and when they came together at the Oval they shared 7 of the first-innings wickets. Bedser, as always, carried his enormous burden superbly, and by gaining mastery over Morris and his fellow left-hander, Harvey, he mus have demolished most of Hassett's batting plans.

An analysis of Australia's batting reveals that I dismissed Harvey and Hassett – who moved from no. 3 to open from the Second Test onwards – six times each, and Morris and Hole, the original no. 1, five times each. Thus 22 of my 39 wickets were against the recognized top four batsmen; their highest opening stand was 65 and the second best 38. Only Hassett (36.50), Harvey (34.60) and Morris (33.70) had averages above 30, an inconceivable failure in the Bradman era.

ENGLAND v. AUSTRALIA
(First Test)

At Trent Bridge, 11–16 June 1953

AUSTRALIA

A. R. Morris lbw b Bedser	67	– b Tattersall	60
G. B. Hole b Bedser	0	– b Bedser	5
A. L. Hassett (Capt.) b Bedser	115	– c Hutton b Bedser	5
R. N. Harvey c Compton b Bedser	0	– c Graveney b Bedser	2
K. Miller c. Bailey b Wardle	55	– c Kenyon b Bedser	5
R. Benaud c Evans b Bailey	3	– b Bedser	0
A. K. Davidson b Bedser	4	– c Graveney b Tattersall	6
D. Tallon (Wkt.) b Bedser	0	– c Simpson b Tattersall	15
R. R. Lindwall c Evans b Bailey	0	– c Tattersall b Bedser	12
J. C. Hill b Bedser	0	– c Tattersall b Bedser	4
W. A. Johnston not out	0	– not out	4
Extras	5	Extras	5

1/2 2/124 3/128 4/237 5/244   249   1/28 2/44 3/50 4/64 5/68 6/81   123
6/244 7/246 8/247 9/248 10/249   7/92 8/106 9/115 10/123

Bowling: *First Innings* – Bedser 38.3–16–55–7; Bailey 44–14–75–2; Wardle 35–16–55–1; Tattersall 23–5–59–0. *Second Innings* – Bedser 17.2–7–44–7; Bailey 5–1–28–0; Wardle 12–3–24–0; Tattersall 5–0–22–3.

ENGLAND

L. Hutton (Capt.) c Benaud b Davidson	43	– not out	60
D. J. Kenyon c Hill b Lindwall	8	– c Hassett b Hill	16
R. T. Simpson lbw b Lindwall	0	– not out	28
D. C. S. Compton c Morris b Lindwall	0		
T. W. Graveney c Benaud b Hill	22		
P. B. H. May c Tallon b Hill	9		
T. E. Bailey lbw b Hill	13		
T. G. Evans (Wkt.) c Tallon b Davidson	8		
J. H. Wardle not out	29		
A. V. Bedser lbw b Lindwall	2		
R. Tattersall b Lindwall	2		
Extras	8	Extras	16

1/17 2/17 3/17 4/76 5/82 6/92   144   1/26   120
7/107 8/121 9/136 10/144

Bowling: *First Innings* – Lindwall 20.4–2–57–5; Johnston 18–7–22–0; Hill 19–8–35–3; Davidson 15–7–22–2. *Second Innings* – Lindwall 16–4–37–0; Johnston 18–9–14–0; Hill 12–3–26–1; Davidson 5–1–7–0; Benaud 5–0–15–0; Morris 2–0–5–0.

Umpires: D. Davies and H. Elliott.

Match drawn.

Fourteen of my wickets came in the opening Test at Trent Bridge, which was much disrupted by rain, including a total washout on the fourth day and no play until after tea on the last. Yet with 7 for 55 and 7 for 44 I felt I had struck an early psychological blow, not the least result of which was the changed batting order. On that first day at Nottingham I bowled as well as I ever did. The pitch was perfect, and I conceded 26 runs from 25 overs, including 12 maidens, for the wickets of Hole, Morris and Harvey. England were held up by Hassett, who was undefeated for 67, and went on to complete a superb fighting century. It was an enthralling duel, so much so that nobody complained that only 157 runs came off 92 overs. Hassett, like Barnes, could be the very devil to get out, as he watched the ball so closely and hardly lifted his bat until he was satisfied he had played himself in. He was an absolute master of the art of slackening his wrists at the moment the ball struck the bat. Consequently he often prevented a snick from carrying to the slips.

Nothing pleased me more during Australia's first innings than the fact that I was able to sustain my attack. At times the ball was wet and hard to grip, but when it dried it swung in the humid air. As the much prized wickets came my way I felt an unashamed exhilaration. My mother, bless her, as level-headed as always, was rung up by a Fleet Street paper asking what she thought of her son taking 14 wickets in a Test match against Australia. 'Well, that's his job,' she replied. 'I don't know what all the fuss is about.'

I think the closest I came to that performance on the first day at Nottingham was in the Second Test of the 1950–51 series at Melbourne, but all – if that be the right word – I had then for ninety minutes' bowling was Morris's wicket. Yet some of the old Australian Test cricketers watching were good enough to tell me it was the best fast-medium bowling they had seen on the ground since Sydney Barnes's famous 9–over spell when he took 4 for 3 in 1911–12.

That series was the summit of my career. My aggregate passed Maurice Tate's 38 wickets in the 1924–25 series in Australia – and we played five, not six, matches, unlike today – and Sydney Barnes's record of 189 Test wickets in all, and at Headingley in the Fourth Test my 6 for 95 in the first innings took me past Clarrie Grimmett's 216 wickets, then a record aggregate for all

Test cricket. Finding myself alongside Barnes, Tate and Grimmett, I felt I had joined an honourable company.

Looking back over my Test career, I reckon my peak period was between 1950 and 1953, between the ages of thirty-two and thirty-six. This may surprise those who hold the conventional belief that a fast-medium bowler has, by his mid-thirties, long passed his salad days. In that period I took part in nineteen Test matches over four series, which is roughly half the number played in today's far heavier international programme.

For the record my figures were:

	Tests	Overs	Runs	Wkts	Avge
1950–51 v. Australia	5	195*	482	30	16·06
(in Australia)					
1951 v. South Africa	5	275	517	30	17·23
1952 v. India	4	163	279	20	13·95
1953 v. Australia	5	265	682	39	17·48
Aggregate	19	898	1960	119	16·18

*Eight-ball overs.

If I had played in forty Tests – the norm today – and sustained an average of 6 wickets a match, my haul would have been 240 wickets, which rather suggests the futility of statistics. To take the argument farther, I took 236 wickets in fifty-one Tests. Had I played in ninety Tests, as some have since, I might have finished with around 420 wickets. I wonder how many runs Bradman would have scored (6996 from fifty-two Tests) or how many wickets Bill O'Reilly would have taken (144 from twenty-seven Tests) in modern Test cricket. The mind boggles, and it is a compliment to Bradman's towering genius that, as I write, Richards, today's champion, has scored 5889 runs from 77 Tests.

It is also interesting that two of my better achievements came well before I was in my prime, while I was still in the process of finding out what bowling was all about: 22 wickets in my first two Tests against India in 1946, a record, and dismissing Don Bradman in six consecutive innings in 1947–48, culminating in the Second Test at Lord's when the Don was only 11 short of what would have been his farewell century in his last Test there.

Proud as I was to earn what *Wisden* described as 'a place in cricket history', I would not have begrudged Bradman a century on such a memorable occasion for he had always been generous in his praise of me, both in private and in public, and I always held him in the highest esteem. He saw to it that he did not fall to me again in that series, which Australia won 4–0. It was the strongest side that I ever played against, superbly led by Bradman. The strength of the batting can be measured by the fact that Bill Brown – on his third tour of England – lost his place after two Tests and yet scored eight first-class centuries. I reckoned my 18 wickets at 38.22, twice as many as Norman Yardley, who surprisingly headed the bowling averages, and Jim Laker were as hard-earned as my 16 at 54.75 had been in Australia in 1946–47.

In 1949, when New Zealand's powerful batsmen drew all four three-day Tests, I experienced the other side of the coin and surrendered my place after the First Test at Headingley (0 for 56 and 0 for 26) to Cliff Gladwin. Cliff, in turn, was replaced by his Derbyshire team-mate Les Jackson for the Third Test at Old Trafford, and he made way for me at The Oval for the final Test. I was one of seven bowlers selected in a desperate bid to break the deadlock, and as I had almost cried off with lumbago I was more than pleased to get 7 wickets.

I always rated my performance against the West Indies at Lord's in 1950 – the year of Ramadhin and Valentine and the West Indies' emergence as a world cricketing power – as one of my best. On paper it was not all that startling with 3 for 60, but the three were the wickets of Everton Weekes, the late Sir Frank Worrell (surely the most elegant of the three Ws) and Bob Christiani, a batsman never to be underrated. And I completed 40 overs in a total of 326. I felt I was on my way as I had developed my leg-cutter and was able to take full advantage of any help from the pitch.

South Africa were the visitors in 1951, and I really came into my own with 30 wickets, helping England to a 3–1 success. At Trent Bridge, where South Africa's hero was their captain Dudley Nourse, who scored 208 despite the handicap of having broken his thumb three weeks earlier, the pitch was affected by rain and I took 6 for 37 in 22 overs in the second innings. At Manchester in the Third Test I took 7 for 58 and 5 for 54, and Jim Laker and I shared 16 of England's 20 wickets. The pitch was damp enough to make the ball lift and turn, and in the second innings I bowled Jack Cheetham, soon to be South Africa's captain, with one of the most effective deliveries I ever bowled. The ball must have pitched six inches outside the leg stump and hit the off. Poor Jack, who had made a fighting 46, was so impressed that he sought out Alex Bannister of the *Daily Mail* and said, 'If anyone tells me that Sydney Barnes was a better bowler than Alec Bedser I shall refuse to believe him.'

Another comment I treasured was written by Johnny Woodcock, *The Times* correspondent and editor of *Wisden*. 'If I could conjure up the perfect day's cricket, it would be played at Lord's (or at Sydney in the days before floodlights) and contain a spell by Alec, head rolling, feet pounding, earth shaking and leg-cutter fizzing, bowling to the Don with Godfrey Evans keeping wicket.'

A less complimentary comment came in Australia in 1950–51 during a warm-up game at Northam, a town 60 miles from Perth. I was likened to a goods engine shunting up and down the nearby transcontinental railway.

By 1951, and certainly when the young Trueman and Statham arrived, England's immense bowling strength of the fifties was emerging. My partner in 1952 was Trueman, and we shared 49 Indian wickets between us in only four Tests – 29 at 13.31 to Freddie and 20 at 13.95 for me. In the last Test at The Oval only rain spared India from a whitewash, but I felt they were not so much short of class as of experience in batting away from their own sluggish pitches. Nor were they accustomed to genuine speed. Trueman frightened them to death.

Nineteen fifty-three was also my benefit year. A benefit was seldom granted before at least ten years' service as a capped member of the staff. It was very much of a gamble, depending on the generosity of the club in setting aside an attractive fixture and subject to the unpredictability of the weather. Surrey generously awarded me the Yorkshire game and the first day fell on my birthday. The sun shone from a cloudless sky and there was a big crowd, some 22,000. Jim Laker and Tony Lock virtually turned it into a two-day match. My benefit realized £12,000, a bumper amount by the standards of the day.

I was perhaps the first Surrey professional to organize my benefit on a scale which has since been improved upon and perfected. Lord Rosebery acted as patron, and an old colleague, George Porter, was the conscientious secretary, with a committee consisting of Andy Kempton, Jack Coventry, Jack Fagan, soon to be a business associate, George Milne, Frank Little and my brother Eric. Frank Sice was treasurer. Surrey also very kindly allowed the first-team players to take part in my six official Sunday benefit matches (the John Player League did not start until 1969).

However, the time was approaching when both Eric and I had to think about branching out into a new career. If we were blessed with sensible parents, we were also very lucky to link up with Jack Fagan. He suggested that we should start a small typewriter and office equipment business with him. He was an old hand in the trade, and we thought that if we ventured nothing, nothing would be gained. We began with a small shop in Woking in the winter of 1954. Jack supplied the expertise and his wife, Florrie, worked in the shop and looked after the books. Our job was to sell typewriters and office equipment.

From 1955 to 1960 we worked all the hours God sent, summer and winter. In the cricket season we would put in a stint before play started and again after close of play. We felt we had to get the business established before we retired as cricketers and while we still had an income from the game. All the profits were ploughed back into the business and Eric's benefit in 1958 provided an extra buffer. Naturally the cricket world gave us some useful contacts, and as time went on we became more knowledgeable and proficient in the job.

Jack Fagan's lifelong experience was of immense value, and we took over another small business in Staines and happily linked up with Reg Edmunds, an incorrigible optimist and an energetic salesman. He gave us a lot of help before he retired. From Staines and Woking the next step was to acquire another small but well-established business – Henry Baker Ltd, in St Bride Street off Ludgate Circus. Our turnover was at once doubled. In 1962, through Jack Fagan's connections with Ronald Straker, a new partnership was formed under the trading name of Straker-Bedser, embracing twenty-five shops in London and the Home Counties, with 180 employees and a turnover of £700,000. By 1971, when

Straker-Bedser was taken over by Ryman, the office equipment chain, the turnover had increased to £1.8 million.

In turn Ryman was bought by Montagu Burton, the clothiers, which meant our swift involvement in an amalgamation and two takeovers in a very short space of time. We found the Burton board very understanding and met many kindly people; Gerry Slater, the company secretary, was particularly helpful and has become a close friend. Despite the changed pattern of our business activities, no obstacle was ever put in the way of my duties as a Test selector or of any other cricket interests. Eric was always willing to cover for me; although Ryman and Burtons never demurred when I was away from the office, I never took holidays as such.

When I was manager of England in 1974–75 I took the opportunity of my association with Burton to arrange for the England touring teams to have a walking-out uniform. I thought the players would look smarter when travelling, and accordingly the teams were provided with blue blazers, with the traditional badge of St George and the Dragon, and grey slacks. Burton's have continued their support without costing the Test and County Cricket Board a penny.

David Evans, the sports-loving chairman of Breengreen (Holdings) PLC, a fast-developing factory, and office cleaning and refuse disposal company, had told us some years before that his door was open to us if our association with Burtons did not develop as we had hoped. It was some two to three years after David had made his offer that Eric and I decided to take advantage of it. Without hesitation David fulfilled his promise to the hilt.

David started life as a schoolboy soccer international and a £7–a-week pro with Aston Villa; he was also on the staff of Warwickshire County Cricket Club. He left Villa to work for a small office cleaning firm for £10 a week, and soon he and his wife Janice were scrubbing floors, armed with buckets of water and long bars of kitchen soap, on behalf of their own business. From that point the growth of a multimillion-pound business, extending to hospitals in Kuwait, the Municipal Palace in Baghdad, and to Hong Kong and Singapore, reads like an improbable romance of commerce. And, incredible to relate, David's company might have closed in 1967 if he had not collected a first-ball duck playing club cricket for Edmonton. As he returned disconsolately to the pavilion everything seemed to be going wrong. His little business was short of capital, there were bad debts, and no one would lend him money. The duck seemed to symbolize his misfortunes as he went for a shower.

In the adjoining cubicle there was a Third XI player who had also got out first ball. They got talking and David poured out his problems, blissfully unaware that his companion worked for Hambro's Bank. 'Come and see me on Monday,' his new acquaintance said. And on Monday Hambro's lent him £45,000.

The £7–a-week Villa pro now employs some 20,000 people and thinks of turnover in terms of millions. He is chairman of Luton Town Football Club and has done an enormous amount for Luton and Edmonton Cricket Club. He captained the Cricket Club Conference team to Australia and returned as manager on another tour. And probably none of this would have happened if David had gone on to add to the sixty centuries he scored in club cricket. He must be the one cricketer who can look back and be heartily thankful for a duck. He is a good friend who has given me full support in my activities as a selector and as manager of England in Australia in 1979–80.

The last thing I wanted to do as a cricketer was to be a waning star, hanging on to the last and, in the end, being told I was finished. I decided to retire from cricket in 1960. One of my most cherished performances was to end my career with 5 Glamorgan wickets for 27 on the sad occasion when I said farewell to The Oval as a player. Nothing hung on the result, and only an hour's play was necessary on the third morning to complete Surrey's victory by an innings and 67 runs. As Surrey captain, I was pleased to end with an impressive team performance at a time when the club was in the process of rebuilding. So the curtain fell on my playing days – a quiet farewell without trumpets sounding, during an ordinary match in front of a few scattered spectators. Just, in fact, how I would have wanted it, for I am sure I would have been too choked inside to have endured a sentimental send-off on a big occasion. The fifteen seasons and four winters abroad, which produced 1924 wickets, 236 of them for England, seem to have passed by in a nostalgic flash. But my cricketing life was always a dream come true, and I have a grateful heart.

7

The Duke and the Ex-Pro

Strange though it may seem, one of my first duties as assistant manager to the late Duke of Norfolk when he managed the MCC side to Australia in 1962–63 was to persuade him to go into the England dressing room. I quickly found that the Premier Duke and Earl Marshal of England was as shy as an impressionable boy in the presence of cricketers of the standing of Ted Dexter, Colin Cowdrey, Ken Barrington, Fred Trueman, Brian Statham and Co. As a moderate club cricketer himself, he felt he had but a humble place in the game's hierarchy and was not entitled to rub shoulders with the cream of England in their own sanctum. I told him that as manager he not only had the right to enter the team's dressing room but was expected to do so.

Frankly, I had expected that, if there were any diffidence, it would come from the players, and so far as I was concerned it was only natural there should be some speculation on the managerial alliance of a duke and an ex-professional. As soon as I got to know the Duke I discovered that he was the last to pull rank. Indeed, with our mutual passion for cricket, we got on famously and formed a lasting friendship. The Duke was easy to get on with and behaved naturally, without a hint of formality. There was never any social barrier between him and the players, who at first had not known what to expect. But on a tour the party should be as one, and the Duke travelled in the same compartments and shared the same dinner tables like any other manager.

In 1962 the winds of change were positively howling through the corridors of Lord's. An all-amateur committee under the chairmanship of the Duke had abolished the amateur status and, for the first time, an ex-professional was serving in a managerial capacity with an overseas MCC side to Australia (MCC were still responsible for tours at the time). My appointment as assistant manager came only two years after I had ended my playing career and in my first year as a Test selector.

At the time of my appointment there was no inkling that the Duke would be manager, and the captaincy was a keenly contested race between Ted Dexter and the Rev. David Sheppard, now the Anglican Bishop of Liverpool. Hot on their heels was Colin Cowdrey. Eventually Dexter made it, with Cowdrey as vice-captain.

Not for the first time MCC had difficulty in finding a managerial candidate with the right credentials and the time to spare. After several fruitless meetings the late Walter Robins, a mercurial character and chairman of the Test Selection Committee, was chatting with the Duke by the fireplace in the committee room at Lord's. Robins, never short of ideas, suddenly turned to the Duke and out of the blue sprang the question, 'Why don't you do it, Bernard?' The Duke, taken aback, promised to talk the question over with the Duchess that evening. She lent her enthusiastic support, and the next morning the Duke reported that he was available. MCC accepted their distinguished volunteer with alacrity and presented the new manager to an astonished press box assembled to report the Gentlemen *v.* Players match.

I was as surprised as any by the news, and as it closely affected me I hastened to find *Burke's Peerage, Baronetage and Knightage* and began to read:

The 16th. Duke of Norfolk (Sir Bernard Marmaduke Fitzalan-Howard, K.G., P.C., G.C.V.O., G.B.E., T.D.), Earl of Arundel, Surrey and Norfolk, Baron Fitz Alan, Clun, Oswaldestre and Maltravers and Baron Herries of Terregles in the Peerage of Scotland, Earl Marshal and Hereditary Marshal of England, Premier Duke and Earl, Lord Lieutenant of Sussex, D.L., J.P. and C.C., Sussex, Mayor of Arundel, Steward of Jockey Club, President Turf Board, H.M's representative at Ascot, Master Holderness Foxhounds (Westside). . . .

At this point I stopped reading. It was enough to take in for one day.

In the speculation surrounding the Duke's appointment there were understandably conflicting views. Some were of the opinion that he would be a mere figurehead, a joke to fair-dinkum Aussies, and that I would end the tour as an overworked wreck. Even protocol came into it. How should he be addressed? There was a wide option, from 'Your Grace' to plain 'Bernard' by the privileged few. The Aussies were, I read, expected to call him 'Dook'. As it was the players called him 'Sir'. All the pre-tour hullabaloo proved to be so much hot air simply because he was natural, considerate and had the ability to put the most nervous at ease. His attitude conquered the friendly and curious Aussies. They took to him in a big way. As the tour progressed I had many a smile at the fears expressed to me by those who were about to meet him for the first time. They did not know the Duke. He was the last to stand on ceremony.

I have to admit, however, that in certain aspects he was a very unusual manager, not to say unique. My brief was to look after the cricketing side of the tour. The Duke's responsibilities covered the general organization, day-to-day management, liaising with the home authorities and officials, flying the flag at the various functions and so on. Soon after his appointment I met the Duke at a tour meeting held at Lord's. Various members of the MCC committees attended. After some discussions I innocently asked whose duty it was to look after the accounts. In those days there were no financial guarantees and an important part of the manager's job was to look after the financial side. Books had to be kept and gate receipts checked. Previously it had been customary to have a co-manager who did nothing else; in fact he was dubbed 'the Treasurer'.

A slightly awkward pause followed my question. Eventually one of the members turned to the Duke and said, 'Bernard, of course you'll do that.' The Duke nodded and nothing further was said on the matter. But it was to prove an overoptimistic division of labour so far as I was concerned. It soon became evident that the Duke had a cavalier attitude towards a chequebook; in addition he was apt to leave the team hotel without cash in his pockets.

When we arrived at Perth to open the tour I thought it would be a good idea to take advantage of the excellent net practice pitches – probably the best in the country. Accordingly I suggested to the Duke that he should take only twelve players for the first two-day fixture at Kalgoorlie, a gold mining town 375 miles from Perth, while the rest of the party remained with me for two net sessions a day. The Duke agreed and, before he left, asked me what he had to do. 'All you have to do is pay the hotel bill by cheque, and put the date, the amount and the name of the hotel on the stub,' I explained. 'Don't concern yourself with the cricket side. The captain will do that', I added.

On his return to Perth I asked him to return the chequebook and how much the hotel bill had been. He had only a vague idea of the amount, and across the stub he had scrawled the one word – 'Kalgoorlie', no figure, no date and nothing to identify the hotel. I had to write to the hotel and ask for a receipt in order to reconcile the bank statement. I realized the Duke had probably not been used to such mundane things, so I thought it prudent not to entrust him with the chequebook again. The financial side of the business was, I fear, not his strong suit, and I had to take over the accounts.

As the Duke had not toured before he had to be shown the ropes, introduced to national and local figures, and taken to and from the various functions. In those times, unlike the present, tours were longer and there were functions that the team were expected to attend, which they did. All sorts of people and organizations, wanting to meet the Duke, tried to contact him through me, and, as the leading lay Roman Catholic of England, he was much sought-after by the Catholics in every state. The telephone scarcely stopped ringing, correspondence mounted, and the volume of work increased to such an extent that I was in constant danger of neglecting my principal job of supervising the cricketing side of the tour. As I was determined that should not happen I was out of bed at 6 a.m. every morning to keep the accounts and other details up to date.

I had a wry smile at the end of the tour when I read the inevitable criticism that I should have devoted more time to the actual cricket and less to other chores. E. W. Swanton, writing in the *Daily Telegraph*, regretted that I had not contributed quite as much as might have been expected as an observer of the players and a teacher in the nets because of 'other calls' on my time, 'particularly in the way of accounts'. He added: 'The Assistant Manager has thrown himself into the financial aspect with much energy and, if he may not have saved the MCC all that many runs, he has gained them a lot of Australian pounds.' If only the critics had better understood my workload they might have held back. As it was,

86

Ted Dexter, the captain, had no complaints – and it was his opinion that counted most.

Kalgoorlie gave the Duke an early taste of life away from the big cities. The small country towns and cosmopolitan Sydney might have been on different continents. From previous visits I knew Kalgoorlie to be an open, friendly town, but in the sixties the hotel, with its corrugated-iron roof and communal wash house, was not exactly four-star living. Apparently it was quite a sight to see the Duke, a towel casually thrown over his shoulder, queueing up services-style for a shave. He took it in his stride, but there was one up-country town where he was far from amused. The heat was intense, the flies a constant vexation, dust flew in clouds, and, it should be added, the locals did everything to please. At the end of the long day the Duke, who had been looking forward to soaking in a hot bath and an early night, was pressed into attending a reception at which he was to be offered a special present. He could hardly refuse, and we all were taken to a destination about 20 miles away. Speeches followed and, with much ceremony and growing hilarity among the locals, the presentation was made. It consisted of an empty jar said to contain 'our fresh air'. The Duke tried his best to raise a smile. Perhaps he was too weary to succeed. If ever there was a joke which sensationally misfired, this had to be it.

The Duke did not always appreciate Freddie Trueman's sense of humour. In the early days of the tour David Sheppard's reactions, rusty after several years' absence from first-class cricket – he was the first ordained priest to play Test cricket – caused him to drop catches. After one such mishap Trueman, the bowler victim, observed to all and sundry, 'If the reverend gentleman cannot put his hands together, what ruddy hope is there for the rest of us?'

Whatever the reason, at the end of the tour Trueman, Ray Illingworth and Barry Knight received only £50 each of their bonus money – a cut of 50 per cent. I knew nothing of the Duke's decision until afterwards. Sir William Worsley, then chairman of Yorkshire, tried to arrange a personal hearing with the Duke, without success. Illingworth must be the only future England captain to have been 'fined'.

As for David Sheppard, his prayers for a safe pair of hands seemed at last to have been answered when Bill Lawry hooked

Barry Knight high to long leg where Sheppard held the ball and, with delighted relief, tossed it high into the air. Alas for David, he had not heard the umpire's cry of 'No ball' and as a result of his exuberant reaction Lawry and Bobby Simpson stole a second run.

Another incident involving Sheppard occurred in a Test at Edgbaston in 1957. Alf Valentine, the West Indies slow bowler, was run out by Sheppard while attempting a short run. When he returned to the pavilion he was greeted by his 'calypso spin twin' Sonny Ramadhin with the words, 'You know what the good book says – thou shalt not steal! Don't you know who the fielder was?'

The Duke's position in the English turf endeared him to the racing-mad Aussies and he was in his element at the major meetings. Invariably I went racing with him, occasions which were a happy diversion from my other duties. While in Perth the Duke leased a horse named Grey Goose with the intention of entering him under his colours for the prestigious Melbourne Cup, the equivalent of our Derby, which brings the whole of Australia to a stop. To the undisguised satisfaction and financial gain of the entire MCC party, Grey Goose won a preliminary race, but, he flattered only to deceive, and dreams of glittering prizes vanished.

I learned from the Duke more about racing than my old Sunday School teacher would have wanted me to know. On the way to the Melbourne Cup I casually mentioned that, although I had lived all my life at Woking, only twelve miles from Ascot and Epsom, I had never been to Ascot or the Derby. 'Oh, we'll have to put that right,' he declared. As he had not made a note of his promise I did not expect anything to come of it.

Next April, some few months later, Eric and I were invited to stay at Arundel Castle. We were having tea with the Duke, and he suddenly said, 'By the way, you want to go to Ascot, don't you? I'll send you the tickets.' Nothing further was said, and as the time for Ascot drew nearer and no tickets had arrived I thought he must have forgotten. But, sure enough, a week before the meeting tickets for the Royal Enclosure, car park and meals, arrived by post. Indeed, every year until his death in 1975 the tickets, duly arrived.

A promise was a promise with the Duke. During the Test at Melbourne he asked to be taken back to the team's hotel a few minutes before the close of play. I thought he must have an important engagement in his suite to drag him from the cricket and asked him why he didn't stay until the end. 'As a matter of fact,' he replied, 'I promised to be back by six o'clock to have a couple of drinks with the chap who looks after my room at the hotel.'

As befitted the organizer of great national occasions and parades, including the coronation, the Duke made almost a fetish of being on time. He was punctual not only to the minute but to the second. When arranging for me, in my capacity as volunteer chauffeur, to pick him up by car, he would nominate the time and add, 'Right, we'll synchronize our watches.'

The almost military precision of his time-keeping was to my liking as I pride myself on being equally punctilious. Car parking was my major headache, and I soon became adept in the art of driving round the block to time my arrival with the Duke's appearance. Never was he other than dead on time, emerging from the hotel door and striding across the pavement. I often wished some of the players could have been half as considerate.

In November the Duke had to return to England for a month on a hush-hush mission, which turned out to be advanced high-level discussions about the state funeral for Sir Winston Churchill. When the Duke came back to Australia he sat with me and talked of the arrangements being made for the sad but inevitably forthcoming event. He told me that he had had a slight disagreement with Dr Ramsey, then Archbishop of Canterbury, about one aspect of the event. 'So I said to him' – and here the Duke turned to me with a smile – 'Who's running this show? You or me?'

The Duke had a very even temper. Tradition was the cornerstone of his life, and traditional beliefs strongly coloured his attitudes towards the playing and conduct of the game. The slightest departure from the highest standards not so much angered but pained him. He was hopeful that with two enterprising captains in Richie Benaud and Ted Dexter the 1962–63 series would be memorable and exciting, and was acutely disappointed when it ended in stalemate, with the players being slow-handclapped off the field at Sydney in the final Test. Unfortunately, the pitch was very slow and the cricket singularly uninspiring. He was privately more than just disappointed.

The Duke travelled light – probably lighter than anyone in the party – with only two ordinary suitcases. He did not have a manservant and did his own packing and unpacking, which can be a boring chore on tour. Early on, being an old hand at the job, I offered to help him, but he politely declined. Every morning before breakfast I went to his room to go over the day's programme and, if he was still in the bath, I would sit on the bath stool while we talked.

He was a light sleeper and in the habit of taking sleeping pills to help him drop off. When he learned that Ken Barrington was also having difficulty sleeping, the Duke told him, 'If you can't sleep, give me a ring and I'll let you have one of my pills.' Barrington took due note and, during the New Zealand leg of the tour, when he was sharing a room with Ray Illingworth, he became desperate for sleep. So, as invited and with the encouragement of Illingworth, who was also being kept awake, Ken rang the Duke's room. It was 3 a.m., and one of the Duke's more restful nights. For once he was in deep slumber and the telephone bell rang for some time before he was aroused. Barrington explained that he could not get to sleep. 'Come up to my room and collect a pill,' the Duke said. Then, fighting what, for him, was an unusually powerful urge to close his eyes and drift into peaceful slumber, the Duke waited in vain for Barrington, who meanwhile had dropped off to sleep. The next morning, when Ken realized what he had done, he spent an uncomfortable breakfast expecting, at best, a rocket or, at worst, a summons to the Tower. Much to his relief, the Duke accepted it in good part; indeed, we all had a laugh together over the incident.

The Duke's daughters, Lady Jane, Lady Mary and Lady Ann, joined the MCC party in New Zealand and were immediately and irreverently dubbed the 'Norfolk Broads' by the players, to the private amusement of their father. As it was their first visit to that lovely and hospitable country, I helped to show them around. Afterwards, much to my surprised pleasure, they gave me a handsome wallet. When I told the Duke his response was, 'I'm pleased. It shows they think of other people, because I did not prompt them in any way to do this for you.'

After the tour Eric and I were invited for the first of several weekend visits to Arundel Castle. We also played for the Duke in some of his Sunday matches. The Duke and Duchess lived in a house in the grounds, but Eric and I stayed in the old castle. I was given what was once the Duke's bedroom – a huge room with an equally huge fireplace invitingly filled with logs hewn from the estate. 'Put a match to it if you feel cold,' I was told. The walls were plain and bare, and the wall separating me from Eric in the next room was three feet wide. To reach him by the communicating door was like walking down a passageway.

For breakfast, served on a hotplate, we joined the Duke and Duchess in their house. When the Sunday papers arrived – the whole range from the heavies to the pops – the Duke read them over the eggs and bacon. 'We always read the papers at breakfast,' he said.

We were treated as friends of the family. There was no side, no ceremony and no suggestion of a social barrier between us. We wandered freely around the castle and estate and watched the horses being trained. We mentioned that the son of a friend of our father had an ambition to be a jockey and to join a stable. To our surprise, the Duke replied, 'Well, if you recommend him, I'll take him.'

I never went to Arundel as guest or player without being awed by a sense of history. The very atmosphere is a breath of England, its rich past and the traditions of an ancient family. The cricket ground is without comparison; since the Duke's death, it is being maintained by the Duchess with the help of a trust formed by Colin Cowdrey and others. When touring teams go to Arundel they must stand breathless. On one side is the backdrop of the castle, and a short walk beyond the boundary lies a vivid patchwork panorama of the verdant Sussex fields. Two generations of Norfolks planned the cricket ground – originally decreeing that it should be as big as The Oval – and planted many of the encircling trees. Above all, I think they put into it their deep love of cricket – a game which had its roots in the countryside of Sussex and the Weald of Kent.

When I first played at Arundel the players changed in a marquee, but a modern pavilion has since been built. To blend with the setting, tiles were taken from old cottages on the estate. Appropriately, bar and dining room are 22 yards long, the length of a cricket pitch. The sheer grandeur and atmosphere of Arundel makes the ground unique, and it stands not only as a proud and dignified testimony to England, but in memory of a simple man born to high estate who loved cricket.

After the MCC tour the Duke wrote of me in words which I ask the indulgence of my readers to repeat: 'Apart from his efficiency and hard work, his devotion to the whole business was quite remarkable. The MCC can never be served better than it was by him.'

To me the Duke was a symbol of the enormous gift to cricket of the amateur spirit of service, by which I mean administrators who place themselves above vested interests and give their energies and time for no other reason than that they love the game. If cricket loses its integrity, money comes to mean everything and cricketers merely mercenaries, it will become just another organization in the world of sport run for the profit motive alone. Maybe such views are anachronistic to many, but there is too much of good and value in cricket for the true traditionalist to watch it drift and perish with complacency.

8

Greig, Botham and Boycott

When, in 1975, Tony Greig followed Mike Denness as captain of England, having been vice-captain in the West Indies in 1973–74 where he emerged as an impressive all-rounder, I suspected that I, as chairman, might have to exert a fair amount of control. Tact and moderation are not words that spring to mind at the mention of his name, and in his early days for England there were signals of concern from high places about his impulsive and occasionally overcombative attitude. *Wisden* noted his 'aggressive and embarrassing mannerisms' on Tony Lewis's tour of India and Pakistan in 1972–73, and in the West Indies 'the doubt caused by his explosiveness when the desire to succeed seemed to overwhelm his judgement.' *Wisden* went on: 'He was very good at creating pressure in others, but he was not always so good at controlling it in himself.'

There was the contentious incident in the first Test of the series at Port of Spain when he ran out Alvin Kallicharran as the batsman began to walk to the pavilion, apparently assuming play had ended for the day. In the strict letter of the law Greig could not be faulted for what was doubtless a spontaneous action; not being present and somewhat confused by the conflicting opinions of 'expert eyewitnesses', I kept an open mind. After a lengthy meeting between the West Indies Board of Control and the Test and County Cricket Board, peace was restored by England withdrawing their appeal, thus relieving the umpires of responsibility and allowing Kallicharran to continue his innings the next morning – a compromise, unsupportable by the laws of the game, but one which may have saved the series from disaster.

I stood by Greig when it would have been more comfortable for me to have taken a different stance, because malice never was the cause of his impulsiveness and I saw in him a dynamism which, if put to proper use, would be of inestimable value to England. I also thought that he was too intelligent not to learn as he went along. Two of his splendid qualities were his spirit and his determination. The tougher the situation the stronger his response and, added to his considerable ability and flair for the big occasion, a talent for leadership emerged. To me he seemed fully aware of his duty to preserve the best traditions of the game.

What I did not appreciate was the depth of his personal ambition. This was the impulsive, headstrong side of his nature. He found it hard to resist the showman in him at times and played to the gallery. In Australia under Denness in 1974–75 he began to point to the pavilion when an opponent was dismissed. At Perth he made the mistake of signalling a 4 when he hit Dennis Lillee to the boundary. Lillee, who was nearing the end of his spell, suddenly found new strength. But the moment that I told him to cut out the provocative gestures he did so, which showed he could take orders – the prerequisite to giving them.

At selection meetings Greig was a firm debater and cooperative, but Len Hutton in *Fifty Years of Cricket* reveals that he was less impressed, and soon realized he had made a mistake in supporting his selection as captain. Hutton, the introvert, soft-speaking Yorkshireman, and Greig, the self-confident extrovert, were the classic opposites. Greig was direct and positive in his opinion, and once a decision was made there was no going back. In some ways his influence over his teams reminded me of Stuart Surridge – a high recommendation – and if he made a mistake he accepted responsibility without a quibble. There was nothing half-baked about anything he attempted; in fact he could have profited from an occasional second thought.

Tactically he did not always take the course I would have expected of an experienced captain, but he was entitled to use his own methods and was not guilty of serious lapses of judgement. At all times he was prepared to listen and I found it easy to discuss things with him. Much of his exuberant personality rubbed off on England's team and was reflected in brilliant fielding standards, which Mike Brearley gratefully inherited and maintained. Despite some gaffes – the promise to make Clive Lloyd's 1976 West Indies 'grovel' was imprudent, to say the least; I'm sure it was a word which just slipped out – Greig was a charismatic figure with good relationships with the public and media. In India, where South Africans can face an icy reception, he was readily accepted, and the very strength of his personality swamped Bishen Singh Bedi, his opposite number, who had a remarkable following. With Greig in the driving seat there was every reason for the growing feeling that England were on course as a major Test power.

My sense of letdown, shared, I am sure, by millions of avid followers and others with merely a soft spot for cricket, went deep when Greig was exposed while captain of England as an active agent in Kerry Packer's plan to take over international cricket and its leading players. It was particularly sickening to know that the great sentimental occasion and gathering of former Test players at the Melbourne Centenary Test in 1977 was used for the secret meetings. Clearly those involved cared little for the past or the present of cricket. The objective was a takeover of the game on behalf of Packer's commercial television network. The fact that the Australian Broadcasting Commission held the existing contract was brushed aside. The core of the dispute was not extra cash for 'downtrodden cricketers', but a threat to the power of the properly constituted authorities who have a responsibility for the welfare of the game at every level. The Test match is but the tip of the structure of cricket at large. The attack on authority disturbed me, and Billy Griffith, then president of MCC, a former MCC secretary and Test player, was right to declare that it would be an absolute disaster for the image to be changed simply to suit television. Greig and Co. shrewdly concentrated on the cash angle for the top players, and persuaded many to believe cricketers were hard done by. He saw himself in the vanguard of a crusade.

As an old pro and an administrator I am completely in favour of rewarding players properly. But the game has to remain solvent and the players worth their pay. I am also implacably against the cheapening of standards for the sake of offering artificial entertainment and turning a few players into an elite at the expense of the rest. There can be no substitute for genuine Test cricket with genuinely selected teams. Bill O'Reilly, the great Australian leg-break bowler, summed up my feelings when he reported a Packer match between Australia and a World XI for the *Sunday Times*. He wrote:

I detested playing in these games, which were arranged under the heading of 'special purpose'. I shall never forget one in which the 1936–7 Australian team returning from South Africa met the Rest of Australia, captained by Bradman, at Sydney in a benefit match for three old-timer Australian representatives. Making an early impression on the opposition I had three wickets for eight runs before Bradman, who had dropped himself down for the occasion, made his way to the wicket. My captain, Victor Richardson, came to me to say 'Tiger, my friend, I have been longing to see you meet up with "little boy" when your blood was up and all cylinders working. Here it is and I must take you off. If you happen to get this bloke out before the luncheon adjournment, this benefit match might as well fold up.' My introduction to Bradman came when his score was 50 and he was on his way to 212. Please do not mention such games to me.

Once Greig was sold on a Packer deal he threw all his boundless energies into his new cause and, if money means everything and any means are justified by the end, he has no room for regret. He says he lost many acquaintances but few friends, and every man has to make his own decisions. I for one could never have taken the course that he did, and a story told by Bob Willis throws some light on Tony's philosophies. In his role of a Packer recruiting agent, Greig approached Willis, who said he doubted if he could be motivated by contrived fixtures between teams from Australia, the West Indies and the so-called Rest of the World.

'The money will be the motivation,' replied Greig.

Fortunately, Willis, Geoff Boycott, Ian Botham, David Gower and others, including umpire Dickie Bird, saw it in a different light and were not lured away from the traditional pastures for the lush Packer meadows.

On the day before the news of the setting-up of World Series Cricket became public in April 1977 I went to Hove to discuss with Greig the MCC team to play the Australians at Lord's, a traditional fixture giving the selectors scope to test out a few fringe players. As the reigning England captain he was asked to name any of the younger players he considered worth a trial. We chatted amiably for some time without the slightest hint from him that anything dramatic was in the wind or that I was wasting my time talking to him. For all I knew, some of the names we mentioned were on Greig's shopping list. Obviously Greig would argue that he was sworn to secrecy, but he could have found an excuse to avoid our little charade. I wonder if Tony gave a thought to the chairman who had stood up for him and was more than a little responsible for his rise to the Test captaincy. In due course I was interested to read Greig's claim that he 'could not trust Lord's.' Trust must always be double-edged.

Packer, with no other responsibilities than to his own organiz-ation, was able to make the propaganda running; I daresay if the affair was rerun the International Cricket Conference would throw aside their velvet gloves. One aspect to amaze me was the emerg-ence of self-opinionated pundits eager for their say, although it was clear they did not understand what was at stake for cricket. Spare me 'instant' authority and the publicity-seeking MP.

After the initial bombshell the immediate concern of the selectors was the possibility of having to decide whether or not Greig and his fellow defectors should be available for selection in the coming series with Australia. My first reaction was to take them off the list, and if it had been my decision alone that would definitely have remained the case. But we were given clear directions, and a difficult moral issue was taken out of our hands. The Cricket Council, however, stripped Greig of the captaincy on the grounds that 'his action has inevitably impaired the trust which existed between the cricket authorities and the captain of the England side.' Freddie Brown, chairman of the Council, added, 'The captaincy of the England side involves close liaison with the selectors in the management, selection and development of England's players of the future, and clearly Greig is unlikely to be able to do this as his stated intention is to be contracted elsewhere during the next three years.'

Greig, having burned his boats, must have expected the sack. I was much relieved by the Council's action and, to judge from the volume of letters I received, not to mention those sent to the authorities and the newspapers, there could be little doubt it was supported by the vast majority of genuine cricket lovers. A few pro-Greig letters reached me, but there was no logical way he could continue as captain.

Our instructions from the Test and County Cricket Board were to pick the England team on merit. Accordingly, Greig, Derek Underwood and Alan Knott were chosen and played their full part in the defeat of Greg Chappell's Australia. Mike Brearley led a united team, and it has to be said Greig was totally unabashed and as cheerful as ever, and put 100 per cent into his play. But it went against the grain to help to pick Packer men, although I realized the financial temptations put in their way. Money not so much talks in modern sport as yells at the top of its voice.

Like the rest of us, Australia's manager, Len Maddocks, a member of Australia's Board and a former Test wicketkeeper, was in blissful ignorance of the undercover activities of the majority of his players when his team arrived in London. To his shocked surprise, no fewer than thirteen of his seventeen players had joined the rebel ranks and, as it was patently obvious that it was impossible and illogical to send for replacements at that late stage, the brutal alternative to soldiering on and making the best of a near intolerable situation was the cancellation of the tour and the Test series. As the public had bought tickets in advance and the Packer rebels had not at that point gone beyond announcing their intentions, the sensible decision was to carry on. Nevertheless, the visiting manager in particular was placed in a very difficult position, and he deserved the highest praise for seeing it through to the bitter end without a major upheaval.

Australia's scars ran deep, and when Kim Hughes tearfully resigned the Test captaincy in 1985, following what he called 'the constant speculation, criticism and innuendos by former players', Peter McFarline, the noted Melbourne cricket writer, made this telling comment: 'If anything, Hughes has been the latest victim of the terrible animosities that arose during the Packer rebellion from 1977–79. There may be rejoicings in the household of his most vitriolic critics, Dennis Lillee, Rod Marsh and Ian Chappell, today, but I hope not.' Hughes, of course, was not a Packer man.

Personally I wondered about the effect of having Greig and the other defectors with their Packer commitments in the dressing room, but I kept my thoughts to myself in that difficult time, and, praise be, the issues which were splitting the game were not to be found in the England side. It might well have been a different story without the calm moderation of skipper Brearley, the native tolerance of cricketers, and the fact that the results were right from England's point of view. If there were any ill feelings they were successfully hidden, which was a remarkable fact in itself considering the bitterness and emotions aroused by the contro-versy. Since Mike Brearley advocated compromise and never said anything provocative, it was all the more difficult to understand why he should later be subjected to so much abuse in Australia. But that was all forgotten in the eagerness to 'promote' a series in the new packaged commercial style. The animosity came from the public whipped up by the media, and not from the Australian cricketing authorities.

At the time of the upheaval I had many distressing letters from old and respected friends in Australia who were dismayed and bewildered by events. One of the several side effects to sadden me at home were the resignations of Billy Griffith and George Cox from the Sussex County Committee after the club reappointed Greig captain. Greig was soon to settle permanently in Australia, and it was incomprehensible to me that two stalwarts of vast experience, completely loyal to Sussex and with so much to offer, should feel obliged to leave. How could Sussex – as later with Yorkshire on a far larger scale – afford to dispense with servants of such rare quality? The game is much poorer for such decisions.

In fairness, I could not fault Greig so far as his playing activities were concerned during that traumatic series, and I remain grateful to him for his eager support during his days with England. In his eighteen months as captain England's fortunes took an upward turn, and Mike Brearley inherited a side with a morale still high and comparatively undamaged by the defections. The other side of Greig, however, was not for me – a view, I am sure, shared by the overwhelming majority of my contemporaries and present gener-ations. I think Tony became overconfident, not the least because of his belief that he could manipulate the media. Of course, he had considerable success in that direction, and still has, and I was told that, after his well-publicized pro-Packer press conference at Hove just after the story of World Series Cricket had broken, he was greatly surprised to find he had not carried the leading cricket writers with him.

As I have said, England were singularly fortunate to have Mike Brearley ready to step in and take charge in a crisis, and the Australian fast bowler, Rodney Hogg, was to make a very perceptive remark. 'I reckon Brearley has got a degree in people,' he said – a neat summing-up of Brearley's scholastic achievements and the sympathetic way in which he handled players. It was with typical consideration that Brearley gave the selectors (Ken Barrington, Charlie Elliott, Brian Close and myself) long warning that he would not be able to go to the West Indies in the winter of 1980–81. We agreed that the time for change should be at the start rather than at the end of the home series with the West Indies in 1980. No useful purpose would have been served by continuing with Brearley and depriving his successor of an entire season's experience. The new captain would consequently not be in the difficult position of going to the West Indies as an inexperienced first-time leader. A tour is hard enough without further responsibilities and complications. Had Brearley been available no change would have been contemplated. There was no secret that the out-going captain, among other knowledgeable critics, favoured Ian Botham, who, as well as being an indispensable all-rounder, exuded confidence and zest, and, what is more, wanted the job – an important qualification.

History unfortunately records that Botham was not a success, but two facts have to be considered. That he was pleased and excited at a new challenge almost goes without saying, and the choice was very limited. Of the names we considered we were not satisfied that Somerset's Brian Rose was quite good enough – and Tests with the West Indies were no place as trial grounds. Keith Fletcher was considered as was Roger Knight, a splendid captain of Surrey, who, in our minds had not progressed beyond county cricket.

As the West Indies provided the immediate opposition in successive home and away series – it seemed a great pity for both countries that the series could not have been better spaced – it was imperative to field the strongest possible side and, looking at the players who appeared to be certain choices, the eye fell temptingly on the young lion Botham as captain. His appointment was far from a snap decision. Part of the duties of selectors is to plan and build for the future and Botham had been marked down as a potential captain. He had already served on the selection committee in Australia. For all that, when the time came we were very conscious of the magnitude of his task, particularly as he had not captained his county. But he was not the first player to be asked to do this. Len Hutton and Peter May are prime examples – neither was captain of his county when appointed captain of England.

It was fairly predictable that having been so often berated for an alleged bias for the senior players and not giving youth a chance, the selectors should be told that Botham was too young, too raw and untried. When it comes to considerations of age I am strictly neutral. Every case is different and my prejudice is for the best available, irrespective of birthdays. While experience can be invaluable, youth as such should not be a barrier to captaincy. Botham, after all, had played in twenty-five Test matches with an assurance and authority far beyond his twenty-four years. Some critics applauded our choice, but when it did not work out the selectors were criticized not only for the original appointment but for the fact that Ian's form slumped dramatically while he was captain. While I concede that his inexperience as a captain began to show when the situation soured, the problems mounted and some critics went over the top. I am not convinced his form deserted him because he was captain. Captaincy did not affect the form of Bradman, Hassett, Hutton, Benaud, May, Sobers and Border, to name a few. The cares of captaincy is an old cliché which has too broad a meaning, and given more normal circumstances I think Ian has the type of personality that can actually thrive on responsibility.

The selectors also came under fire for a decision to make his appointment match by match in 1981. The reason was his personal form. Faced with the fact that our principal all-rounder was not producing results, it would have been unrealistic to have guaranteed him a place over a six-match series. It was stretching credulity to the limit for critics to say he was not performing with bat and ball regularly because he was uncertain whether he would still be captain in the next Test. What sort of a man did they think Botham was? No captain has a divine right to be selected for a whole series, although at times it might be a wise course of action. If they read the game's history those critics would find many precedents for the practice. Even Don Bradman was selected match by match, an arrangement which did not seem to affect his run output! Peter

May, too, was selected for one match when he was first made captain.

Also, it should not be overlooked that Botham was given the captaincy in all three Prudential Trophy single-innings internationals (which England disappointingly lost) as a lead-in to the Cornhill Test series. At the time of his appointment the possibility of a decline in his performance was taken into consideration, but if it did happen, we hoped that it would merely be a temporary problem and disappear the more accustomed he became to the job. We took into account Ian's attitude and felt he was the last person to be intimidated by the odds against him. But we never visualized a situation in which his form would fade so emphatically. Talk of caging a lion by making him captain must have produced many a smile from many former successful captains. In 1980 Ian was not as fit as he might have been. He was a bit overweight and had a niggle in his back, which probably handicapped his bowling to a degree.

Only Ian can say how much he was affected by his back complaint. Many players in my day played on with aches and pains and still maintained their level of performance. Presumably he considered himself fit enough to play for he never said he was not. In the end it is the player who knows whether he can play effectively. In five Tests he bowled only 131 overs, admittedly more than any other English bowler, but that must be compared with 230.5 by Michael Holding, 212.4 by Joel Garner and 172.3 by Malcolm Marshall. If Ian looks at his figures for the summer of 1980 – 224 overs for Somerset in the County Championship – I am sure he would be honest enough to recognize he did not bowl enough and that fact had a direct bearing on his performance. In contrast, he did a lot of bowling for Somerset immediately before the 1981 Test at Headingley, which I am sure helped him to rediscover his rhythm, swing and nip off the pitch in the Test itself. The extra work was exactly what he needed; there is no substitute.

Ian was desperately unlucky in the West Indies and I am with manager, Alan Smith, who said he did better than well to keep the side together in face of unnatural adversities. The misfortunes to descend on him would have stretched the character of a Brearley. There was the numbing blow of Kenny Barrington's sudden death, and the militancy of the Guyana Government when Robin Jackman replaced Bob Willis, who had to return home with injury almost by return flight. Ian thus tragically lost both a much loved assistant manager, who was a friend, confessor, adviser and staunch ally of every player, and his vice-captain and strike bowler, and ran headlong into a political row over which he had no control and in which he was the innocent victim.

Back home against the Australians in 1981 he was hurt by the pointed silence of MCC members when he returned to the pavilion after collecting his second duck in the Lord's Test. Presumably the mood of the members was a protest at the shot which had caused his downfall rather than against Botham himself. Ian was understandably also incensed by taunts and abuse directed by a mindless few against his family. After Ian himself and his immediate family, I doubt if his disappointments were more keenly felt than by the selectors, who had invested in his character and intelligence. We knew what his failures meant to him; we sympathized; we knew he had it in him to achieve our highest hopes; but we saw a dream fading and our plans falling apart. It was as worrying to us as it was to him.

Ian's position had reached crisis point during the Lord's Test. How quickly the fates decreed his nadir should be followed by the summit of his fortunes! As Ian's form lurched downwards and England finished one down with four Tests to go, a change of leadership became a stark necessity, not the least reason being to spare him further embarrassment. Mike Brearley was in our contingency plans, and he appeared to the selectors as the one captain with a proven record for a short-term rescue operation and – what was absolutely vital – with an understanding of Botham to spark him into life as the team's essential all-rounder. Botham had to play his full part if the series was to be salvaged and the Ashes retained. One important ingredient in the Brearley-Botham association was Botham's respect for Brearley.

Selectors in the natural order of things are the anvil for the hammer of every critic, and I have no complaints, but there are occasions when they are human enough to pause for self-congratulations when they get it right – even if no one else notices! I suggest we did get it right in 1981 by standing fast, refusing to panic, and making a cool assessment of a heated situation. Whatever mistakes we made, we could not be held responsible for the dropped catches which were the direct cause of England's defeat in the First Test at Trent Bridge. The restored partnership of Brearley and Botham, to be seen as conductor and virtuoso, proved to be exactly right. I doubt if there would have been an overloud chorus of protest if Botham had been dropped after his low point at Lord's; in fact many critics were saying he should have been left out. We could have lost faith in him and dropped him, but without exception the selectors believed in his ability and believed that he would resurface as a star before the series ended. Naturally there was regret that he had to go as captain.

Unfortunately Botham complained in his book *Ian Botham: The Incredible Tests 1981** that I had let him down and spoiled an amiable parting — surely not a parting but a redeployment of resources from which he richly benefited — by revealing that he was sacked as captain. When I saw Ian to tell him that the selectors had decided to replace him, he preempted my words by saying he had decided to resign the captaincy and added he would feel better if he announced that he had resigned. I replied, 'By all means, if that's the way you want it. You say it that way.' Which he did.

At a press conference following the match I was put on the spot with the unequivocal question: were you going to drop him from the captaincy? The fact was that we had decided to replace Ian and if I had said no it would have been a direct lie. As everyone present seemed to know the true answer or was capable of the intelligent guess, I could not see any advantage being gained in telling even a white lie (which I am sure would not have been accepted), evasion (not my style) or remaining silent (tantamount to a tacit admission). Had I not been pressed for an answer I would have kept quiet, and I naturally regret Ian felt badly about it, but the truth was bound to come out sooner or later. A far more important fact was the selectors standing four-square behind him and keeping him in the team when it would not have created a sensation if he had been left out of the next Test.

Success often hangs by a thread. There would have been no celebrations and no legendary deeds by Botham if he had been discarded; nor if Bob Willis, who took 8 for 43, the best figures ever by any bowler in a Test at Headingley, had missed the match

*Pelham, 1981.

which turned the tide so sensationally for England. He was not in the original twelve selected. Our information at the selection meeting on Friday, 10 July, was that Willis had a virus and because of it was not playing for his county. Therefore his fitness for the Test, starting on the following Thursday, was in serious doubt. By a happy coincidence Warwickshire were playing at The Oval over the weekend. As the team was not to be announced until the Sunday, I saw Willis at the Surrey ground. He was surprised when I told him he had not been considered for the Test on the grounds that he was unfit and particularly as he was not playing in the current match. He assured me he was resting from the county fixture and would be fit for England. Agreeably surprised, I rang Mike Brearley and the other selectors, who agreed that if Bob was fit he would play. I told Bob, 'If you play tomorrow in the Sunday League and bowl your eight overs straight off and show you are fit, you will be at Leeds on Thursday.' Bob duly played. Actually he bowled seven overs with 2 for 17, but that and his assurance were good enough for me, and I scrubbed out the name of a bowler, who fortunately had not been told of his selection, and substituted Willis.

Without Bob's inspired bowling of 15.1 overs on the last morning of the Headingley Test, England, astonishing winners by 18 runs after odds of 500 to 1 had been offered against them at the end of the third day, would have gone two down in the series. And without Botham's unforgettable 149 not out the position would not have been set up for Willis to complete *one of* if not *the* most spectacular comebacks in the long history of international cricket. Yet if the selectors had lost patience with Botham or not followed up the reports on Willis, neither would have played!

There was a near parallel to Bob's case when Richard Ellison was advised by physiotherapist Bernard Thomas not to risk playing in the Edgbaston Test in 1985, the famous occasion when the Kent bowler wrote himself into the record books and won the Man of the Match award with 10 wickets for 104 in the defeat of Australia by an innings and 118 runs. Richard had a chest virus and was taking antibiotics, and it says much for his spirit that he shrugged off sound advice in his determination to play. The importance of his contribution was reflected in his award despite David Gower's

215, an achievement which normally would have meant automatic selection.

The difference with Willis, of course, was that Ellison was selected for the Test in the face of an almost hysterical demand by some critics for Gloucestershire's David Lawrence, whose performances put him in the front rank of current speed bowlers. We did not doubt David's pace, only his accuracy and inexperience at that stage of his career. We also anticipated the ball would swing at Edgbaston, and argued that good, controlled swing, of which Ellison was as fine an exponent as any in the country, would be more effective than out-and-out pace. Moreover, Ellison has the ability to swing an old ball. Ironically, Allan Border had said after the previous Test at Old Trafford that England were a good side lacking a strike bowler. The emergence of Ellison after a lengthy lay-off with injury must have come as an unwelcome surprise to Border. And, if I may be allowed to say so on behalf of Peter May and his team of selectors, it was not a bad choice either.

Only selectors, past and present, who have agonized over team problems can appreciate the overwhelming relief and satisfaction when all the parts slot into a winning pattern as it did in 1981. It was all the more satisfying because I feel we made the best use of frugal resources. To watch Botham's Olympian batting, the devastating spells of bowling by Willis and Botham, to appreciate Brearley gently but firmly coaxing miracles from his players, and finally Alan Knott justifying our reluctant decision to sacrifice the admirable Bob Taylor in the cause of strengthening the batting, made all the hard work, frustration and worry no more important than a puff of wind in high summer.

Selectors soon learn the wisdom of patience and to expect no more of a player than to give his best at all times. They cannot demand more, but at Headingley, Edgbaston and Old Trafford in that golden summer which began so unpromisingly we were given everything – and much more. What might have been a disastrous flop suddenly became a glittering triumph, enthralling the nation, and refocusing attention on the game to the extent that Botham was elected BBC's Sportsman of the Year, in preference to the record-breaking Sebastian Coe. To beat the Australians at any time is an achievement, and the way it was done in 1981 could not have made my last year as chairman more memorable or satisfying.

When Botham was scoring his century at Old Trafford in the Fifth Test my mind flickered back to a comment in an Australian newspaper in which an eminent bowler wrote that Ian couldn't bat his way out of a paper bag. The day after Botham's achievement John Woodcock's respected opinion in *The Times*, which gave half its front page to the innings, was that his century at Old Trafford was the most brilliant of its kind of all time. I would put it this way: there can never have been a more brilliant innings. Those who were privileged to see Botham at Headingley and Old Trafford will surely never forget the experience, and young men will be proud to tell their grandchildren they were there.

Ian, at his best, is a jewel; he has the effect of exhilarating and quickening the pulse more than any other contemporary batsman with the exception of his great friend Viv Richards. He makes the shrewdest judges stretch their imaginations to find comparable talent, and has the same magical touch as Keith Miller – the ability to do something positive and exciting as batsman, bowler and fielder. He is the one latter-day Jessop who would, at his peak, be certain to find a place in the best England XI during my time both as player and selector.

Brearley, not one to go overboard with hasty words, had this to say: 'Great is not a word to be used lightly. Great can be applied to Botham as it has been to Dr W.G. Grace.' Curiously, until 1981 many Australians seriously underrated Ian, perhaps because he did not do much in Melbourne grade cricket when he was there on a Whitbread scholarship. One of his early coaches at Lord's assured me that Ian had possibilities with the bat but none with the ball. Kim Hughes, Australia's captain in that historic series, was left to say, 'Anyone who tries to tame Botham, or forces him to play in any other way, deserves to be lynched.'

Botham's several major assets include an unusual physical strength and a willingness to take on the opposition and prove he is the better man. Willis had much of the same fierce resolve to be the best the moment he stepped on the field for England. 'A light seems to burn within him,' as his father Ted once wrote in *The Cricketer International*. I have to admit Botham's full-blooded approach to life added to my grey hairs when I was chairman. When he resumed his soccer career for Scunthorpe United between tours and the cricket season, I had nightmares of a 'Compton knee' or of England's irreplaceable all-rounder being stretchered off. He also lapped Silverstone at 140 m.p.h., took up solo flying, and turned down £10,000 to shave off his beard when Gillette sponsored the sixty-over competition – a sum which a goodly number of players do not make in their whole career.

To expect conformity from Ian would be to expect mercury to stay still in a test tube. He goes by his own rules and was destined from the start to be involved and interested in everything, to travel in the fast lane of life. It is hard to imagine him batting as well again as his century at Old Trafford, but on that one innings alone – even forgetting his many brilliant match-winning performances as a bowler – he took his place alongside the immortals.

I never knew, and I am no wiser today, precisely why Geoffrey Boycott cut himself off from England for three years. The critics described it as a self-imposed exile and assumed, like most inside the game, that he was offended when the Test captaincy, on which he had set his heart, went to others whom he saw as lesser lights not as well qualified for the job. In the absence of an explanation from Geoffrey we shall have to be satisfied with opinion rather than fact. When he discussed his position again, in the unlikely venue of a car park at the Watford Gap service station on the M1, he offered no reason, and I thought it prudent not to press the point. All I wanted was an ending to a bizarre complication in the job of selecting the strongest possible side to take on Greg Chappell's Australia in 1977 – the year of World Series Cricket when victory over a Packer-dominated side would taste all the sweeter.

The Boycott saga began in the comparatively benign atmosphere of a Test with the friendly Indians at Old Trafford in 1974, a series which took on extra significance with England building up a team for the winter tour of Australia and New Zealand. For one of those reasons which crop up in cricket and are not easy to explain, Eknath Solkar dismissed Boycott four times in six innings for England, MCC and Yorkshire. Instead of shrugging it off as one of those things, Geoffrey, the perfectionist, got it into his head that he had a weakness against left-arm over-the-wicket swing bowling. Solkar did not take another wicket in the three-Test series and conceded 125 runs from forty-four overs, such was the menace he presented. In the second Test at Lord's Solkar bowled only six overs, and England scored 629; Dennis Amiss made 188, Mike Denness 118, Tony Greig 106 and John Edrich 96. I could only imagine Geoffrey's feelings when he looked at the England score.

Boycott missed a seat at the feast in 1974 because he had told me at Manchester he did not wish to be considered for England for the rest of the summer (the second half included three Tests against Pakistan) as he wished to concentrate on captaining and playing for Yorkshire. Much as I wanted him to carry on, there was no alternative but to agree. Players are invited to play for England; there is no contractual agreement to force them to play against their wishes. My committee of Ossie Wheatley, Brian Taylor and Jackie Bond were as disappointed as I was, but it was accepted that Boycott was probably not in the right frame of mind for Test cricket. We left it at that, confident that all would be satisfactorily resolved by the end of the summer and he would be available for Australia.

During the season I was appointed tour manager to Australia and New Zealand and Boycott was duly selected, with Mike Denness continuing as captain and John Edrich as vice-captain. Geoffrey, who had averaged 58.09 for Yorkshire, did not respond immediately to his invitation sent by the Test and County Cricket Board. As the days passed my suspicions grew, and a month before the party was due to leave he withdrew. So many stories and theories circulated that it needs to be said that Boycott did everything by the book and in the proper way at a meeting with Donald Carr, secretary of the Test and County Cricket Board, and myself as chairman of the selectors. He also sent a letter to me explaining that he had gone to the West Indies the previous winter against his better judgement, and had he taken that tour off he might have been in better shape to have faced the home season.

As it was, he continued, he had thought of retiring at the start of the 1974 season, which would have meant quitting the game at around the same age as Peter May and Ted Dexter (Geoffrey was then thirty-four). I remembered a comment made at Old Trafford: 'This fellow is worrying himself into premature retirement.' To his credit, Geoffrey was mindful of his responsibilities to his widowed mother and asked me not to think he was taking a selfish view.

He added he was 'desperately sorry' to miss the tour. A rest, the selectors thought, would enable him to look forward to the 1975 season with zest and confidence restored.

Although Geoffrey seemed to be assailed by an unjustified self-doubt, the final paragraph of his letter suggested that it was no worse than a passing phase and, disappointing as it was, I expected his early return. His position as opening batsman was left open provided his form warranted selection over other candidates. Certainly the door was not closed on his England career, as, of course, subsequent events confirmed. His withdrawal from the touring party was accepted on the undertaking that he would not play elsewhere during the English off season, and I was therefore surprised to be contacted in Australia by Donald Carr with the news that Boycott had applied for permission to go on a short private tour of South Africa. His request was turned down on a matter of principle, with the Test and County Cricket Board stating: 'When Boycott declined to tour Australia and New Zealand with England he made it quite clear that he had no intention of playing any cricket at all during the winter. The selection committee, and subsequently the Board, accepted his decision on that basis.' In declining his application I felt the Board were protecting Boycott from himself. Imagine the furious public reaction if he had played on an undemanding visit to South Africa while the official team were being blitzed to pieces in Australia!

In 1975 the first major task was to rebuild from the battering of Lillee and Thomson in time for the Prudential World Cup. Four Tests were also to be played against Australia, who clearly had a psychological trump card. I was delegated to sound out Boycott, who immediately put paid to any hope of his immediate return. Without offering an explanation, he told me he was not available for selection. The first reaction of the press – not to mention my colleagues, Sir Len Hutton, Ken Barrington and Charlie Elliott – was that he had played his last Test match for England. Apart from the natural frustration at the continued absence of our no. 1 batsman in such an important season, my personal feeling was that it was tragic that such a dedicated and talented professional should fall victim to a personal torment so deep as to divorce himself from a world gathering of cricketers. I still find it difficult to accept that he really wanted to cut himself off. But there it was, and for whatever the reason he missed an exciting event and four eventful Tests. He was missed, particularly in the semifinal of the Prudential Cup, narrowly won by Australia at Headingley. *Wisden*'s blunt comment was that it was high time he came to terms with himself. He could not complain of the editor's impatient words.

A year later I again contacted Boycott with the same result. He had retreated into his defensive shell so far as the Test team was concerned. The selectors, rightly in my opinion, decided it would be wrong to approach him again that summer, especially as I had always made it clear to him that he had only to ring me if he changed his mind or wanted to discuss his position. No such call was made, but my conscience was clear as I had done all that could reasonably have been done to maintain contact. It became a little irksome to be urged to plead with him to return every time England suffered defeat or a batting breakdown and to read of offers to mediate between Geoffrey and myself. The would-be mediators missed the point entirely, for it was now up to him to make the first move. Indeed, that was our parting agreement. One of the selectors, in an excess of zeal and, I am sure, for the best motives, ignored the collective agreement of the committee and approached Boycott during a county match at Worcester. Geoffrey's answer was as before. The selectors also bore in mind that if Geoffrey was pushed in his prevailing mood he might quit the game for good – a possibility in his mind as revealed in his letter declining to tour Australia.

A tantalizing aspect of the difficult situation was that his form for Yorkshire in the three years he was out of the England team hardly suggested a player with technical or any other problems, and in 1976 his 1915 runs with an average of 73.65 made me suspect his old thirst for runs might bring about a thaw in his attitude.

The first hint of a change of mind came in May 1977 with a telephone call to my home from a Yorkshire journalist asking if I would meet Boycott. I said of course I would, and Geoffrey subsequently phoned me. As he was in Yorkshire and I live in Surrey, a halfway rendezvous was arranged on the motorway at Watford Gap. Feeling rather like an overconspicuous special agent, I duly arrived. When Geoffrey appeared I suggested we talk over

111

a drink or a coffee, but he considered that to be too public and preferred the privacy of my car. We talked for about an hour and a half and, in the language of diplomats after a conference of heads of state, our discussion was wide-ranging on matters of cricket – and, I suppose, fruitful. I made it abundantly clear there had never been any prejudices against him whatsoever, the selectors were all old pros like himself with similar social backgrounds. Geoffrey, as I saw it, laboured under the misconception that the selectors and hierarchy were somehow 'agin him', which was nonsense.

The England captaincy, which the entire cricket world assumed, in the absence of a denial by Geoffrey, to be the bone of contention, was mentioned, but, to the best of my recollection, it was not the central issue of our talks. Indeed, I would not have allowed it to be, for the choice of captain is not at any time a legitimate area of discussion between a chairman of selectors and a player, no matter how eminent he may be. If the player is invited to give his opinion, that is another matter entirely. I reminded Geoffrey that the selectors had never wanted him to be out of the side, had always regretted his absence, and if he made himself available again the slate would be wiped clean. I also pointed out that my presence was a guarantee of my personal goodwill and that of the selectors. Finally I told him, 'You have said in the past that you don't want to be considered, and that you would tell us if and when you changed your mind. I have told you of our position. The ball is now in your court.'

We parted after agreeing that I should contact him by phone after forty-eight hours, and when I did so he told me that he was available for selection. Geoffrey could not, however, expect to walk into the team right away, and he returned for the Third Test at Trent Bridge (Ian Botham's first) and scored 107 and 80 not out. He batted on all five days of the match, a total of twelve hours. Bliss for Boycott, eminently satisfactory for England and the ever patient selectors. England won a nerve-wracking climax as storm clouds built up, but that was but the rehearsal for Boycott's triumph in the next Test on his home ground of Headingley. All the lost years passed like a distant, easily forgotten dream as he scored 191 and claimed the distinction of becoming the first batsman in history to complete 100 first-class centuries in Test cricket. The crowd were enraptured; you could sense the waves of affection and pride in the moments of his sublime triumph, and in a way, I wish for Geoffrey it had ended there with the cup of his reputation overflowing. England had won the first Test at Old Trafford without him, but his entry came at exactly the right moment to tilt the balance against Australia. His fame soared to new and deserved heights.

On the evening of Boycott's 100th Test Ian Wooldridge, the *Daily Mail's* celebrated columnist, wrote, 'There are some who should have it on their consciences that Boycott had been by-passed for Test captaincy.' I saw Boycott and the Test captaincy from a different standpoint. My conscience would have been pricked only if the various selection committees under my chairmanship had appointed him as captain without a genuine conviction that he was the best available man for a highly demanding job – particularly for someone with major responsibilities as a player, as Sir Len Hutton will willingly testify. It is easy to submit to popular clamour, and I have never felt the need to defend the fact that not one but several sets of experienced old players arrived at the conclusion that other candidates were more suitable for the captaincy. Selection would be child's play if the leadership automatically went to the leading player of a side regardless of other factors. Sometimes the best player has the best qualifications to lead; sometimes he has not.

Geoffrey's claims were always considered at the appropriate times, conscientiously and at length, and were given the same fair airing as all the other candidates'. And it goes without saying that no barriers were put in the way of his selection outside the selection room. Selectors, appointed by the counties for their specialized knowledge, are left to make their own decisions, and if they are shown to be persistently wrong in their judgements they can be sacked. This is not to deny the existence of private lobbying on occasions. There was strong behind-the-scenes lobbying for Colin Cowdrey to take England to Australia in 1970–71, but it did not succeed. Ray Illingworth, the man in possession, was appointed, a case which must serve as proof positive of the integrity of selectors. I can honestly claim that no committee under my chairmanship bowed to lobbying or outside pressures from any source, and that includes the newspapers. The moment a selection panel is blown

113

off course by the winds of opinion – changeable at all times – it is on the rocks.

Boycott, I have often read, was not given a fair crack of the whip, but for a shrewd man in pursuit of a legitimate ambition he made some surprising decisions. One was to decline to go to India and Pakistan in 1972 when it is logical to assume he would have been vice-captain with his foot firmly on the ladder of promotion. Clearly he could not be considered if he was not available for selection, and when he came back others had entered the lists. In 1981–82 he failed to last Keith Fletcher's visit to India and Pakistan as he was 'physically and mentally tired', a condition which did not prevent him from going on a private tour of South Africa, and which eventually led to a three-year ban from Test cricket. It is surely one of the oddest decisions ever made by a player of his class and standing.

Geoffrey also had eight years as captain of Yorkshire without tangible success and, when his successor John Hampshire resigned after two years, the county did not revert to him but appointed Chris Old.

Any suspicion that his voluntary exile was held against him must have disappeared when he was appointed vice-captain to Mike Brearley for the 1977–78 tour of Pakistan and New Zealand in the winter after his great comeback against Australia. On the eve of the third Test at Karachi Brearley broke his left arm and was obliged to return to London. Boycott took over for one Test in Pakistan and three in New Zealand, without, it has to be said, gaining the recommendation to retain the post from the manager-selector Ken Barrington. By the next home season Brearley was fit again, and it was only fair he should reclaim his position. In any case, Brearley was held to be the better leader with the gift of getting the best out of his team.

There is so much to admire in Boycott that it is a thousand pities he should be a controversial figure. His dedication is not matched by any of his contemporaries, and he is conscientious and pains-taking to a remarkable degree. His devotion to stockpiling runs tends to make him a man apart. He needs the long hours in the nets to maintain his high consistency for, without continuous hard work it is questionable whether he could have continued to produce impressive results year after year. No one can deny his technical

114

excellence, staying power, single-minded resolve and physical courage. A sneer circulating around Packer-time that he ducked out of meeting Lillee and Co. can be contemptuously dismissed. He had his share of fast bowling, bumpers and intimidation, and was always too good a player to be afraid.

But Boycott was not blessed with the natural genius of Hutton, Compton, Hammond or May, and in his pursuit of technical perfection, success and aggregates he smothered some of his innate gifts. Every now and again he lifts his veil of defence to reveal vintage strokeplay and a masterful authority, but at times he relapses into a one-gear run machine, content to accumulate runs and allowing himself to be tied down by mediocre bowlers. As Bill Bowes once wryly observed when we were discussing the challenge of bowling to Bradman, a bowler's nightmare is to have his best delivery smashed to the boundary. He then asks himself: what on earth can I do now? The truly great carry the fight to the opposition, win the psychological battle and dominate. If there is a chill in a bowler's heart when his best ball is attacked equally there is hope when a half-volley is not punished, and for a batsman of his class Geoffrey has mostly been too ready to grind along at his own pace. Maybe in another era, when the ever loyal Yorkshire public had a wider choice of heroes to worship, Boycott could have developed under a less glaring spotlight. As it is, the Boycott cult among sections of Yorkshire's following has not, in my opinion, been wise or healthy, and certainly not in the player's own best interests.

My fellow selectors and I always bent over backwards to try to understand his contradictory and enigmatic personality, and to make allowances for what I believe at bedrock to be a sensitive nature longing to be liked. Without exception every selection committee I served with valued his quality as the foremost English batsman of his time – how could they not do so! – and appreciated the strains and pressures his application and style imposed upon him to maintain his performances. 'Forget cricket when you have a day off and enjoy yourself on a golf course' was Sir Don Bradman's advice to his teams on tour, and he could never be accused of taking his tasks as captain and player lightly. I fear Geoffrey never discovered the knack of relaxation. 'Our eminent eccentric' was how Frank Keating described him in the *Guardian*. When I was manager on tour, Geoffrey would inevitably be apart from the rest in the airport lounge or hotel, a loner, seemingly writing interminable letters. In our man-to-man dealings I always got on pretty well with him and we never fell out.

There is more to captaincy than a knowledge of tactics. As Tony Lewis, who had considerable experience at Glamorgan, made it clear in *Wisden* in 1979, a captain needs to be father confessor, nurse, teacher, preacher and collector of the beer kitty, as well as a professional hard dealer for his players' rights. Of Boycott's dismissal as Yorkshire's captain Lewis wrote:

The committee [Yorkshire's] bombarded from outside with poison darts, was itself defended by an illustrious cohort of former Yorkshire Test cricketers, and eventually the truth emerged that Yorkshire's current players had done much to force the issue by threatened mutiny. Boycott, they said, had not understood their aspirations as young professionals. They found a senior champion in John Hampshire. It was all very public and personal, but most crucial of all to Boycott's fate was his record. In the eight years of his reign Yorkshire had won nothing. He blamed the committee.

Later in his perceptive article Lewis added:

There are two facts that most senior players I have talked to are agreed upon. Captaincy is two people. It is the captain and the trusted senior player. For example, it looked as if Geoffrey Boycott was doing it on his own in the end. Remember Roy Marshall behind Colin Ingleby-MacKenzie and Peter Sainsbury with Richard Gilliat at Hampshire. Ray Illingworth behind Brian Close at Yorkshire, Don Shepherd with both Ossie Wheatley and myself at Glamorgan, Keith Fletcher behind Brian Taylor at Essex, and so on. That is how it looks best. Otherwise your house is in flames and you are the last to know it.

Tony might have added Alec Bedser to Peter May – a little piece of Surrey history which gave me a new insight into the many demands of captaincy.

And there, in an oversize nutshell, was a cogent answer to those who believe Boycott was unjustly passed over as captain of England. Being the pragmatic professional that he has always been, I am sure he accepted the honesty and integrity of the various

116

selection committees, although he retains the privilege of thinking to his dying day that they were wrong.

9

A Manager's Lot

Senior players of an MCC party touring South Africa between the wars once told me that the only conversation they had with their manager was when he put his head in their carriage window at Waterloo Station and announced, 'Hello, chaps. I'm your manager.' He then promptly disappeared in the direction of the first-class compartments. No doubt an exaggeration, but in the days when the ties of Empire were cemented by cricket an England manager had duties other than looking after the players. He left that side of the tour to his captain, who had the senior pro as his right-hand man. During my two difficult tours in Australia as manager in 1974–75 and 1979–80 I sometimes wondered how some of my predecessors of more circumspect eras would have reacted to the changed times and attitudes.

My deep and abiding affection for Australia's sporting public since my first tour with Wally Hammond in 1946–47 was, I admit, put to the test on occasions. In 1974–75 England ran headlong into the full fury of Dennis Lillee and Jeff Thomson, who proved to be Australia's most hostile fast bowlers since Ray Lindwall and Keith Miller. Too many bumpers were allowed and, inevitably, there was a heated atmosphere. If Tim Caldwell, chairman of the Australian Board, and I had not been old friends and able to exert a restraining influence, the situation might have got out of hand. England, too, were cruelly hit by injuries. And the 1979–80 tour presented particular problems as it came immediately after the patched-up truce with Kerry Packer. In the previous season Mike Brearley had humiliated Australia, who were without their Packer players, by 5–1, and England now became the guinea pigs in a hotch-potch itinerary of three five-day Tests with Australia, a triangular single-innings tournament with Australia and the West

Indies, and a number of night matches. Pop-style gimmicks, with players and officials being manipulated by so-called marketing projects and television companies, made many genuine cricketers and followers of the sport weep for lost traditions.

I had two patient and understanding captains in Mike Denness and Mike Brearley – and, heaven knows, they had pressures of their own – and two splendid aides in Alan Smith and Ken Barrington.

Lillee and Thomson were magnificent in 1974–75 and, as chairman of the selectors, I was subsequently surprised to read in *Wisden* that England's party was chosen on the assumption that Australia would have no fast bowlers. No writer with a modicum of understanding of the game and selection could make such an assumption and issue such a curious statement. Australia is always likely to turn up a fast bowler. Already we knew that Lillee was making superhuman efforts to get fit after a back injury which had threatened his career and Thomson had played in only one unsuccessful Test against Pakistan. The England team, as always, was selected as the strongest available. The best players should, under normal conditions, be able to cope with the unexpected. Only Geoff Boycott was unavailable as he was then in what the newspapers described as his self-imposed exile, but his presence would not have materially altered the pattern of the series.

The hard fact was that Lillee and Thomson were brilliantly aggressive, even if, in the words of the late Jack Fingleton, they got away with murder in the number of bouncers they bowled. Lillee had saved himself for England. Two years before he had rescued his career only by his fierce dedication, hard work and determination, and a willingness to wear a plaster cast. In the season of 1973–74 he had patiently held himself back, and a surge of pent-up energy was subsequently released which enabled him to bowl flat out with English batsmen at the other end of the wicket. In common with most, I have deplored the incidents which Lillee has got himself into, but as a fast bowler he has my complete admiration. Thomson's ability to make the ball rise steeply from little short of a length at top speed was a devastating weapon. Later in his career he had bursts of his old speed, but never again did he match his consistency in that series, possibly because of recurring injuries. The best batsmen of any age would have been

119

sorely troubled by these two superb bowlers, and, indeed, by the whole Australian attack.

The pitches helped them – how they had changed from the shirtfronts all too familiar to me in 1946–47 – and Max Walker, with his cut and swing, was the ideal back-up. The Chappell brothers, Ian and Greg, Ashley Mallett and Ian Redpath also made a habit of taking breath-taking catches. The standard of catching in the area of the slips and gully was of the highest. No fewer than 23 of the 58 wickets shared by Lillee and Thomson were held from first slip to gully. In all, thirty-eight catches were made, not counting the eighteen by wicketkeeper Rodney Marsh, and many were inspired. Even what are usually termed straightforward catches at slip needed some holding, so fast did the ball leave the bat.

At the same time, although courageous, England's batting was short on technique. Too many were guilty of not getting behind the line of the ball, which was one reason for the inordinate number of slip catches. There have been worse sides than that led by Denness, but Lillee and Thomson, the pitches and the injury crisis were too powerful a set of circumstances to overcome. Australia were supreme and England vanquished.

The sixth and final Test at Melbourne, which began with Australia 4–0 in the lead and England understandably in disarray, was proof, if proof were needed, how much Lillee and Thomson dominated the series. Thomson was absent with a shoulder injured playing tennis, and Lillee retired with a bruised foot after bowling only six overs. England, who had enjoyed only one century stand in the previous five Tests, now had stands of 149, 192 and 148, Denness, so out of touch that he had dropped himself from the Fourth Test, scored 188, and Keith Fletcher, spared the torment of nonstop bouncers, 146. England, whose previous highest total was 295, made 529 and won by an innings and 4 runs. There could hardly have been a better tribute to the deadly duo.

Before Melbourne it was said that England's batsmen were shellshocked by the bouncers. The phrase was apt, but I do not go along with the opinion expressed by some pundits that England brought it upon themselves by starting a bumper war in the state matches leading up to the First Test at Brisbane. Peter Lever, it is true, bowled a few bumpers in the accepted way of a fast bowler, but the number was far from excessive and they did not frighten any of the batsmen. The bumpers would have come from Lillee and Thomson whatever happened in the early matches of the tour.

As always, the definition and control of bumpers were contentious issues, and umpires everywhere were reluctant to exercise their powers. Every endeavour has been made to define in black and white a bumper without general acceptance. England tried to get the world to agree to restricting the number to one per over, but the West Indies would have none of it, and there has been no shortage of suggestions to meet the problem – a line across the pitch, a longer pitch, and so on. My personal feeling is that, as with all laws, it eventually comes back to the captain and players performing within the spirit of the game. If that is not possible in these days of big financial incentives and advanced national pride, the umpires and captains need to be stronger. The experienced cricketer intuitively knows the dividing line between fair and unfair play, and if he steps over it he ought not to complain if he takes the consequences. I deplore the tendency to blur the line, to make wild, concerted appealing in the hope of intimidating the umpire, and to claim catches which the fielders must know are extremely doubtful. If, in recent Test series the world over, the umpiring has not been up to scratch, the players ought, in part, to blame themselves for unfair appealing.

One of the worst moments of the 1974–75 tour occurred during the Sydney Test. There were far too many bumpers and the atmosphere became overcharged. When Geoff Arnold, England's no. 11, went in to bat he was given a short-pitched first ball by Lillee, which passed just in front of his nose; Marsh, standing a long way back, held the ball at head height. Arnold had a narrow escape. If the terrifying delivery had struck his head – and it was in the days before helmets were worn – there was no way he could have avoided serious injury or even worse. The England dressing room was amazed, and my personal opinion was that it was nothing short of disgraceful. Dennis had all the armoury and skills at his command to dismiss a no. 11 without reverting to bouncers. An aggressive temperament is part of a fast bowler's make-up, though I have known many to do very well without it.

Even before the series started Lillee had fired a psychological salvo. Straight on cue his book *Back to the Mark* appeared on the eve of the opening Test at Brisbane, and he made no bones about his intention to aim at the batsman's ribcage. Some felt that the Australian Board might have picked up the gauntlet in the wider interests of cricket. Others felt that all is fair in love, war and Test cricket – the last two are often inseparable – but I thought it was provocative and unnecessary. But there, I was one of the old stagers, and it was popular stuff lapped up by the mob, whose chant of 'Kill, kill, kill' as Dennis ran into bowl was not the prettiest sound I have heard on cricket grounds. Maybe cricket reflects the general violence of the age, but I will always contend that Dennis was one of the greatest fast bowlers and had such high tactical instincts that he lowered himself to try to scare opponents out, especially the tailenders.

The wonder was there was not a serious injury during the Brisbane Test as I can only describe the pitch as diabolical. It was far below the lowest accepted standard for a Test match and I cannot recall, other than unplayable stickies after violent storms on the same ground, so many deliveries misbehaving as in the opening spell by Lillee and Thomson. The bounce was particularly erratic at one end where England lost 16 of their 20 wickets, and Australia 8 out of 15. The fact that Thomson, with his slinging action, was not sure where he would pitch the ball made it worse for the batsmen, and one short-of-a-length delivery flew over Dennis Amiss's head and was still rising as it passed over Marsh like a comet. With one bounce it crashed against the sightscreen. The pitch would have been bad enough for bowlers of orthodox pace; against Lillee and Thomson it was nothing less than frightening. I doubt if any batsmen, not even Wally Hammond, whose genius on the Brisbane sticky in 1946 was a revelation, could have hoped to survive for long by accepted methods.

Tony Greig's 110 must surely be the best and bravest innings of his career. His method was entirely his own. Making the maximum use of his height he improvised by standing away from the wicket and using his bat in the manner of a flail at every ball wide of the off stump. Standing 6 feet 7½ inches tall, he was able to slash at rising deliveries. The other batsmen were obliged to take hurried evasive action from the same type of ball. The harder Tony flashed, the faster the ball flew off the bat and eluded the cordon of slip and gully fielders at various heights and angles. Lillee and Tommo must have been more than frustrated. I always respect the batsman who can invent shots and a technique to meet an unusual situation. Denis Compton was a prime example; like Greig, he was prepared to take risks and carry the attack to a surprised opposition. In the second innings Thomson found the answer with a lightning-fast, swinging yorker, the delivery which brought Ray Lindwall such just fame.

Brisbane's pitch problems had started ten days before the Test was due to start. The pitch itself was prepared by the redoubtable Lord Mayor of Brisbane, Clem Jones, who had taken over after he had sacked the groundsman. Clem's reputation in Queensland as a politician who got things humming was second to none, but he took on more than he bargained for. No doubt he was a splendid mayor, but a Test groundsman he was not. Nor did he have any luck. Two days before the game the ground was flooded – a not unusual event at Brisbane at that time of year – and between the dismissal of the groundsman and the flooding the ground had apparently been largely neglected. There was even doubt whether a pitch could be made in time. At least it was in Clem's favour that the match stayed at Brisbane, but when I went to the middle only forty-eight hours before the start there was no visible trace of the site of the actual pitch. All that could be seen was green grass and mud. When Neil Harvey, chairman of Australia's selectors, arrived, his first question was, 'Where's the pitch then, Clem?'

The Lord Mayor of Brisbane had a plasterer's trowel in his hand which he used to smooth the surface mud and level out the ground. After the levelling out, a roller was used, but in the tropical climate the grass grew apace with the result that many indentations were left. Ultimately it was a pitch famed only for its treachery. The same for both sides? Naturally, but England did not have Lillee and Thomson, they lost the toss and batted when the pitch was at its worst, and the injury jinx began with two major casualties: Dennis Amiss broke his thumb and John Edrich a finger. Some teams are fated, and surely this one was, for John also broke two ribs in the Sydney Test, Bob Willis suffered from sore knees from November onwards, and David Lloyd and Mike Denness were other casualties. Only Tony Greig and Alan Knott remained free from trouble and played in all six Tests. Injuries can be the curse of a touring side, not only causing headaches in team selection and disrupting the best-laid plans, but sapping confidence and morale.

Even as early as Brisbane, because of injuries, the tour committee felt the need to send for a batting reinforcement and, to judge from the surprise that it caused, only the committee took into account Colin Cowdrey's vast experience – he had been the junior member of Len Hutton's side which retained the Ashes twenty years earlier. But he was only a few days short of his forty-second birthday and some of the Australian writers had fun at his expense. Without hesitation Colin answered our call and, in doing so, he equalled the record of six tours to Australia held by Johnny Briggs, the Lancashire slow left-arm bowler and batsman of the last century. Considering the time it took to get to and from Australia in the 1890s Briggs must have spent a large part of his short life at sea.

Colin arrived straight from an English December in the early hours one morning, shrugged off his jet lag and spent four exhausting days under the hot sunshine in the nets. It would have been an ordeal for someone half his age. One of the willing bowlers was Graham McKenzie, among Australia's best fast bowlers, who spent several years with Leicestershire. Later, when I was in Barbados, I could not help comparing his attitude with that of some of the local boys. Someone had put them up to asking for money to bowl at England batsmen. At one time there were scores of bowlers only too happy to join in the net practices and try their luck against top players from abroad.

The injuries continued. By the eve of the Second Test at Perth Peter Lever had back trouble, Mike Hendrick went down with a throat infection and, with Dennis Amiss and John Edrich already casualties, England were down to an unlucky thirteen, including the reserve wicketkeeper, Bob Taylor. We congratulated our prudence in sending for Colin, who had to go in at no. 3 although he had not had an innings since the end of the home season in September. Incredibly, thanks to the work he had put in and his innate gift of timing, he was still able to make shots against Lillee and Thomson, scoring 22 and 41. He showed what an advantage a batsman possesses if his technique is correct with the bat coming down straight and the full face of the blade facing the ball. Nothing rattled him.

At the end of the first over against the dreaded Tommo, Colin, extended his hand and made the classic remark, 'I don't think we have met. My name's Cowdrey.' What the fire-eating Thomson thought of that can only be left to the imagination. And one of my chief worries had been that Cowdrey might have been hit and injured by the fast bowlers!

Unfortunately Colin found it hard to live up to his early promise, although he was dreadfully unlucky in the Third Test at Melbourne, where he had played a truly masterly innings of 102 on a bad pitch on his first tour. England's historic victory in 1954–55 is always linked with Frank Tyson's rout of Australia on the final day, but, memorable though that performance was, it is often forgotten that nothing would have been possible without Colin's innings. It was so brilliant that I fear we consequently expected too much of him. He had all the hallmarks of greatness, with oceans of time to make his strokes, and there were times when I bowled to him and felt he ought to be the greatest batsman in the world. Yet on another day he could be comparatively easy to contain, and he remained something of an enigma. On Colin's first tour of Australia I asked Sir Don Bradman his opinion of him and he replied, 'I can't quite make up my mind.' Much the same could be said at the end of his career, distinguished though it was. One always had the feeling that he could have been even better had he been a bit tougher, less modest, or found it less easy in his days at Tonbridge as a cricket prodigy. But for all the niggling suspicions I would have jumped at the chance to have had a batsman half his class in my later years as chairman of selectors!

Another crisis on that injury-bedevilled tour arose at Sydney before the Fourth Test when Mike Denness, who had not reached a half-century in thirteen innings, broke the news that he had decided to drop himself and pass the captaincy on to John Edrich. I disagreed with his decision. 'Stick it out. Think again' was my candid advice. In my opinion it was wrong for the captain to abdicate his position on the grounds of lack of form. Unselfish it might be and, as he saw the situation, in the best interests of the side, but I did not consider it right for the captain of a touring team to opt out on the grounds of poor personal performances. Mike is a man of high principles and, conscious of his batting failures, thought that England would fare better without him. Yet I did not believe he was all that much out of touch; he was capable of finding his form at any time – as indeed he did. For the Sydney Test the leadership passed to John Edrich, who understandably was not madly keen to take on the extra responsibility. He was already to the front of the firing line, but he accepted his temporary job phlegmatically and without complaint. The Edrich cricketing family have an enviable reputation for courage. John added to it, and showed, like Greig, a heart of a lion in the moments of crisis on the tour.

Australia called on only two umpires in the series, Tom Brooks, a former New South Wales fast bowler, and Robin Bailache, then only twenty-seven, for all six Test matches. The Australian Board argued they were the best available and there was no advantage in having a panel system. Reviewing the series in *Wisden*, John Thicknesse acknowledged the burden of standing in all six matches in a difficult series and concluded: 'Yet, when all their difficulties are added up, it must still be said that their umpiring fell short of required standards.'

I had a large measure of sympathy for the pair. They took on probably more than was right to expect. At the same time more protection should have been given to England's batsmen, who wanted to know why amid the barrage of bouncers, the bowlers were merely 'spoken to' instead of receiving direct warnings and, accordingly, being subject to the penalties laid down in Law 46 which deals with the persistent bowling of short-pitched deliveries. The dangerous climate of excitement and partisanship during some periods of the Tests must also be remembered. Fast bowlers seem to raise the blood temperature, and I again turn to Thicknesse: 'When Thomson and Lillee were bowling, the atmosphere was more like that of a soccer ground than of a cricket match, especially at Sydney, where England's batsmen must have experienced the same sort of emotions as they waited for the next ball as early Christians felt as they waited in the Colosseum for the lions.' Thicknesse rightly felt that it would have needed umpires of much self-confidence to have interfered with this Roman holiday.

It is hard to avoid the pretentious observation that cricket was never meant to be played in fervent hothouses of aggression, and all too easy to make umpires the scapegoats. In my opinion the captain is more culpable if he allows his bowlers too free a rein. He has the power to defuse inflammatory situations, but, having said that, I admit to little faith in the desire of so many captains to control what they see as an advantageous position. In fact, if a bowler is cautioned, the first to arrive on the scene is often the captain to defend his bowler and protest at the umpires' action.

What would have happened if Lillee and Thomson had been penalized by the umpires defies imagination. Sadly, too often umpires have to put up with verbal abuse at all levels of the game, and it is an unhappy reflection of our times that Brooks, an upright and honourable man, announced his retirement during a lunch interval in the England-Australia Test at Perth in December 1978. Fortunately England were not implicated. No doubt the time will come, God forbid, when decisions are made – or confirmed – electronically or by action replays projected on a giant screen to be seen by all on the ground. I doubt if all arguments will be satisfied even then.

After Australia the comparative calm of New Zealand can be a soothing therapy, although the crowds in the big centres are getting noisier.

Curiously the most serious accident of the tour came in the relative tranquillity of Auckland with New Zealand's no. 11, Ewen Chatfield, the victim of a strange mishap. He was struck on his head, via his bat, by a ball from Peter Lever, generally held to be a bumper but which arrived at about chest height. Chatfield fell on his back almost swallowing his tongue and a tragedy was averted by Bernie Thomas's prompt arrival at the crease. The England physiotherapist gave first aid and Chatfield was taken to hospital. Lever was so distressed that he twice visited the hospital in the afternoon and remained inconsolable no matter how hard we tried to impress on him that he was not to blame.

Rain ruined the Christchurch Test, and it was impossible to play on the first, second and sixth days. As New Zealand relies heavily on revenue from representative matches to finance her cricket, I was approached with a request to make up for lost time and gate money by playing on the rest day. I saw no objection, but, to my dismay, some of England's players opposed the plan, complaining they were at the end of a gruelling tour and were physically and mentally spent. I listened to the arguments and decided we would play, and added that I did not think it too much of a hardship as they had not had to perform for two days. To be fair spirits were low after being beaten by Australia and the players wanted to get home, but I thought it was not much to expect. Also, I believed that New Zealand deserved to be helped out. Top players sometimes overlook the fact that a large part of their livelihood springs from Test matches and tours, not to mention their commercial spin-off value, all against countries largely run by dedicated unpaid officials willing to give up their leisure for the benefit of the game at all levels. The same, of course, applies to England.

An example of the other side of the coin came when Keith Fletcher's side, which had hardly had a birthday in India in 1981–82, flew back to India from Sri Lanka to take part in a benefit match organized for Gouind Bawji, a humble bearer who had looked after every touring international side in India since 1950. Dressed in his uniform of khaki trousers and a tunic bearing the official badge of the Indian Board of Control, he and his assistants transported the baggage from ground to ground and acted as dressing-room attendants. One of the sights of an Indian tour was to see him stretched outside the team manager's hotel room on his bed roll ready to repel unwanted visitors and to answer every call from manager and players.

During my second tour of Australia as full manager in 1979–80 I pinched myself to make sure that I was in charge of a national cricket team and not a touring pop group on one-night stands. There were thirty-one air flights and fifty-two coach trips, starting in early November and ending in the first week of February. From Melbourne the team flew to Bombay to meet India in a Golden Jubilee Test match which, to my gratification, an extremely tired England won by 10 wickets, thanks to an extraordinary all-round performance by Ian Botham, who scored 114 out of a total of 296 and took 6 for 58 and 7 for 48. I had feared that England would be too shattered to do the occasion justice. Bob Taylor's enthusiasm and concentration had not deserted him either as he established a new world record with ten catches.

To understand the situation in Australia, it is necessary to return briefly to the agreement reached nine months earlier between the Australian Board and Packer's World Series Cricket organization. Packer's company, PBL Sports Pty Ltd, had been given the important concession of the exclusive rights to promote the Board's official programme, both in televising and merchandizing, which in practical terms meant that Packer had largely got what he wanted – exclusive rights for his Channel 9 television network. Once the scheduled visit by India was cancelled and replaced by a series of Test matches between Australia and England and Australia and the West Indies, with the three countries also involved in a one-day tournament. The agreement meant that the Packer razzamatazz would continue. To quote Peter Smith in *Wisden*, all was 'neatly parcelled to present a cricketing package suitable for maximum exploitation on television.' My guess is that Packer's interest in cricket was stimulated by the exploits of Lillee and Thomson against Denness's side in 1974–75.

In the end, as someone with a close and nonstop love affair with cricket at the highest level over four decades, I gave my personal opinions on the new-style presentation and programme. Few, I venture to say, were in disagreement. We now live in an age of television and instant cricket, but if this type of complicated itinerary persists I see short careers for the internationals and a completely new game.

Unfortunately in the understandable haste to end the financial haemorrhage on all sides, the International Cricket Conference accepted the agreement with World Series Cricket only in principle. It meant that the still unresolved issues were left to the 'goodwill' of Australia, and the tour conditions were still not finalized when Brearley's team, including one ex-Packer man, Derek Underwood, left Heathrow. Complications arose as, in the short time available, all the details could not be ironed out. The Test and County Cricket Board, naturally anxious to avoid committing England *carte blanche* to way-out innovations, were not to blame, but the practical result was that Brearley and I were obliged to try to work out some of the thornier issues on the spot, until George Mann, chairman of the TCCB, arrived in Australia. Normally all the i's would have been dotted and the t's crossed long before the team's departure.

At once Sydney's newspapers branded the team as 'whinging Poms'. Usually there is a reasonable interval between England's arrival and some actual cricket before that old cliché of a headline is trotted out. The Sydney *Daily Mirror* announced 'Moaning Brearley flies in'. In short, it seemed that Brearley was to be made the whipping boy by the media over matters that had nothing to do with him. Until I read that headline I had innocently assumed that England, in taking India's place and agreeing to take part in an experimental programme, was helping to heal cricket's wounds and doing her best to help Australia, where the original dispute started over commercial television rights. On such unpromising beginnings the tour was launched and an innocent Brearley was cast in the villain's role.

There were several conditions England could not accept. The most important was putting the Ashes at stake. England held them by virtue of Brearley's victories at home in 1977 and in Australia in 1978–79. I defended the decision not to play for the Ashes for three reasons: one, there were only three Test matches instead of five – there had been six in the previous season; two, it was unreasonable for one country – Australia in this instance – to have two successive series at home; three, the first Test in Perth was to be played without the visiting side having the customary opportunity to play on the ground before the Test. The dispute concerning the use of the name of the Ashes bordered on the ludicrous, but the TV boys badly wanted the label to improve the prestige of the series. Finally Australia gave way. Other issues were coloured clothing (modelled by Tony Greig) for the night matches and the markings to control field placings, which proved to be a good idea and were later adopted for our own single-innings matches in England.

The TCCB had accepted in principle an itinerary which included eleven one-day fixtures – there were actually nine in the end – and referred to the 'abnormal conditions', a description of commendable restraint so far as the captain, managers and players were concerned. Because of the nature of the proposals everything was done in a rush. England's one-day games were sandwiched between state fixtures over four days and Test matches over five. Not to put too fine a point on it, the tour became a mad helter-skelter, and lest any might imagine I overreacted I quote from Bob Simpson, Australia's former captain:

The programme for the Australian cricket season must never again be designed with the interests of television considered above those of the players and cricket itself. While appreciating that television is of prime importance to Australian cricket, I believe the interests of cricket and

130

television are best served by a programme that allows the best cricket to be played.

Simpson rightly went on to say that the smorgasbord of cricket in the season had confused rather than stimulated the appetite of the Australian public. It was very soon evident that the style of cricket, the hours of play, and so on, were arranged to coincide with television promotion, which of course was part of the deal, and the feeling grew in the England camp that they were being exploited most of the time. There was also much resentment at the eternal sniping at Brearley. On the field he was booed when he fielded the ball, booed when he reached his 50 at Melbourne, and booed when he led England onto the field. *The Age* of Melbourne, regarded as a highly respectable paper, said no England captain had attracted such hostility since Douglas Jardine. If true, and there seemed ample grounds for believing it to be so, it was totally undeserved and was nothing short of whipped-up hysteria. There had been no hint of similar feelings a year before. The ill will passed all limits and entered the unsavoury realm of persecution. In another editorial *The Age* dismissed English cricket as the odd man out in international cricket – 'out of step, out of date and rapidly running out of time'. If insisting on high values and standards is getting out of date perhaps the plea should be guilty. What 'running out of time' meant I do not know, and the charge rang hollow in 1981, and even more so when Allan Border's teams ran into a series of defeats and Australia's cricket was at a low ebb.

One came to the conclusion that part of the public and media had been brainwashed by events, and my respect for Brearley grew. A lesser man might have cracked. Brearley emerged stronger and more dignified than could have been expected, and was a great credit to his country.

Until the tour England had never played floodlit cricket. My sole experience of it had been in 1952 when Eric and I were umpires in a benefit match for Jack Young, the England and Middlesex slow left-arm bowler. The venue was Highbury football ground, the teams were Arsenal Football Club and Middlesex, and it was believed to be the first occasion that cricket was staged under floodlights. Afterwards the Middlesex skipper, Walter Robins, made the interesting prediction, 'Serious cricket is possible under

131

lights. We might be doing it in twenty years time.' Eric and I thought it was a substitute for the real thing. Now here was I as manager of England with official matches to be played under floodlighting in Australia. Curiously it was not thought necessary for England to have any experience of this new form of the game before their first match. I insisted that we must have some practice under lights, and two full-scale practice matches were played in which I acted as an umpire. England's players quickly adapted, finding it easy to follow the flight of a white ball. As umpire I also had no difficulties. As a spectacle floodlit cricket has its attractions, but it is clearly more suited to Australian conditions than English. Australia, which had the advantage of warmer weather, does not enjoy the long light of an English evening. I find it hard to visualize pylons desecrating Lord's, Old Trafford and other famous English grounds as they have Sydney and Melbourne. Once Sydney's ground was beautiful to behold and marvellous to play on. Now the light from Sydney's massive pylons turns night into day, attracts myriads of insects and local residents complain of an 'environmental disaster'. Because of the extra wear and tear, the square, which is not very large, deteriorated during the Packer era, and footballers who went with England to Australia recently complained of the mound which had built up in the middle of the ground where the wickets are pitched.

England's consolation for losing the Tests was to be beaten finalists in the knockout competition. An England v. West Indies final was probably not what the Australians had in mind when the tour script was written.

So within a year of England's 5–1 victory in Australia, a 3–0 defeat was suffered by virtually the same team under the same captain. The margin of victory of both series was doubtless exaggerated, but Australia were patently stronger with the return of the Packerites, including the Chappells, Ian and Greg, Dennis Lillee and Rodney Marsh. The most profound change was in the captaincy, and while Brearley had been tactically superior to Graham Yallop, Greg Chappell was a better player, more versed in captaincy, and had a better set of players. The loss of Mike Hendrick and Geoff Miller, who had shared 42 wickets between them a year before, was keenly felt, but their absence was balanced by the withdrawal of Rodney Hogg, the taker of a record 41 wickets in 1978–79, while Thomson bowled only 32 overs. One was left speculating on the possibilities of an attack led by Lillee, Thomson and Hogg. Perhaps an embarrassment of riches.

Australia's winning margins were comprehensive enough to brook no arguments, but, as always, if things go wrong on tour they go wrong in a big way. If England had won at Sydney in the Second Test it could have made a big difference to the result, but the crucial toss was lost and the advantage went the other way. The ground was flooded by a violent thunderstorm and the groundstaff had been given the day off to celebrate the New Year. As a result, the pitch was open to the elements. Further rain on the following two days left the pitch damp when the Test started, fifty minutes late. Greg Chappell put England in and took only forty-three overs to bowl them out. If Australia had batted first it might have been a different story. The damp pitch helped the ball to move a lot and I am sure we could have dismissed Australia for a low score. The series could have been squared and the final Test taken with a team in renewed heart. A lot of 'if's' to be sure, but that is the way of the game.

Constant travel and the changing forms of cricket took its toll. The side became weary and certain the odds were stacked too high against them. As a general criticism, however, I am sure there could have been more application by the batsmen. Geoff Boycott and Graham Gooch, after a sloppy start, were the exceptions, and, indeed, I never saw Boycott more positive and generally bat better, particularly in the limited-over matches. By attacking and getting on top of the bowlers Geoff revealed strokes he had probably not used in fifteen years.

Gooch also hit with power with that heavyweight bat of his. When he got down to it he was not only a much improved player, but a leading batsman of the season. David Gower was unable to conquer some shortcomings in his footwork, and his performances dropped a long way from the previous tour in which he had been outstanding. All the potential was there, including his exquisite timing, but at that stage of his career I felt he needed more application and concentration. There was an idea to use Derek Randall as an opener, inspired by a double century and a century against Middlesex for Nottinghamshire late in the English season in that position, and reinforced by an innings of 97 off Queensland in the opening fixture. Unfortunately, from then on he declined rapidly, and Lillee had only to come on to get him out. Even his fielding, which was always such a recommendation, suffered from a lack of confidence. Derek's cheery presence and fielding always made him a welcome member of an England side and one to whom the selectors always turned readily, but he became such a fidget at the crease, sometimes making as many as four movements before the ball reached him, that he became a technical disaster.

The absence of Hendrick and the temporary eclipse of Bob Willis, who bowled only ninety-eight overs in the three Tests, upset the plans of the selectors to use Graham Dilley, the strapping young prospect from Kent, as the learner bowler. He was pitched into two Tests and, as could only be expected, was not ready. The fault was not with Dilley, but with the structure of English cricket. At the time there were restrictions on the first innings in the Championship, which more often than not led to a spate of declarations in an effort to get a result one way or the other. In short, some matches became three one-day affairs within the framework of the three days. The result was that Dilley had never spent a full day in the field until he went to Australia and had never taken a second new ball. Dilley batted for some three and a half hours for 38, then, after bowling eight or nine overs, he told me he was physically shattered. In the one-day games, to which he was more accustomed and in which he could pace himself as he knew how many overs he was likely to complete in a spell, he was impressive.

I left Australia with the conviction – and reported to the TCCB accordingly – that the programme was too severe and that cricket must not be wholly subservient to television's needs. Clearly the experiment was valuable in a negative way in that it should have served as a lesson. A limit must always be placed on the non-cricketing aspects of promotion and promoters left in no doubt as to their secondary role. Otherwise the tail wags the dog and Test cricket, as we know it, will exist only in the memory. If the Ashes are to have meaning they can only be fought for over a series consisting of the traditional five or six Test matches and on an alternating home-and-away basis. Australia, I feel, needs to address herself to these and similar problems perhaps more than any of the major cricket-playing countries.

Nor was I a convert to the new forms of the game. One of the handicaps of the 1979–80 planners was that they must have had only a modicum of knowledge of the requirements of cricket and cricketers. The best cannot emerge from a tour so overcrowded that a large percentage of the time was spent in aircraft and coaches, checking in and out of hotels with such speed to make it hardly worthwhile unpacking suitcases. The Australians themselves might as well have been on tour abroad for all the time they spent at home. At one point England flew the 3000 miles from Perth to Brisbane, and from Brisbane to Sydney, and back to Brisbane on the following day – and all for limited-over one-day games. Add the time spent on the move, getting the luggage on and off planes, and waiting at airports, and at least another five-day Test could have been played!

In the final analysis the whole experience developed into a blatant example of overkill, with the public saturated with too much cricket both on the field and on the screen. Time and time again friends told me they were sick and tired of having some form of cricket thrust before their eyes on television. They said they wanted to return to the simpler days when interest was centred on a Test series for the Ashes or against the West Indies. I heard a lot about the 'new' public and less about the 'old' – those real followers of the game who saw through the artificialities and were soon to be rewarded by the great 1981 rubber in England.

Lest I should be thought to be on my own I turn to Peter Smith of the *Daily Mail* for his personal view of the tour in *Wisden*.

Forty-eight hours before England's cricketers flew out of Melbourne for the last time Alec Bedser was asked by the Australian authorities to present his considered view of the experimental twin-tour programme, the first product of the marriage between the Australian Cricket Board and World Series Cricket which had taken place some nine months earlier. He gave it a definite 'thumbs down'. It was a strictly personal view, sought not in his capacity as England's tour manager or as chairman of England's selectors, but from a man who has had the closest possible association with the game through four decades. He received majority support from those who had the best interests of the game at heart, particularly Australian cricket below Test level. This had been swamped by the accent on Test and one-day internationals, neatly parcelled to present a cricketing package suitable for maximum exploitation on television.

Privately, at least, the Australian players agreed with Bedser. With a

135

programme of six Test matches – three against England and the West Indies – plus the triangular one-day competition for the Benson and Hedges World Series Cup, the Australian players became very much a touring side against their own country.

England's cricketers were just as unhappy with the complicated programme of matches that brought a constant switch from one-day to five-day cricket with a few three-day matches in between. It could be claimed that England's verdict was coloured by their three-nil defeat in the Tests, but Clive Lloyd, the West Indies captain, was just as critical immediately after his side's two-nil series win – their first in Australia at the sixth attempt – and their victory in the World Series Cup.

It was not only the match programme but the whole atmosphere that the England players found disagreeable. Their captain, Brearley, was the subject of a disgraceful campaign wherever he went, and a large section of the Melbourne crowd was so abusive that the Australian team manager, John Edwards, was moved to issue a statement in which he said they made him ashamed to be an Australian. The childish behaviour of Lillee during the aluminium bat affair during the first Test in Perth, and his baiting of Brearley during a one-day international at Sydney, proved as distasteful to them as the treatment they received from the crowd in the early night games under the Sydney floodlights when they became the target of an assortment of missiles.

At the end of the tour I offered my private views to the Australian Board of Control in a friendly spirit of constructive criticism. Some of the eleven points raised were:

In a dual tour it might be better to run the fixtures separately with one international side playing its Test matches in one half of the season and the other in the second half, with a special period set aside for one-day internationals.

The programme did not give teams enough cricket outside the Tests and single-innings matches. Players not in the Test side had little chance to get net practice, and those out of form had no opportunity to get into form.

There is a danger of overemphasizing the one-day game and of ignoring its effect on standards as well as on Test cricket. Is there a danger of one-day games taking over traditional Test cricket?

In such a full programme the Sheffield Shield competition was pushed very much into the background. Is this good for the development of future Australian cricketers?

136

Personally I was in favour of reverting to a full tour each of Australia by England and the West Indies with appropriate one-day games. Country areas could then be visited. I always felt this aspect of touring to be important, although it is not always favoured by modern players.

Having made these observations I wondered if I represented a voice from the past. Now, several years later, it seems to me Australia is still searching for the right blend of cricket to satisfy both the public and the need to maintain their traditional playing standards.

The question of how much limited-over cricket should be played without eroding the standard required at Test match level has always been a bone of contention. As it is an inescapable fact that the longer the match the greater are the skills required, I have consistently maintained there must be a sensible balance between the one-day competitions and the traditional three- and five-day matches.

On this subject I got into a little hot water after addressing what I was told would be a private function in New Zealand in 1975. I was assured the Press would not be present. Unfortunately a version appeared in newspapers that I put England's defeat in Australia that winter down to the effects of limited-over cricket 'which I did not watch'. My comments were taken out of context, and it was absurd that it should be construed to suggest I made a blanket criticism of what is now an acceptable form of modern cricket.

As a result I was suspended by the sponsors Gillette for three years from acting as an adjudicator in the Man of the Match award. I was also publicly rebuked by my old friend Doug Insole, then chairman of the TCCB. I am sure it was all a misunderstanding.

Ironically eleven years later a committee of enquiry set up by the Test and County Cricket Board concluded that limited-over cricket has been the main cause of the decline in batting and bowling standards, a finding long shared by most old players. Which does not mean they are unmindful of its public appeal and financial benefits.

10

The Captaincy

If my arm were to be twisted for me to name the best of more than a full team of England captains whom I helped to choose from 1962 onwards, it would be Mike Brearley, the quiet persuader, who twice took over and triumphed when anything less than strong but sympathetic leadership could have led to disaster. Brearley was always in danger of being considerably underrated, possibly because he was perhaps half a class below the most exacting Test batting standards (although he averaged 68·33 in the county averages when he was first selected in 1977), possibly because he was self-effacing, without the extrovert Tony Greig's up-and-at-'em approach, and lacked the presence that some one like Freddie Brown or Ted Dexter commanded. And possibly he did the kind of things away from cricket which the public do not associate with their sporting heroes, like taking a first in Classics and a 2:1 in Moral Science (which he described to me as a century in the first innings and 80 not out in the second) and coming joint first in the Civil Service examination; or being a Samaritan at Cambridge and helping disturbed adolescents.

The secret of his strength as a county and an international captain is not difficult to find. He had that indefinable gift of earning personal respect and getting the best out of his team. His selfless attitude was evident when I rang him in 1981 to ask if he would come back as captain after the Lord's Test. England were in some need of uplift, and failure could have been a painful postscript to Brearley's career. He would not have been remembered so much for his achievements in his first spell of captaincy but as an example of the dangers of 'making a comeback'. There was not much I could offer him except to put his reputation on the line, but his response was immediate. 'I'd be delighted', he said, and from those few words sprang a miracle, with England spectacularly winning the series and the Ashes and a reborn Botham and Bob Willis rightly winning places in Test history.

I remember, too, with gratitude the calm control Brearley brought to the dressing room at a time of crisis and acrimony when he succeeded the sacked Tony Greig. Not only was there Greig, but two other defectors in Derek Underwood and Alan Knott, and the selectors knew that, just as Mike could handle that potentially difficult situation, so could he ease Geoff Boycott back midway through the series as tactfully as if Yorkshire's prodigal son had never been away. A third trial of his strength of character was to be the butt of personal attack in the first post-Packer Tests in Australia. Needless to say, he survived with much dignity. A lesser man might have capitulated, packed his bags and caught the first jet home.

There was a bit of nonsense by Bob Willis, who went into print in the *Sunday Express* to say that, as vice-captain in Australia in 1979–80, he was obliged to act as the go-between Brearley and myself on the grounds that our age difference made us incompatible. The headline read: ' "How I tried to bridge the 'Gap' between Bedser and Brearley" – by Bob Willis.' Bob contended that Mike and I were 'not quite on the same wavelength' and did not seem to get on personally, a view which more than surprised me. I supported Mike in every important issue throughout a difficult tour, and was with him totally on his reaction to some of the conditions of the tour which had not been finalized before the party left. All in all, I thought we got on very well together, not only in Australia but throughout our association as captain and chairman. Of course there was a generation gap as there has inevitably been between captain and manager on so many tours. Mike and I might not have agreed exactly on the question of player power or on some of the long-established conventions, but we always had more in common than in contention. I would be strongly suspicious of a relationship which was so cosy as never to provoke a difference of opinion.

I was in the habit of reading, especially in one newspaper, that Brearley had got his way in the selection of Test teams. The implication that Mike dominated the meetings, insisting on having the final word, was quite wrong. As would be expected, he was articulate and logical in presenting his case and listened courteously to contrary opinions. Never once was there the slightest hint of what might be called his pulling intellectual rank, as I have heard suggested. Naturally there were occasions when the selectors fell in with his wishes, and others when they disagreed and Mike did not get what he wanted. On marginal issues Brearley, like all captains before him and since, was likely to be allowed his choice. That is the unwritten law of selection, for the last thing selectors aim to do is saddle a captain with players he strongly feels he does not want.

It was very much to Brearley's and England's advantage that he was a mature thirty-four when he followed Greig and had been thoroughly prepared and groomed for the national captaincy. He was the first to lead Cambridge University for two successive years since F. S. Jackson in 1892–93, and he had taken an MCC Under–25 side to Pakistan where he outshone Dennis Amiss and Keith Fletcher, then regarded as England's two leading young batsmen. More importantly, he had captained Middlesex for five years.

No doubt some will infer that I have a bias for university-trained captains, but there are no hard and fast rules to appointing a captain, even at Test level. Invite the average cricket lover to compile a list of natural leaders and it would be surprising if Douglas Jardine, Gubby Allen, Percy Chapman, Freddie Brown, Peter May and Walter Robins were not included. Yet not one was captain while at university. However, all were well primed for the Test captaincy when the time came, although Robins always insisted that he served as a mere caretaker. Having played at Oxford or Cambridge was an advantage, but in those days the university blue often went on to county cricket and many became captains.

At the time of Brearley's appointment four of the county captains were from overseas; Keith Fletcher and Lancashire's David Lloyd had been in the firing line against Lillee and Thomson and their selection was not considered appropriate at that juncture; Ray Illingworth, Brian Close, John Edrich and Warwickshire's David Brown were well advanced in their careers; and Geoff Boycott had not yet returned to the fold. Norman Gifford and Richard Gilliat were considered, but Gilliat, although he came close, had not progressed beyond county cricket. Brearley was the natural favourite and it was gratifying that he did so well. His contribution was summed up in a perceptive comment from Keith Miller, who wrote that an all-rounder was not necessarily a batsman-bowler. Brearley was an all-rounder as an excellent captain who was able to get his players to do their best for him, a useful batsman and a first-rate slip fieldsman.

The best captain makes the most of his resources, but the best is not enough if the odds are too great. Much as I admire Mike Brearley, his outstanding record against Australia would probably not have been quite the same in the Bradman, Lindsay Hassett, Richie Benaud eras, or possibly against Ian Chappell. Ray Illingworth beat Gary Sobers's West Indies team in 1969, but understandably could not contain the Rest of the World XI in 1970. He was no worse a captain in defeat than he had been in victory. Maybe Gary, with such an embarrassing array of talent at his disposal was not seriously put to the test in 1970, but if I had to choose between the two, I would go for Illingworth as captain. Both Illingworth, with John Snow in 1970, and Brearley, with Ian Botham and Bob Willis in 1981, made exemplary use of match-winning fast bowlers and had the gift of carrying their teams with them.

In recent years Clive Lloyd has been far and away the most successful international captain, but, without underplaying his personal influence, it is hard to imagine even a moderate captain going far wrong with the all-round talent at his disposal. 'There are a hundred more waiting to fill our shoes' was Clive's ominous warning to world cricket – a boast I am inclined to believe after seeing Antigua in action in Bermuda in 1984.

There have been better tacticians than Lloyd, and at times I felt he could have curbed the over-enthusiastic use of bumpers and short-pitched bowling by his attack. Despite the powers vested in umpires, captains exercise the major influence in controlling intimidatory bowling. It has been said that captains cannot be expected to control the length their bowlers use, but this argument is nonsense. If a bowler cannot, or will not, bowl a fair length, he should be taken off. It is as simple as that.

Obviously I want to see the day return when there is competition for the captaincy as there was in 1962 when Walter Robins's committee could speculate between Ted Dexter, Colin Cowdrey and David Sheppard. Sheppard's return after a lengthy absence was seen as a sure sign that he was earmarked for the post, a view which Robins did not discourage in his conversations with the leading writers. It must have been his way of keeping the pot boiling, but so far as I was concerned it was a choice between Dexter and Cowdrey, and, unless I am very wide of the mark, Robins himself regarded Dexter as first choice. Robins was an individualist and regarded as unorthodox, but in the sense that he set the highest store on a positive approach at all times and would never accept the second rate he was very orthodox. He once went into the Australian dressing room during a Test at Lord's and told them he hoped they would win as they were playing the more aggressive cricket. The Aussies found it difficult to credit that an Englishman could express such views, but I am sure he was absolutely sincere for that was his approach to the game. I often suspected he came out with outrageous views merely to stimulate discussion, and there was nothing he enjoyed more than a lively argument. Give me a man who tells a joke against himself – and Robins had a veritable fund.

A brilliant fielder, Robins made one of his rare mistakes in missing Bradman at a critical juncture of the 1936–37 series which Australia won after losing the first two Tests. At the end of the over Robins went to his skipper and close friend Gubby Allen to apologize. 'Terribly sorry', he said. 'Oh, it's allright, old boy' was the calm response. 'You've only lost us the Ashes.'

Always quick to counter what he thought to be unfair criticism, Robins stood up for Ted Dexter when he was flayed by critics and public alike during the third Test with Australia at Headingley in 1964. England scored a modest 268 but appeared to be heading for a useful first-innings lead with Australia crumbling at 187 for 7. Fred Titmus was bowling his off breaks superbly when Dexter decided to take the second new ball in the hope of bringing the innings to a speedy end. Peter Burge was 38, and, with the help of Neil Hawke and the late Wally Grout, he went on to make 160. The last 3 wickets added 211, Australia gained a lead of 121 and, on the strength of a 7–wicket victory – the only Test of the series to finish with a clear result – took the Ashes.

Dexter took the full brunt of England's fury. 'He couldn't skipper a rowing boat,' declared the late Brian Sellers, the plain-speaking former Yorkshire captain. To be candid, it was hard to defend what transpired to be an error of judgement, but taking the new ball in the circumstances Dexter found himself to be in was one of those decisions which can turn out to be absolutely right or disastrously wrong. Personally I believe he should have left Titmus to complete his job, but Dexter could not have expected Trueman would bowl what *Wisden* described as a 'generous supply of long hops to Burge' – a notably strong hooker and puller. Robins believed Dexter had been let down by his fast bowlers and snorted with indignation as he read the next morning's papers. When at last he found a view in the *Daily Mail* to support his contention he walked round the ground to the press box to congratulate Alex Bannister.

One of the instinctive acts of captaincy is to let well alone or slip in the right word to a bowler at the right moment. Sir Donald Bradman, who scored 212 in Australia's second innings in the crucial Fourth Test at Adelaide in 1937, knew he had to dismiss Wally Hammond on the final morning if England were to be beaten and Australia draw level in the series. He opened with the left-arm googly bowler Fleetwood-Smith and told him, 'I want you to bowl the best ball of your life to get Hammond out.' Fleetwood-Smith did exactly that and England were beaten by 148 runs. Some might retort, 'Lucky old Braddles.' Another time Fleetwood-Smith would have bowled a long hop and been hit for 6. But there is a lot to the psychological handling of bowlers and encouraging every member of the team to pull out some extra effort where it is most needed. Bradman challenged Fleetwood-Smith and found the response he wanted. I would have relished playing under Bradman, particularly in my early Test days.

George Mann, under less pressure in South Africa in 1948–49 than Norman Yardley had been as Hammond's successor, was a good example of the old-style captain who got the best out of his players without seemingly trying to do so. He let the 'professors' get on with the job without interference. I was happy to bowl, and he was happy to let me bowl. Our captain-player relationship was as simple as that. In the comparatively innocent days of 1948–49 there was not the rancour of outside interference as there is today and George, who never put a foot wrong, had a manner which reduced every order to a polite request. Yardley, Mann and the bluff Freddie Brown had distinctive styles, and they were not afraid of losing, which has become a curse of contemporary cricket.

To me Brown had a special appeal, born of our partnership in Australia in 1950–51, when he was captain at the age of thirty-nine and with Trevor Bailey and Doug Wright we shared a heavy workload. Switching from leg breaks to medium-pace swing, Brown took 18 wickets in the series. He started as an opening bowler at Leys School, Cambridge, and was advised by the coach Aubrey Faulkner to take up leg-breaks and googlies as the best way to a blue at Cambridge. Although I did not take kindly to being on a losing side in Australia in 1950–51 and felt so much could have been achieved with a stronger side – how much he influenced the selectors to send so many inexperienced players I do not know – Freddie Brown did a wonderful job for England and his vigorous leadership was undoubtedly a turning point in England's post war recovery. Ironically he is probably better remembered for his 4–1 defeat in Australia than his 3–1 home victory over South Africa in the following summer, but he put English cricket on course again and, with a splendid new stock of young players coming through, handed over a winning combination to Len Hutton in 1952. He also made a major contribution to the successful years which followed.

As a player I found Brown an ideal captain. Unlike Hammond, he willingly discussed tactics and, like Surridge, he brushed misfortune aside with an air of perpetual optimism. He regarded me with the understanding of one bowler for another and never interfered with my tactics or field placings. Between overs I would tell him where I wanted my field and he would invariably reply, 'I'll leave it to you.' In other words, he trusted me to get on with my job, which is exactly as it ought to be between a knowledgeable skipper and a thinking bowler, as I tried to be.

Some players found Brown's bluntness hard to take but I found him exceptionally easy to get on with. His image as an affable, forthright bulldog figure in flannels was right as far as it went, but it should not disguise the fact that he had a far deeper understanding and judgement of tactics than some captains who have gained a reputation for such accomplishments.

He respected ability and despised slackness, which he neither understood nor tolerated. The merest hint of anything but maximum effort brought a sharp reprimand, and at least one noted international I could mention owes him much. On the other side of the coin, he was even quicker to praise and to trust, as I discovered at Adelaide, where midsummer can be excessively hot and the nights an ordeal of sleeplessness. During the Test match there some friends offered to put me up at their home in the Mount Lofty range, which was up to 15 degrees cooler than the hotel where the team stayed. When I asked for permission to sleep away from the rest of the party the captain said, 'Of course you can'. I appreciated his trust, and my summing up of Brown would be equally direct – straight, honest, flexible (an admirable trait in a captain), a man's man and a first-rate captain and leader.

Look at Freddie Brown on the field and you could almost read his thought processes. He went arrow-straight to the point and was disarmingly uncomplicated. Look at Len Hutton to try and read his thoughts, and you were seldom the wiser. He was a much more private person, given to guarding his inner feelings, with basically a sensitive and worrying nature. Len was brought up in a hard Yorkshire school, at a time when to see play from the pros' room at Lord's it was necessary to stand on a chair or on tiptoe. For all his triumphs as a batsman he needed considerable adjustment to take the reins of captaincy. It must have been a great strain and he never quite reconciled himself to the national captaincy although he was better than well received by the public at large and his performances were unanswerable. He freely admitted in his recent book *Fifty Years in Cricket* that his playing career was shortened by maybe two years by the problems he faced in the West Indies in 1954. 'It was a close call that I was well enough to go to Australia in 1954–55,' he wrote.

Perhaps deep down Hutton, like Sir Jack Hobbs, would have preferred to have been left to the pursuit of batting perfection unburdened by the extra responsibilities of captaincy. The cares of office did not weigh lightly on his shoulders and he was acutely aware that as the first professional captain to be appointed this century he was a sitting target for snobbery and vulnerable to the backlash of the diehards. He also had a native Yorkshire caution, found difficult decisions hard to take, and had a constant private battle with his never robust health and his weakened left arm, the legacy of a wartime accident. It was never an easy ride for him and the responsibility he had as prime batsman and captain, plus the criticism he attracted from some quarters, took its toll.

I have often wondered if Hutton had not been injured in the war, if he had played as long as Sir Jack Hobbs, and had not had the pressures of captaincy, what his final record might have been. The real yardstick of his lofty class was his 2428 runs against Australia at a time when they had Bill O'Reilly, Ray Lindwall and Keith Miller to name but three – and in 1948 when the new ball could be taken after only fifty-five overs. When you bowl at a champion only 22 yards away you know what you are up against, and there was never any doubt in my mind when I bowled at Len that he was indeed a champion. He must surely be the finest of all Yorkshire batsmen with his classical technique and his natural patience and concentration. If there was one possible chink in his armour it was his pick-up, which began in the direction of gully and left him a little open at times to the late in-swinger or the well-bowled off break. I can claim to have given him a little trouble in this respect, but all things are relative and by no means can it be described as a technical weakness.

Hutton needed iron willpower and character to overcome the pressures upon him, which never seemed far away even when he hit a winning trail. On that score alone he could not fail to win admiration and, when I hear modern players saying we old hands cannot hope to understand the pressures of today, I feel like referring them to Len. There are misconceptions about pressures. A line needs to be drawn between the challenge to character and temperament awaiting every player in a Test match – and that is something which starts afresh with every new match – and being in the public eye. Bradman had his private life almost ruined by a measure of fame which has not been accorded to one player before or since. He was seldom spared the blaze of publicity and it was a miracle how he coped with it. But there are what might be considered self-imposed pressures in modern cricket induced by spin-off interests such as endorsing equipment, lending one's name to newspaper articles, advertising, public appearances and a host of other activities which are classified as 'useful little earners'. If a player chooses to become a minor industry, backed by an agent and an accountant, that must be his personal decision and I do not blame him for making hay while the sun shines. There is a limited time at the top. But his commercial value depends on his performances on the field and being constantly in the public eye. Thereby hangs the pressure and the strain. It would be an interesting experiment if a leading player eschewed all commercial temptations and concentrated on his cricket. Would he be a better player without his self-imposed pressures? This aspect of pressure is comparatively new as in my time the stars were often exploited and poorly rewarded. Bradman, Compton, Hutton, May, to name but four, coped astonishingly well with the strains associated with great performers, although perhaps at a cost for Hutton. All would have made fortunes in the modern set-up.

Evidence of Hutton's natural caution was reflected in the composition of England's teams in 1953 when the Ashes were recovered after nineteen years. To enable him to play an extra batsman he took the field in three of the five Tests with only four bowlers. In the First Test at Trent Bridge there was Bedser, Bailey, Wardle and Tattersall; in the Third at Old Trafford, Bedser, Bailey, Wardle and Laker; in the Fourth at Headingley, Bedser, Bailey, Lock and Laker. At Headingley there were six batsmen – Hutton, Edrich, Graveney, Compton, Watson and Simpson – supported by all-rounder Bailey, who was later to open the innings for England, and wicketkeeper Evans, who was not lightly to be dismissed as a batsman. For all that, England were dismissed in the first innings for 167 by Lindwall, Miller, Davidson and Ron Archer. Allan Border's Australians also favoured a four-man bowling attack in the 1985 series in England, but it does not alter my opinion that four bowlers over five days is a risk and defensively minded.

Years later when Len joined us as a selector his comments and opinions were never expressed without a careful examination of the arguments. They were always worth listening to and were often accompanied by a knowing grin. Few have had deeper feelings for cricket or a better understanding of tactics. Len had wisely listened to older heads on the selection committee when he was first made captain and there was much wisdom in his contribution at all times.

Much of the flack directed at the captaincy during the Hutton era died away with the coming of Peter May, Colin Cowdrey and Mike Smith. They were less vulnerable. Denis Compton and Trevor Bailey dropped out of contention; indeed Denis's failure as Freddie Brown's deputy left the way clear for Hutton. Bailey, who had been Hutton's vice-captain in the West Indies in 1954, sacrificed his chance of succession, as I understand it, with the premature publication of some articles. In those days there was a two-year embargo. Nowadays articles and comments are permitted during a tour, which seems to me to be too liberal a concession. Denis would have made an interesting captain, but Bailey must have been a considerable loss. In an examination covering tactics, field settings and the range of captaincy, he would have come close to the top of the class. There was not an aspect of the game he failed to investigate and act on his findings. He was more than a useful all-rounder in the top flight, a fighter with the gift of rising to an occasion, but if I have a doubt it is that he might have proved to be too defensive and cautious.

Peter May's modesty and calm manner deceived many into thinking he was not a natural leader. Tell that to his contemporaries and they would reject the charge immediately. A real captain has no need to make it clear with extrovert behaviour who is the boss. Knowing Peter as intimately as I do, I can write with honesty that as both captain and player he had few peers. As vice-captain to him at The Oval I saw his total dedication and depth of character. He was a good captain because he led by example, carried out his duties without fuss, and was a loyal friend of every player in the dressing room. Very much a players' captain.

My personal experience of his tactical expertise was limited as he was away leading England for half the season, but I saw enough to convince me that he was one of England's better captains. Richie Benaud placed him in front of Len Hutton, but such evaluations are a matter of opinion. I would be satisfied to give both a high ranking. Peter did not have an easy time. In the six years he was captain he had forty-one Tests, including thirty-five in succession until he was laid low by a particularly painful illness and had to return from the West Indies in 1959–60. Typically he kept the illness and the pain to himself. When he could no longer hold out, the rest of the team were surprised to learn how bad his complaint was. Equally unluckily, he was in the thick of the throwing and dragging controversy in Australia in 1958–59, and his side, which looked so powerful on paper, was cut to ribbons.

Peter was put in an invidious position, especially as the home critics generally stoutly defended the suspect bowlers. The situation should never have been allowed to develop, but that was no consolation to Peter, who could either protest officially, which would have been construed as sour grapes from a losing captain, or suffer in silence and tacitly suggest nothing was wrong. It is another argument that England's cricketers on tour take what they believe to be injustices too much to heart. I think Ian Meckiff and Gordon Rorke did infringe the law, and at the end of the series throwing and dragging, which troubled the whole game, was effectively dealt with by legislators. A bit late for Peter, though!

Peter never put himself above advice. He listened to chairman Gubby Allen in 1956 when Cyril Washbrook was brought back to turn the tide against Australia, and he had a receptive ear at The Oval. His question to me, 'What do you think, Alec?' became a catchphrase in the dressing room. The important fact was that we pooled our ideas and worked as one. As a tactician Peter played straight down the line, being neither daring nor overcautious. Sound and orthodox he might have been, but he was not so conventional as to be dull. He was creative enough to follow the inventive Stuart Surridge – a far from easy transition period for both captain and players. The door was wide open to invite unfavourable comparisons, but Peter was wise enough to anticipate the possible difficulties.

When I listen to pundits listing the qualities of the perfect captain I seldom hear one virtue mentioned. That is selflessness. Peter had it in abundance and it helped to bind the dressing room together. His first thought was for his players in a sincere and unaffected way. A good spell of bowling, or an innings would bring an encouraging 'Thank you'. To merit his simple acknowledgement of a performance was like a professional accolade. Nor would the public know how often he shielded his struggling batting partner from difficult bowling. In effect it was team work of a high order, and it was impossible to play with Peter and remain oblivious of a rare personality.

Colin Cowdrey was the enigma of my time. As Sir Robert Menzies put it, 'Cowdrey is handicapped only by a charming and inveterate modesty; he doesn't know how good he is!' In the post Hutton-Compton era only May was his superior, and he should have made the captaincy his own and achieved his ambition to lead England in Australia. He was, of course, very unlucky not to have done so for there seemed no obstacle in his path for the 1970–71 tour. He had been vice-captain in Australia in turn to May, Dexter and Mike Smith before I was chairman of selectors. In the West Indies in 1967–68 he was highly praised in *Wisden* for his 'flawless captaincy' and victory over Gary Sobers, and he came through a tour of Pakistan marred by persistent rioting and civil disorder with his reputation enhanced. His handling of almost unprecedented problems, both on the field and politically behind the scenes, was exemplary. The captaincy crown was on his head, without a pretender in sight, and I felt content that my spell as chairman would start with a major bonus of settled leadership.

But in late May 1969 Cowdrey ruptured an Achilles tendon in a John Player League match at Maidstone, and the saga of Cowdrey and Illingworth for the captaincy in Australia was about to begin. If his injury was to prove a catastrophe for its distinguished victim it was an unpleasant shock for me and my co-selectors Don Kenyon, Alan Smith and Billy Sutcliffe.

Ray Illingworth had just started a new career having left Yorkshire, after eighteen years, to take over the captaincy of Leicestershire. It was no secret in the game that Ray had been an invaluable tactical adviser to Yorkshire captains and had a good cricket brain. Within weeks of taking over at Leicester the grapevine was alive with commendations of his skills as a captain. His personal form was also good, and with Cowdrey on the sidelines the need for strong leadership was made all the more necessary by the loss of the heart of England's batting. For one reason or another Cowdrey, Barrington, Milburn and Graveney had gone. England's batting never quite recovered from the losses.

Clearly Illingworth answered the selectors' immediate requirements, and Cowdrey's large body of supporters, extending far beyond the borders of Kent, had reason to believe the appointment was nothing more than a temporary expedient. But Illingworth, seeing himself as more than a caretaker, brilliantly took his chance, beating the West Indies and New Zealand in a split season in 1969. There was a groundswell of criticism, the chief thrust being directed at the slow tempo of play, but *Wisden* for one doubted if there would have been a difference under Cowdrey.

Cowdrey now had a clear rival, and it did not need much prescience to foresee the classic seeds of controversy. Some of the heat went out of the growing debate of two strong claimants with the crisis that winter over South Africa's impending tour of England, but it returned again when the Rest of the World XI, captained by Gary Sobers, took South Africa's place. Ironically the party included five South Africans. Cowdrey's comeback campaign had the worst of starts with 152 runs from thirteen innings, and both he and Geoff Boycott asked to be excused from the first match at Lord's on fitness grounds. England could ill afford to be without two leading batsmen against the combined bowling talent of Australia, the West Indies, South Africa and Pakistan and were trounced by an innings. Illingworth, however, made 62 out of 127 in the first innings and 94 out of 339 in the second. In the next match at Trent Bridge, won by England, Illingworth scored 97 out of 279, and, match by match, he strengthened his grip on the captaincy. To my mind, unlucky as it was for Colin, it would have been a rank injustice if at that point Illingworth had been asked to move aside as he had done everything the selectors had asked of him. In two summers he had shown an unmistakable flair for sensible and firm captaincy with a high degree of tactical skill and awareness. No one was more alive to Colin's position than I was. To be pushed into second place once again was a cruel twist of fortune, but it could not have come as a surprise to anyone of neutral mind when Illingworth's appointment to captain England in Australia the following winter (1970–71) was confirmed during the third match with the Rest of the Word at Edgbaston. Colin had made a splendid effort in the second innings, but by then the die was cast.

I have read accounts of what was purported to have taken place when the selectors' decision was made known to the two candidates. Some did me less than justice, and to put the record straight I give the simple facts. As was his right, Illingworth was told in the privacy of an office which Warwickshire had put at my disposal. I realized the news would be painful to Colin so I arranged to see him also in an office. Alan Smith, one of the selectors, was also present. The allegation that Ray and Colin were told of the decision in the dressing room within earshot of other England players was not true. Nor was it a compliment to my courtesy and my understanding of the feelings of the two players.

As I feared, Colin was very disappointed and asked for time to consider his position as the vice-captain elect. Naturally his wish was granted. As I look back this was possibly a mistake. I should have stipulated an answer within forty-eight hours. The selectors fully appreciated Cowdrey's feelings of frustrated ambition. Apart from his tremendous ability they recognized his past services both as a captain and vice-captain and that he was always the perfect diplomat.

At a personal level I was a friend of both players, but ignoring the lobbying – which was strong – and the personalities, the selectors in the end had to make a hardheaded, unsentimental answer to the question: who would serve England's interests better in Australia? Cowdrey's innate caution had to be set against Illingworth's hard, practical realism. Illingworth was already reshaping the destiny of Leicestershire.

One of our fears was that Colin, as a Test Captain, had given the impression of lacking confidence and firmness in arriving at an important decision. As the days passed after Edgbaston without any response from him, he seemed to be supplying proof of that very misgiving. By now the selectors were caught in a veritable crossfire of opinion. Colin's supporters were unhappy, Ray's well satisfied; there was criticism heaping on our heads for giving Colin time to think over his position, and those for and against Colin's inclusion in the team if he was not to be captain.

While I sympathized with Colin I began to think that if he had suffered such a knockout blow in being passed over for the captaincy and did not want to tour under Illingworth, he should have pulled out at once, or at least within forty-eight hours. To let the matter hang fire did not help anyone. In the end Colin accepted the vice-captaincy. The selectors felt an unnecessary complication had arisen because they had tried to ease the pain of disappointment. I know Colin had set his heart on the ultimate distinction of taking England to Australia. The prize had been snatched away from him when it was within his grasp, but the fact had to be faced that Illingworth was the man in possession and he had not let England down. In fact, he had proved his qualification for the job on hand. Four years later, however, I was to be profoundly grateful when Colin flew to Australia to answer my SOS as a manager facing an injury crisis.

Although Illingworth returned with the Ashes in 1971 he was not everyone's hero and my own position as chairman of selectors was put on the line. I am not sure to this day if the two facts are related, but the predictions in some newspapers of my removal proved to be wrong. Some light was thrown on the situation in E. W. Swanton's book *Gubby Allen – Man of Cricket.** He wrote:

An unexpected call on his [Allen's] services was made in the spring of 1971. The TCCB Cricket Sub-Committee nominated him, ten years after his retirement as chairman, to serve again as a selector. Gubby, while far from enthusiastic, said he would do the job if there was a strong wish that he should. However, the 1970 selectors, under Alec Bedser, the sitting chairman, had picked the side which under Ray Illingworth had just won back the Ashes in Australia. As soon as Gubby learned that the wisdom of a change was disputed and that Alec was keen to carry on, he saw to it that his nomination was withdrawn.

Presumably had Gubby returned as a selector he would have taken the chair. As it was I continued as chairman and Illingworth as captain. It was a good working relationship.

Illingworth's unshakable resolve and strong Yorkshire sense of independence trod on some sensitive toes, and he met with a measure of hostility even before he set foot in Australia, which I thought was harsh, particularly as the allegations were mainly on hearsay. He was said to be too defensive – a daring charge since Bill Lawry was Australia's captain – and made excessive use of leg-side field placings, then a somewhat contentious issue. I would never rate him as any more defensive than other captains of his day. One of his main strengths was his refusal to be intimidated or blown off the course he had planned to take. He was not afraid to be wrong and deserves a high ranking among England's postwar

*Hutchinson-Stanley Paul, 1985

captains. To win the last Test at Sydney without Geoff Boycott, who had broken his left arm, and John Snow, whose fast bowling separated the two sides in the series, with a broken finger midway through the match, was one of England's epic victories.

As captain Ray could be criticized for not bowling himself enough, but, considering the resources available to him, his achievements were considerable. There was a touch of Hutton in his strategies, shrewdness and tenacity but, at the age of forty-one, following a crushing defeat by the West Indies under Rohan Kanhai in 1973, the time had come for him to make way for a younger captain. I did not expect a fighter of Ray's calibre to agree to the selectors' assessment of the situation, but he accepted it gracefully. He was certainly not made the scapegoat for a debacle at Lord's where the West Indies won by the embarrassing margin of an innings and 226 runs. Only once before, when Wally Hammond's side were caught on that impossible sticky wicket at Brisbane, had England taken a worse beating. Morale was beginning to be put to the test and Ray's own form was not what it had been.

After long deliberations we – my co-selectors were Ossie Wheatley, Alan Smith and Brian Taylor – concluded it was psychologically ripe for change and to relieve Ray of his burden. Our choice fell on Mike Denness, who had carried on Kent's newfound winning ways impressively and had been vice-captain to Tony Lewis in India and Pakistan in 1972–73.

Originally Lewis had been earmarked as Illingworth's successor. He had all the right credentials as captain of Cambridge University and Glamorgan and as a batsman of consistently good performance. Our intention was to give him as much experience as possible under Illingworth, and accordingly he was selected to play in the first two Tests of the home series with New Zealand in 1973. Unfortunately he had to pull out of the Second Test with injury and was able to play in only three Championship games all season. Before the end of the summer we asked Lewis to try himself out on the field, but it was a failure and he dropped out of the running for the captaincy. What was Lewis's misfortune became Mike Denness's opportunity.

Before the First Test there was a Test trial at Hove between Lewis's MCC touring team of the previous winter and the Rest. As there was often little first-class cricket played in the opening weeks to guide the selectors, I had persisted in my efforts to revive the fixture after twenty years. Some critics played down its value, but that was not my opinion. Commenting on the end of the Illingworth era, *Wisden* thought the selectors were wise to appoint a county captain enjoying success, in contrast to Yorkshire, who under Geoff Boycott were 'down in the doldrums'.

Unfortunately Denness had withdrawn from the Test trial with injury and did not play in any of the six Tests during the season against New Zealand and the West Indies. To the public Denness's appointment may have been unexpected, but he was the no. 2 to Lewis, a position which Boycott could have occupied if he had toured India and Pakistan in 1972–73. I think Lewis, ever mindful of what Don Shepherd, his senior adviser at Glamorgan, had meant to him, would have been happy to have Geoffrey at his side. And I have little doubt that the selectors would have agreed, but Boycott, whose spleen had been removed as a boy, had doubts that his health would stand up to a tour on the subcontinent. He declined the invitation to tour, and it becomes a simple fact of history that, had he gone and made a success of the vice-captaincy, he, and not Denness, would in all probability have been captain in the West Indies in 1973–74.

Boycott's consequent withdrawal from the 1974–75 party to Australia which Denness captained and I managed left Denness with the uneasy suspicion that he might have been the unwitting cause. In his book *I Declare** Denness writes:

I was disappointed that Boycott dropped out, for he was one of the best players in the world, and obviously had something to offer us in Australia. We picked the best players we had in the hope that they would be keen and enthusiastic enough to play for England. Whatever his reasons, it was very sad that Boycott was not part of the England set-up. The story appeared, not necessarily originating from Boycott, that the reason he did not want to go was because I was captain. Until Boycott confirms this there is nothing I can say about it. Even if it was true I would not be able to answer it.

As chairman of selectors, committed to the never easy task of finding the best side to represent England, I scarcely need to add

*Arthur Barker Ltd., 1977

155

that I shared Denness's sentiments. I would go a shade further and doubt if anyone regretted it more, apart from Geoffrey himself.

Boycott was much missed in Australia, but I doubt if two Boycotts would have redressed the imbalance between the sides. There seemed no end to Denness's misfortunes, and it spoke volumes for his character and courage that he should recover his form after Sydney and enjoy a storming run-in both in Australia and New Zealand.

Even his home series with Pakistan produced a bomb scare at Headingley and an intemperate outburst during the Lord's Test by the touring manager, Omar Kureishi, who is better known as a broadcaster. There had been a violent overnight storm and Kureishi accused the MCC, the ground authority, of 'an appalling show of negligence and incompetence in not covering the wicket properly.' The late Jim Fairbrother, the head groundsman and his staff, had battled throughout the small hours drenched to the skin at the height of the storm trying to stem the flood cascading from the roof of the grandstand and down the slope towards the pitch. The Pakistan players themselves accepted that every reasonable precaution had been taken, and it was interesting that almost to a man they sought out Fairbrother to tell him not to be concerned about the complaint. Although Denness was not directly involved, protests of that nature can be upsetting.

Perhaps Mike used up too much of his share of the luck on his first venture in the West Indies in 1973–74 where, after being outplayed for the first three Tests, he returned with a drawn series. England's performances resembled a high-wire act in a gale-force wind, but although he wobbled close to catastrophe on several occasions, the tenacity and skills of Dennis Amiss, Tony Greig and Keith Fletcher staved off two defeats. The Fourth Test at Guyana was wet and drawn, and in the opening days of the final match at Port-of-Spain the West Indies again had the better of it. Then, against all reasonable odds and logic, England snatched a remarkable victory largely on the broad backs of Boycott, who scored 99 and 112, and Greig, with his newly adopted style of off breaks. By any yardstick it was an astounding turnabout. Unfortunately Greig was never able to bowl half as well again as a spinner, and I have an uneasy suspicion that in the euphoric surprise of his deeds Boycott's contribution did not get the recognition that was his due.

Clearly some credit must go to Denness for his resolve and resilience, and not least for his ability to seize on the growing frustrations of his opponents. Evaluations of his tactics and general leadership were, however, confusingly mixed. He followed by comfortably disposing of India in 1974, whose record of one defeat in the previous eleven Tests led them to being hailed at home as 'world champions', and held the much superior Pakistan well enough to forestall any possible criticism.

If a man's true identity is most evident when the going is tough, Denness, it must be said, emerged from his ordeal in Australia in 1974–75 with great credit. As manager I was closest to him in his most trying moments, and he never lost his humour or dignity. His reputation as a 'bad communicator', which was said to be a reason for his dismissal as captain by Kent, was never apparent to me. Nor was he the taciturn Scot. Rather, my impression of him centres on his friendly and approachable disposition, and, as far as I was concerned, he was very easy to get on with.

The rigidity of his tactical ideas did not always meet with approval, but I am inclined to regard a leader with a mind of his own more favourably than one swayed by the opinions of others. How perverse, therefore, that his consultations with other members of England's side at Edgbaston in 1975 in the First Test with Australia should lead to his undoing. I know I shall be reminded that a captain makes his own luck – surely a half truth – and that Mike ought to have heeded the long-range weather forecasts before the match. The worst happened. He won the toss, conceded first innings, and almost as soon as England's innings started the pitch was drenched by a thunderstorm.

According to his book, Denness talked with his bowlers and none was against putting Australia in to bat. He revealed: 'Other senior members of the side were also asked for their views – some were in favour and some were against it.' Mike has always acknowledged that the final decision was his, although the reaction of the bowlers was sufficient for him to make up his mind. I rather think the weakness of his case was that 'some were against' the idea. Therefore there had to be doubts, and to take the kind of gamble that he did the odds ought to be well in favour of the risk.

As Dr W. G. Grace once said, 'By all means think of putting the other side in. Think about it – and then bat.'

Talking to Mike before the game the question of putting in Australia if he won the toss never arose because it never occurred to me. A captain has to make up his own mind, right or wrong, and I always made a point of never interfering, though, if ever I was asked to give my opinion as player or selector I gave it to the best of my ability. I was taken aback, therefore, to read in an Australian paper that I had told Denness when to declare in another Test match at Edgbaston and he 'did what he was told'. Nothing could have been farther from the truth. If Mike, or any other captain, came to me seeking advice, that was entirely different, but he knew and I knew that the final decision was his.

Denness's growing problems were compounded by a report in a morning paper in which a selector said he and his colleagues were unanimously of the opinion that England should have batted first. The selector in question subsequently apologized to Denness and, as chairman, I had to step in as peacemaker. That morning Mike and I sat and talked outside the England dressing room until it was time for him to take the field. Mike was understandably upset, and I was vexed by a situation which should never have arisen. Our conversation centred on the report. Unfortunately the writing was on the wall for Mike, and I never found it easy to tell a friend whom I admired that he was to be replaced by a new captain.

Denness, it ought to be stressed, was not punished for one mistake, but, equally, had he not made it and England won – a distinct possibility if they had batted first – there would not have been any cause for a change. Taking the broader view, things had not run kindly for Denness and the selectors thought the team would benefit from a new initiative at the top.

My overall verdict was that Mike did a good job for England both on and off the field, and it would be manifestly unfair to remember his term of leadership by his one final disaster. He deserves much better. When I wrote a commiseratory letter to him I recalled a happier letter I had sent to him twenty-two years before. It was to congratulate him on winning a cricket bat as a prize in a competition run by the old *Sunday Chronicle* for a performance when he was a scholar at Ayr Academy. As a bowler!

I appreciated reading in his book that he bore no ill feeling towards me for losing the Test captaincy – indeed it was a committee decision – and that he noted I took a disproportionate blame for what went on during our association as captain and chairman although I had no control over much of it. I presumed this to be a reference to the selection of teams. The lot of the chairman is to take criticism on behalf of the selectors, deserved or undeserved. I have no serious complaints either way, and selection is often a matter of individual opinion. Without a genuine love for cricket no selector in his right mind would consider taking the job, and I can say in truth that I have yet to encounter one who shirks his duty or lacks dedication and enthusiasm. Fools we might appear to be on occasions; but never knaves.

11

Times of Change and Challenge

Raich Carter, the renowned soccer international, once said that old footballers ought to be shot – mock-serious words that strike a chord of sympathy in many a professional sportman's mind. Cynics might suggest that cricket's alternative to the merciful bullet is a place on the Test selection committee since its members are invariably in the sights of snipers. But, lest any doubts should arise from my levity, I hasten to put on record that I would gladly relive both my careers – as a player and as a selector.

Both occupations gave me exceedingly good times, occasionally disappointment and frustration, but I was as keen and as proud to be a selector in 1985 as I had been in 1962, the year of my first being appointed. For me there is no greater distinction than to play for my country, and then to be able to put something back into the game.

Compared with modern problems, being a selector in 1962 was a sinecure. My distinguished predecessors like Sir Pelham Warner and Walter Robins – he was wont to disappear to the cinema if England were faring badly or the play did not come up to his ever high expectations – would be astounded at the mileage I have covered in a season as chairman and the amount of time I have given to the job. At one time a Test side was simply phoned through to the Press Association, which distributed it to the newspapers, without official explanations of changes, injuries and so on. Now the media are rightly encouraged to make contact and every critic expects the chairman to be at the end of a telephone, both before and after selection. The chairman's work has mounted season by season, and Robins saw nothing like the amount of cricket that I did. For one thing, he probably could not have spared the time from business; for another, attitudes have turned upside down.

As a player in 1946 I scarcely met the then chairman, Group

Above: A moment I shall always savour: returning to the Trent Bridge pavilion after a match aggregate of 14 for 99 against Australia, 1953, my peak season in Test cricket

Below: David Wynne, working on a sculpture of me. I am told I was the first cricketer to have this distinction while still playing

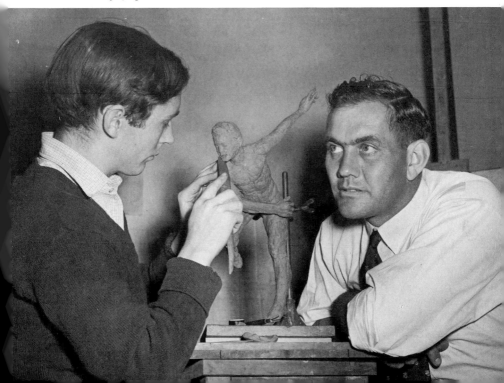

Above: Surrey, 1956, the season in which we won the championship for the fifth year in a row and beat the touring Australians by 10 wickets. Standing *(left to right):* Andrew Sandham (coach), Bernie Constable, Ron Pratt, Mike Willett, Ken Barrington, David Fletcher, Tony Lock, Peter Loader, Tom Clark, Micky Stewart, Dennis Cox, Derek Pratt, Jim Laker, Roy Swetman, Sandy Tait (physiotherapist). Seated: Eric Bedser, myself, Marshal of the Royal Air Force, Lord Tedder (President), Stuart Surridge, B. K. Castor (secretary), Peter May, Arthur McIntyre

Below: England's triumphant side which won the Ashes at The Oval, 1953. Standing *(left to right):* Trevor Bailey, Peter May, Tom Graveney, Jim Laker, Tony Lock, Johnny Wardle, Freddie Trueman. Seated: Bill Edrich, myself, Len Hutton (captain), Denis Compton, Godfrey Evans

Top left: I owed a lot to my wicketkeepers. Godfrey Evans' agility and anticipation was unmatched. Here he leaps high to take a hurried return in a Test match with Australia as Ron Archer scampers home. Brian Statham is the fielder

Top right: My old rival and friend Arthur Morris, Australia's opening batsman. We had many duels and I always thought honours were shared in the end

Below: Arthur McIntyre's outstanding keeping was a feature of Surrey's high performances in the field. They set new standards for county cricket in the fifties. Arthur was also an attractive batsman, here scoring to leg against Middlesex. The wicketkeeper is John Murray, who also played for England, and became a fellow Test selector

Above: The late Duke of Norfolk, MCC's manager in Australia in 1962-63. I was his assistant manager – an alliance of the Premier Duke of England and an old pro which intrigued the cricket world. We got on famously. At first the Duke was too shy to enter the dressing-room

Below: Selectors at work! Choosing MCC's party to tour Australia and New Zealand, 1965-66. Seated around the table at Lord's *(left to right):* Don Kenyon, myself, Mike Smith (the captain), Doug Insole, S.C. ('Billy') Griffith (MCC Secretary), 'Gubby' Allen, Freddie Brown, Peter May

Above: My big fist clutches a snick from Middlesex's Sid Brown, clearly to the approval of my captain, Michael Barton and Arthur McIntyre. I enjoyed fielding at slip or gully where I took the majority of my 290 catches

Below: Perhaps my most notable innings – 79 against Australia at Leeds, 1948. I enjoyed batting. Ron Saggers is wicketkeeper, with Ray Lindwall at slip and Ernie Toshack at short leg

Geoff Boycott, a dedicated batsman, who opted out of Test cricket for three years during my term as chairman of selectors. We met to discuss his return at Watford Gap Service Station on the M1

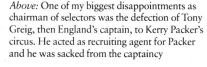

Above: One of my biggest disappointments as chairman of selectors was the defection of Tony Greig, then England's captain, to Kerry Packer's circus. He acted as recruiting agent for Packer and he was sacked from the captaincy

Above: Mike Brearley, who replaced Botham, was a magnificent leader of men and I had the highest respect for his captaincy. He was also a useful opening batsman and is seen here cutting the West Indian fast bowler Andy Roberts at Lord's, 1976

Below: An incident during Ian Botham's remarkable innings in the third Test with Australia at Leeds, 1981, the series in which England made an historic recovery to win the Ashes against all odds. As chairman of selectors I had the disagreeable duty of telling him that we were replacing him as captain

All good things must come to an end. I return after my last match in 1960 against Glamorgan at an almost-deserted Oval. Only an hour's play was necessary on the third morning to complete an innings victory by Surrey. A quiet farewell but I was grateful I did not have to share my sentimental occasion before a large crowd

Captain A. J. Holmes, a former captain of Sussex, not because he was neglectful or socially aloof but because contact with the team was not considered part of his duties. He followed the conventions of his time and stayed clear of the players, leaving the dressing room to the captain and the players to get on with the job. I believe this policy to be fundamentally right. From the legendary Lord Hawke, the first national chairman in 1899 and probably the most misunderstood figure the game has known, the broad policy has been for the selectors to select, the captain to captain, and the players to play. I saw the position of chairman inexorably move to being effectively that of a manager for a home series. Team selection is but the starting point for a range of duties undreamed of in the not so distant past.

Modern trends were set in motion by the indefatigable Doug Insole, who succeeded Gubby Allen and was one of my colleagues in 1962. The chairman-cum-manager is now expected to run the whole show, from looking after the players to making sure the hotel accommodation is satisfactory. The players are not slow to make it known if anything falls short of their expectations. The job also includes contact with ground officials, making sure there are net facilities before and during the match, arranging the customary eve-of-Test dinner, which usefully brings the players together to discuss tactics and raise morale, and the important liaison with the press, television and radio. If there are injuries fitness tests have to be arranged; the team has to be finalized and judgements passed on the pitch.

Often the ring of a telephone a day before the match brought news of an injury. Most clubs are conscientious to a degree, but surprisingly there have been cases of neglect which meant a lot of unnecessary work. At least I was spared the shock of a predecessor who saw Harold Gimblett arrive for a Test match at Trent Bridge with a carbuncle on the back of his neck and unable to look in any direction but straight ahead!

Players, inevitably, have come to expect more and more to be done for them. In my time as chairman I saw players become less self-reliant, and my colleagues and I on various selection panels have wondered if such attitudes affect performances in the middle where mental stamina and a resourceful determination are crucial. The point arrived when players scarcely needed to think for them-

161

selves. Just occasionally I would like to hear some appreciation expressed to committee members, administrators and ordinary enthusiasts who do so much voluntarily in their own time and are inspired only by a love of cricket.

In 1980 I spent ninety-two days, and in 1981, the year of the dramatic Ashes victory, over a hundred days attending selection meetings, studying form in all parts of the country, attending Test matches and one-day internationals, having discussions with my fellow selectors before the actual meetings, and with the captain, administrators at Lord's, county team managers, umpires and others whose opinion I valued. Running a Test team is such a time-consuming task that only the dedicated should dream of taking it on. I make these comments not as a complaint but as an observation. When I accepted the job I knew what was required and I enjoyed it all very much.

Understandably it is not easy to find four selectors with both the time to spare and the qualifications. In my last two years as chairman I had Ken Barrington, who had a garage to run, Charlie Elliott, with a hotel to supervise, and Brian Close and John Edrich, who had business commitments. We were prepared to give all the time necessary to do the job properly, and with a hand of four the workload could be spread. Basic expenses are met and a small compensation made for time lost, but basically it is a job for the volunteer, someone who seeks neither financial reward nor popularity. He becomes inured to criticism, some of which can be singularly uninformed, and realizes that the best selection committee, like an umpire, is the one that makes the fewest mistakes. For mistakes are inevitable. The supreme moments, like the victories over Australia in 1981, are more than ample compensation for the times when the best-laid plans go wrong.

Each April my first task as chairman was to assemble the newly elected committee (which is elected annually) for preliminary discussions and to draw up a list of candidates, where they were to be watched and by whom. It is a distinct advantage to have selectors from different parts of the country, but the ideal is not always possible. Even the simple exercise of scouting for talent can be complicated by bad weather, prospective batsmen getting out first ball, bowlers not being asked to bowl, and so on. The early fixtures are dominated by the Benson and Hedges Cup matches, and a combination of rain and cup ties can lead to the unsatisfactory position of players having to be judged for the opening Test of a series on an absurdly low number of innings or overs bowled. Gone are the days when in-form batsmen saw as their early-season goal 1000 runs before the end of May. Performance in one-day matches can be misleading: field placings are generally defensive, batsmen are not crowded, a bowler causing trouble has to come off after his allotted number of overs, while bowlers intent on keeping runs down often make dismissals a secondary priority. A key fact of cricket is that the longer the duration of a game the higher the basic skills need to be, and restricted matches mean restricted information available to the selector seeking class.

Cup finals in front of a full house at Lord's and with a television audience of millions are exciting occasions, but they can be a trap for the selector, public and even the players themselves, who might be tempted to imagine a good performance automatically means selection for a Test or a tour. Mr Selector has to remind himself not to be carried away, as limited-over cricket does not require the same skills as the five-day Test. Both critics and public tend to overlook this basic fact.

An example was Hugh Wilson's 4 wickets for 56 for Surrey in the 1979 Benson and Hedges Cup final. On the evidence of his performance the selectors were urged by the media to gamble on this young fast bowler for the winter tour of Australia and New Zealand. I was less convinced as I had already had a private session with Hugh at The Oval and thought he had a long way to go before he became a Test fast bowler. He later left Surrey for Somerset.

The choice of captain is the committee's first hurdle, and thrice-blessed are those fortunate enough to have a tried and proven leader who can be allocated the whole series. Even better if there is a Mike Brearley or a Clive Lloyd, for continuity is paramount. Constant changes of leadership breed uncertainty and dissension. Selectors have to think ahead, and try to groom a captain, but there are unfortunate times when no obvious leader is available. Mike Brearley left an enormous gap in 1980, and, as usual, the selectors were bombarded with advice and subjected to a measure of lobbying behind the scenes. Speculation is always rife in the newspapers and letters from the public arrive by the score.

Ideally the captain should be elected for a series, but new leadership is something of a gamble and selectors court disaster if they do not leave room to revise their plans. A captain's automatic right to serve on the committee, which is appointed by the Test and County Cricket Board, goes back to 1902 when Archie MacLaren was shown his team minus Sydney Barnes, Charles Fry and Gilbert Jessop. 'My God, look what they have sent me,' he expostulated. MacLaren thereupon insisted on having his say in future selections and since then every captain has been coopted.

I am far from convinced, however, that the presence of the captain serves the best interests of team selection. Over the years I invariably found captains to be the most cautious members of the panel, particularly when it came to the introduction of young or new players. By and large they are a conservative breed, intensely loyal to old team-mates – a highly commendable trait – and closely involved with the team. At times it must be difficult for them to stand back and have an objective view. They are also conscious of the fact that they are the likely can-carriers if experiments fail. They forget that the selectors are equally exposed.

The last thing selectors want to do is to send into the field a team which the captain does not feel reasonably happy with. It is a very delicate and debatable area, but the argument abruptly ends when it enters the realms of tactics, strategy and approach to every game. The captain has to be in sole charge, which is the most cogent reason why I oppose the suggestion of a supremo. You cannot have two captains, a manager and a captain, on the same bridge.

Long before my time there was a classic confrontation between Sir Pelham Warner's three-man committee and skipper Bob Wyatt over the choice between leg-break bowlers Tom Mitchell of Derbyshire and Walter Robins for the Test against South Africa at Lord's in 1935. Wyatt held out for Mitchell, and the meeting, which began at eleven in the morning, ended at seven in the evening with the selectors bowing to the captain's wishes. As it happened Mitchell was not a success and England lost for the first time at home to South Africa. Afterwards the chairman received an unsigned telegram which read 'Robins Robins Robins Robins Robins Robins'. 'And I didn't send it,' Robins used to chuckle.

Tony Greig showed the strong hand which used to be held by

the captain when he suddenly sprung it on the meeting that he was keen to recall Brian Close, then forty-five, to play against the West Indies in 1976. Greig argued that Brian was still among the best batsmen in the country against fast bowling, which was the West Indies' attacking strength. Sir Len Hutton, whose quiet deliberation contrasted with Greig's confident approach, was unavoidably absent due to an urgent last-minute business matter in Germany, and the voting was split 2–2. At the time the captain had the casting vote. Brian was chosen and held his place for three Tests without really solving the problem.

In 1977 I asked the Test and County Cricket Board to change the standing procedure with regard to the captain's powers. My proposal had the backing of my fellow selectors. The Board's instructions laid down that 'in the event of a no-majority agreement the captain's wish shall prevail.' After a lot of consideration my committee felt it should be the chairman who should have the casting vote should it be necessary. The TCCB agreed to alter standing orders. In point of fact a situation rarely arose during my spell as chairman when a vote was necessary. Sticking points usually ended in sensible compromise. Without give and take it would be well-nigh impossible for a five-man committee – augmented for the selection of overseas tours – to operate.

A general impression exists that the chairman virtually picks the side or exercises his considerable pressure. It is not the case at all. There were times when I accepted majority decisions, and I hid many a wry smile when I was held personally responsible for selections.

The Australian method of naming the captain from the chosen side appeals to many in England who assume that within the eleven there is one player with every qualification to be leader. What if there is no such individual? Nominate a second-best leader or drop one of the team to make way for a captain? If there is an obvious captain in the side he will be automatically chosen, so we are back where we started, with the difference that the captain could not be co-opted to the selection committee before the team was selected and thus would have no say in his team.

Australia's selectors usually have a pretty good idea of the captain they want long in advance of his actual appointment. Ian Johnson, Richie Benaud and Ian Craig were quickly earmarked for promotion, while Don Bradman and Lindsay Hassett could not have been challenged. I doubt if the Aussies ever wrote eleven or twelve names and then asked, 'Who shall we have as captain?' Rather, they start with someone who will be the captain and build the team round him, but they do not coopt the captain in team selection meetings. They did so for a short period but soon dispensed with the idea. With only six state teams to choose from, Australian selection is far easier, and their system of grade cricket, now threatened by nonstop Test and first-class matches, used to ensure a potential captain's progress from school to state level. Obviously a prospective captain will be asked his opinion of various players.

As the term implies, grade cricket was an effective selection process aimed at the ultimate objective of fielding Australia's best possible team, but, in the long term, it remains to be seen whether the system will survive the Packer revolution. Australia's Board were much criticized for their agreement with World Series Cricket, but, as I was given to understand, they were given a licence by the other countries to take unilateral action if they thought it necessary in order to survive. Initially the Board did take on Packer, and as a consequence they were reduced to fielding virtually a Second XI in Test matches and the public were bombarded with anti-establishment propaganda by the press. England's Board approved when the unwelcome decision to call it a day was taken in what was a painful financial fight for both sides.

The agreement has undeniably led to big changes in the structure of Australia's domestic cricket. Top players demanded high rewards, and the Board had no choice but to pay up. The next development was the granting of contracts to a so-called squad of Test players. This has created a professional group who depend on cricket for their living, a situation far removed from the old system in which the Australian player had to have a job outside the game. The difference is that, unlike England, Australia cannot support an entirely professionally orientated programme, and with the broadening of the international stage – necessary to pay the professionals' wages and to meet marketing tie-ups with television and commercial interests – the Test men cannot always be available for their state, let alone appear in grade cricket.

The situation endangers the very basic strength of Australian cricket, which could end by being top heavy. The effects may not be felt immediately, but, as England have found with an imbalance of one-day matches and too many foreign players, a day of reckoning inevitably arrives. Grade cricket was the nursery of Australia's hopes, with young players having the chance to pit their skills against the best in the land. With Test and state players in regular competition the standard had to be high, and because of this there was the opportunity for the youngster with talent to mature quickly. Today's grade products do not appear to me to be of the class they used to be, and Australia might be stretched to preserve her reputation for developing and giving youth its chance. There were reasons for Australia's attitude. The grade system and conditions led to talent emerging more quickly but the normal career did not last long because a career outside cricket had to be made. So simple economics helped to push the young player forward into the state and Test scene.

In 1979–80 I heard complaints from elder cricket statesmen that a closed-shop situation was developing and that injuries were being hidden from selectors. Obviously the circle of Test players are now going to hang on as long as they can and play as often as they can. The average age of Australia's teams in the post-Packer era seemed to rise, and it could be that if another Neil Harvey emerges he might have to wait longer to go right to the top.

Fears that Australia have taken the wrong road with the restructuring of their cricket in the aftermath of Packer are widely held by many of their most famous old players. Not unexpectedly, Bill O'Reilly leads the attack on what he describes as the 'bunch of assassins bent on its extermination'.

'Ever since the 1977 Packer revolution the standard of Australian cricket has catapulted to rock bottom so far as real skills are concerned,' he thundered in an article. 'Candidly I say that there is not one Australian presently in our national side who would have seriously been considered for a place in any Australian side at any time during the 1950s and 1960s.' He argues that there is an obsession with 'pyjama cricket' – the variety of the game in coloured clothing under floodlights – and Australia needs to be rescued in order to return to first principles. Words straight from the heart, and words which carry sentiments felt by so many of us both during and after the Packer intervention. There has to be a price for such grave tinkering with the game to jazz it up for television presentation.

Criticisms that England have a tardy attitude towards young players are not justified by facts. Although captains are inclined to bank on experience, England have not been backward in seeking new blood, and, as in the cases of Ken Barrington and Graham Gooch, young players are not permanently discarded if they do not succeed at once. Selectors have to judge genuine class before a young player is promoted, not an easy thing to do, and timing is of the essence. Australia were able to cushion Neil Harvey in a batting line-up which included Arthur Morris, Sid Barnes, Don Bradman, Lindsay Hassett and Keith Miller, a vastly different prospect from the ordeal of having to face fast bowling in a struggling side. Perhaps it was singularly fortunate that Peter May was not one of the young batsmen sent to Australia in 1950–51, but given time to develop. It is unfair for a player to be put to a searching examination of his ability and temperament before he is ready to cope, particularly when playing in a poor side. But if the cupboard is bare it sometimes has to be done.

Selectors expect to get it in the neck when playing standards slump, and I was amused to read in 1981 that Doug Walters's omission from the Australian team to tour England was described, in the Australian Parliament no less, as 'outrageous'. Walters was then thirty-five – not that I believe that to be too important – but there had been a time when in Australia anyone over thirty was approaching senility in the cricketing sense. Nor had Doug been a success on previous visits to England. Yet one MP advocated the sacking of the selectors and said it was the 'greatest disgrace in the history of Australian sport'. Three MPs joined in a demonstration march in Canberra.

I do not remember an equivalent outburst at home, but in 1984 the selectors shared puzzled amusement at the story that Chris Broad, the big opening batsman, had moved from Gloucestershire to Nottinghamshire to have a better chance of catching the selectors' eyes; and that within two months he had proved his point when he was chosen to play against the West Indies. Nottinghamshire was described as a more 'fashionable' county which might surprise Wally Hammond, Charlie Barnett, Tom Graveney, David

Allen, John Mortimore and Arthur Milton, who did not find playing for Gloucestershire a handicap to a Test cap.

The less romantic fact was that, until 1983, when he averaged 42.44 in the County Championship, Chris had three moderate seasons with averages of 26.93, 29.66 and 25.92, figures which were hardly likely to excite attention. When he did start to come good and get among the runs he was watched and noted, and it could be that his game improved with the move from Bristol to Nottinghamshire. But the move itself had nothing to do with his selection – he 'caught the selectors' eyes' when he began to get better scores.

It should go without saying that for those selecting national sides there is no such thing as a 'fashionable' or 'unfashionable' county. If a player is good enough he will break into Test cricket, but before he does the first requirement is to succeed at county level. When a player is advocated for a place someone must be dropped. Back-seat-advice usually suggests who should play but hardly ever says who should be left out. Only eleven can play. A player only moderately successful in the Championship is scarcely likely to do better in the highest stratum where the bowling is better and batsmen are harder to dismiss. Believe me, selectors could not care less where a player is based so long as he fulfils the requirements of class and temperament. The crux of the matter is what players are available.

I wonder, too, if some writers would have the nerve to put their theories into practice if they were selectors. Cricket selection has a lot in common with politics – it is easier to put everything right in opposition. In office it is a different ball game. In 1984, when the West Indies were unstoppable, one old England batsman said the selectors *must* find better England players. What were we expected to do: coopt the magician Paul Daniels? If the England and West Indies selectors had changed places, would the result have been different? Patently not. At least the stage has not been reached to match the sight many years ago of some disgruntled Indian fans parading a banner with the words 'DEATH TO THE SELECTORS'!

India is one country where pitches and conditions are not likely to vary to any marked degree. Experience of the slow, turning wickets and the large, excitable crowds – which seem to have dropped off somewhat since Tests have been televised – is therefore invaluable. But in 1976–77 and 1984–85 the selectors had the additional responsibility of having to choose players who had to go on to Australia after a tour of India – in the first instance to the Melbourne Centenary match and later to the single-wicket tournament. To have a double horses-for-courses policy embracing such differing conditions was not possible, but I think we managed compromises, even though defeats were incurred in Australia. Tony Greig's side magnificently rose to the occasion at Melbourne in 1977 although physically and mentally drained, not only by their exertions in India but by their brief visit to Sri Lanka in oppressive pre-monsoon heat.

When the 1976–77 party was announced one critic made the flat accusation that the selectors had made a number of chronic errors – if memory serves me right no fewer than six wrong selections – and I was interviewed on a BCC news programme as if this was a fact rather than an opinion. I pointed out that my fellow selectors, Sir Len Hutton, Ken Barrington and I had 212 caps between us, and Charlie Elliott had umpired in around fifty Test matches since his retirement as an opening batsman for Derbyshire. There was not much Charlie did not know about cricket and cricketers, and Barrington had the extra bonus of specialist knowledge as a former tourist to India. We did our homework and confirmed that, contrary to a widely held belief, pace bowling was not a hopeless cause in India. There had been West Indies wicket-takers and four years previously, on Tony Lewis's tour, 48 wickets had been shared by England's pace bowlers. India had a traditional weakness against speed, and to back Bob Willis, John Lever – whose left arm provided variety and a different line – and Chris Old, England had Derek Underwood, who could win a match on his own. Derek had long shed the reputation of a slow-to-medium left-arm bowler carried around like an umbrella as an insurance against rain.

Underwood finished with 29 wickets against a combined 56 by Willis, Lever and Old, but Lever (twice) and Willis made significant breakthroughs in the first three Tests, which were won by margins of an innings and 25 runs, 10 wickets and 200 runs. No previous touring team had taken the first three Tests in India.

We had selected as many of Lewis's party as was possible on form, including the Leicestershire wicketkeeeper Roger Tolchard. His selection caused some eyebrow raising but, as he was one of the few batsmen in the county circuit with nimble footwork against quality spin, we thought of him not only as Alan Knott's under-study but as a possible first-choice batsman. The theory worked for he played at no. 5 in the Second Test at Calcutta, where all grass was removed from the pitch by the ground staff armed with household scrubbing brushes. Tolchard scored 67 with methods expertly improvised for a wicket on which it was impossible to drive, and his stand of 142 for the fifth wicket with Tony Greig (103) broke India's back. That one innings justified our theory. All selectors score notable 'own goals' at one time or another, and they have to be tolerantly aware that these are far more likely to capture publicity than the successes.

The changing styles and patterns of county cricket in the seventies, which led to complications for the selectors, can be illustrated by some of my comments made at various times. In 1976 I wrote as follows:

Steps have been taken to control the number of overseas players who participate in the county programme. It has been realized by all what effect the preponderance of overseas cricketers has had on the development of our own players, but a further factor I feel is evolving is that more and more international overseas cricketers are being appointed as captains of county sides. There is a danger that too many counties may appoint players who are not eligible to play for England and so restrict the training of future English Test captains. Whilst appreciating it is a matter for the counties as to how they operate their own affairs, I feel this should be pointed out.

In 1979:

It was pleasant to see the advance of the younger players, Gower, Gooch and Botham. There are a number of other young batsmen who are 'knocking at the door' of international honours and continue to show improvement. In general there are several potentially fine batsmen but the same cannot be said for young bowlers. Every effort must be made at county level to find and encourage young bowlers. The 'international cupboard' could be bare in a year or two if these are not forthcoming.

Also in 1979:

It is again pointed out that the dominance of overseas players occupying

171

the principal batting and bowling positions must have its effect on the development of English cricketers. It will have been noticed that in the first 25 of the batting and bowling averages almost 50 per cent in both sections were overseas players. This must restrict the number of English players having opportunities to develop. . . . I saw a tremendous amount of cricket during the summer and regrettably, in my opinion, the average standard of English county bowling has deteriorated. The control of length and direction often left a lot to be desired.

In 1980:

The younger batsmen in the country are developing – if a little slowly – to Test Match standard. The same cannot be said of the opening bowlers. We are in a period where there is a dearth of potential international opening bowlers. Fast bowlers, in particular, can arrive quickly – but they must be given a chance to do so. Last season some 15 to 17 overseas bowlers were opening the bowling in English first-class cricket. That is almost 50 per cent of the opening attacks.

My postcript to the excessive employment of ready made imported talent is simply this: if, to their numbers, one adds those not of Test material, the injured, and others either over the hill or unready, the selectors have precious little choice – and certainly no scope to build intelligently for the future. In the land of plenty – it should be with the amount of cricket played from schools upwards – there has too often been famine. In the area of opening bowlers during the period reviewed the choice was very small, and the prayer was for the fitness of Ian Botham, Bob Willis, Chris Old and Mike Hendrick – a prayer not always answered. There is, therefore, much satisfaction at the emergence of a young bowler of the calibre of Neil Foster, whom I saw when he started for Essex and dismissed Bob Woolmer with a perfect out-swinger. His side-on action and instinct to attack the off stump was impressive from the start. I hope he does not fall into the modern habit of bowling too short of a length.

When options are small, selectors need to resist a temptation to gamble with immature players, but there have been occasions when there was no alternative but to use a Test match as a trial ground. I was far happier going for experience to meet an emergency. To general surprise David Steele was brought in for his maiden Test at

Lord's in 1975 after Australia had won the first match. David was approaching his mid-thirties and with his prematurely grey hair and rimless glasses he deceived all who judge by appearance. The selectors were looking for a proven county man with the right methods, an ability to play fast bowling, guts and the character to take on Dennis Lillee and Jeff Thomson. He proceeded to fulfil all requirements with a positive relish which warmed the public's heart. But he could not have performed his deeds without his long years with Northamptonshire. His skills and spirit were burnished by experience.

It used to be rightly said that the youngster needs a three to five years settling-in period as a grounding for first-class cricket. Batsmen can make a more instant impact – one has only to cite the examples of Len Hutton, Denis Compton, Peter May and Colin Cowdrey – and an out-and-out fast bowler can come swiftly on the scene as did Frank Tyson. For all that, the average bowler – and particularly the spinner, who should mature with age – needs time to fashion skills, and there cannot be any substitute for skill at any level. I never bowled against any of the great batsmen and thought they had anything but the right basic techniques, nor have I known bowlers of true merit to lack control of length and direction.

The introduction of limited-over cricket – there is an important difference from the one-day matches in which I played – worried me and the majority of my contemporaries raised in the old school who believed that standards were being eroded because the modern player was denied a proper apprenticeship. Bad habits can be easily formed. As Andrew Sandham once said, 'I feel sorry for the newcomers today. They have to play so many forms of cricket in so short a time.'

As limited-over cricket is a hit with the public and an economic necessity, whether it should be played or not is a dead debate. Clearly it forms an important part of the domestic and international programme. The only question needing an answer is: how *much* should be played? I believe there is a happy medium in everything and it should be possible to keep the public and the county treasurer satisfied and maintain playing standards. I remember Bill O'Reilly watching England bat against New South Wales at Sydney in 1975 and saying, 'You know, limited-over cricket is either going to produce the finest players yet seen, or the worst.' I knew what he meant and if I had my way the limited-over game would be banned at school and junior level because it gives boys the wrong idea of what cricket is all about.

When Ray Illingworth was Yorkshire's manager he told me of his concern that the leagues had reverted to limited-over matches. He would see young spin bowlers of real promise at the winter nets, but they would seldom get a look-in during the season. The clubs preferred a battery of medium pacers.

I am not opposed to *all* limited-over cricket and *all* overseas players, but I am concerned about future standards. Hence my welcome for the inquiry set up in 1984 following England's first-time defeats in Pakistan and New Zealand, and a whitewash by the West Indies at home. The improvement of the West Indies, New Zealand and Pakistan has, ironically, been in large part due to the experience their leading players have had in English county cricket. A committee, under the chairmanship of Charlie Palmer, was duly formed with the official words, *'in view of England's recent dismal performances'.*

Ironically, no sooner had Palmer's nine-man committee started work than England enjoyed the heart-lifting experience of successive victories in India, where it is no mean achievement to win, and at home to Australia, with David Gower's inspired team regaining the Ashes and taking the final two Tests with innings margins. However, not only had it been felt necessary to investigate the quality of all grades of cricket in England, but Geoff Cook, the chairman of the Cricketers' Association and captain of Northamptonshire, had urged his members to look to their laurels; the reticent and highly respected Bob Willis and Bob Taylor, who had given so much for so long, had also felt obliged to admonish some of the players for their indifference to defeat.

The reversal of fortune showed dramatically how things can change, for the better or worse, inside a year. The same can be said of players, and the old adage of success breeding success is as true as it ever was. The result in India was a great fillip to morale and a credit to the captain and team management who had the side working together. In some ways it is an advantage after a heavy home defeat to go away to a totally new environment and to face fresh challenges, and the way the England team stood as one in the difficulties they encountered both on and off the field was in the best traditions of English cricket.

Another important factor in the marked improvement of the team was the batting, and the selectors enjoyed the luxury of having the first six batsmen almost unchanged for the entire six-match series. What had been our constant anxiety became the least of our worries, and was in no small part due to the return of Graham Gooch and the confirmation of Tim Robinson's class. Also vitally important was the fact that the batsmen were mature cricketers; they had all served their time in Test cricket.

Gower could also reflect that those who had previously cast doubts on his quality as a captain and in mid series called for his dismissal ended the 1985 season singing his praises and celebrating his big scores. David is a steady young man and the last to be unduly influenced by any extremes of opinion. The selectors held firm in their belief in him. We were handsomely repaid.

One decisive bonus for England over Australia was the unquenchable spirit of Ian Botham. In this respect I am not thinking so much of his bowling, dangerous batting and catching, which alone is capable of turning a match, but of a quality which shapes the character of every truly great bowler: his ability and willingness to keep trying, and never to be satisfied with less than 100 per cent effort. In the Oval Test Botham was as fast as any bowler on either side throughout the series – no doubt helped by the excellent pitch prepared by Harry Brind – and, whatever his persistent critics might have to say about him, they can never charge him with not giving everything he has for the side. That alone endears me to Botham the cricketer. The zest bottled up after a winter's rest fizzed like uncorked champagne and, apart from setting a refreshing example, underlines my contention that the top players become jaded by too much Test cricket and nonstop touring. However, much as I admire Botham, I was somewhat taken aback to read his agent being quoted as saying 'Botham is bigger than the game.' That, in my opinion, is manifest nonsense, and Ian himself would be the last to believe it.

We have been in a catch–22 situation in many ways, and as a selector and as a member of the Surrey committee, I have seen both sides. On the one hand there is a struggle to remain viable and retain local interest by succeeding in one of the four limited-over competitions. On the other hand is the need to have a truly representative Test side. There is a danger of one prospering at the expense of the other. There has to be a proper and sensible balance and, as a large proportion of every club's income comes from the Test and County Cricket Board's shareout, a strong Test team is not only a matter of national pride but makes sound business sense.

There will, of course, always be ups and downs, times of good teams and of not-so-good teams, but it is an unarguable fact that the choice of players of true class has narrowed and standards have declined. Time and distance have always lent enchantment, but when I became a selector in 1962 the range of choice was much wider. Chairman Walter Robins was able to indulge in a plan to give Ted Dexter and Colin Cowdrey two Test matches each in the home series with Pakistan in order to compare their leadership qualities before nominating the captain in Australia in the following winter. The selectors also had Ken Barrington, Geoff Pullar, Fred Trueman, David Allen, Fred Titmus, Tony Lock, Peter Parfitt, for ever plundering the Pakistanis, and the all-rounder Barry Knight.

Robins's predecessor, Gubby Allen, for whom I have the utmost admiration, had enormous talent available in the fifties, particularly in the bowling, and whenever I was reminded by well-intentioned friends of England's bowling plight before the party was chosen for the tour of Australia in 1982–83, I was apt to forestall criticism by whipping out some comparative tables I had prepared. Statistics can be misleading, but the facts of the situation at that point told the true story.

My first exhibit was of the season's averages for the leading eleven English bowlers before Len Hutton's side was picked in 1954. It read:

	Overs	Wkts	Avge
Statham	615	92	14.13
Appleyard	1027	154	14.42
Loader	699	109	14.57
Jackson	939	125	14.60
Bedser, A. V.	957	121	15.10
Laker	966	135	15.17
Trueman	817	134	15.48
Wardle	1262	155	15.80
Lock	1027	125	16.00
Gladwin	1082	136	16.70
Tattersall	1040	117	16.81

Six of the above – Jim Laker, Tony Lock, Fred Trueman, Les Jackson, Cliff Gladwin and Roy Tattersall – were left behind. All in recent years would have been automatic selections. Frank Tyson (78 wickets) and Trevor Bailey (101 wickets), who helped to win the series were forty-fourth and forty-fifth in the table!

The second list is taken from the national bowling averages published in newspapers in 1982, at a time when the selectors were getting down to the business of finding an attack to retain the Ashes won by Mike Brearley in 1981. Of the first twenty-five, the seven players eligible to play for England are shown in capitals.

	Overs	Wkts	Avge
Hadlee (NZ)	338	52	14.42
COWANS	138	26	15.42
Marshall (WI)	600	97	15.82
Le Roux (SA)	344	53	16.03
GATTING	97	14	16.50
Daniel (WI)	374	58	16.53
Imran Khan (Pak.)	426	56	17.17
SAXELBY	185	28	17.28
Hendrick	244	26	18.19
Clarke (WI)	563	77	18.64
Taylor	434	54	19.72
JESTY	229	31	19.77
Roberts (WI)	281	36	19.80
Lever	409	59	20.86
Underwood	572	66	21.60
EMERY	471	63	22.04
Phillip (WI)	482	69	22.10
STEELE	317	34	22.17
Gooch	198	20	22.45
GREIG, Ian	416	54	22.81

The list includes Hendrick, Taylor, Lever, Underwood and Gooch, who were banned for travelling to South Africa on an unauthorized tour, Mike Gatting, who is primarily a batsman, Ian Greig, who had been dropped after a trial of two Tests, David Steele, approaching the end of his splendid first-class career, and Kevin Saxelby, who was not always certain of a place in Nottinghamshire's side. Other than to point out the disproportionate numbers of overseas bowlers, little more need be said. Bob Willis, England captain in Australia and spearhead bowler, ended in fifty-seventh place.

The third chart shows the county record of the England bowlers at the time of the third Test with Pakistan in late August 1982.

	Overs	Wkts	Avge
Botham	374	40	29.12
Marks	541	50	30.18
Hemmings	431	42	24.88
Jackman	521	59	24.03
Willis	323	37	27.24

Given the difference in programmes since the advent of one-day cricket, there can be no comparison between the choice open to the selectors in 1954 and in 1982, and no need to search for reasons why England won one series and lost the other. But the effectiveness of selectors cannot be judged solely on whether England wins; if the talent is not available they may be doing a good job in keeping a series reasonably close. Bricks were never made without straw.

For all the batting ability at his disposal, Gubby Allen ended his seven-year spell urging England to be more aggressive, and Robins with the support of the rest of us – Doug Insole, Willie Watson and myself – declared that no candidate would be considered unless he had a positive attitude. Today such sentiments might be dismissed as lofty ideals but the game has not changed so much as to rewrite basic truths, and one of the most profound is that attitudes make or break an individual and a team.

It is interesting to compare the captaincy options open to selectors since my first year in 1962, my first as chairman (1969) and my last in that office (1981):

	1962	1969	1981
Derbyshire	Donald Carr	Derek Morgan	Geoff Miller
Essex	Trevor Bailey	Brian Taylor	Keith Fletcher
Glamorgan	Ossie Wheatley	Tony Lewis	Malcom Nash
Gloucestershire	Tom Pugh	Tony Brown	Mike Procter (SA)
Hampshire	Colin Ingleby-Mackenzie	Roy Marshall (WI)	Nick Pocock
Kent	Colin Cowdrey	Colin Cowdrey	Asif Iqbal (Pak.)
Lancashire	J. F. Blackledge	Jack Bond	Clive Lloyd (WI)
Leicestershire	David Kirby	Ray Illingworth	Roger Tolchard
Middlesex	Ian Bedford	Peter Parfitt	Mike Brearley
Northamptonshire	Keith Andrew	Roger Prideaux	Geoff Cook
Nottinghamshire	Andrew Corran	Sir Gary Sobers (WI)	Clive Rice (SA)
Somerset	Harold Stephenson	Brian Langford	Brian Rose
Surrey	Peter May	Micky Stewart	Roger Knight
Sussex	Ted Dexter	Mike Griffith	John Barclay
Warwickshire	Mike Smith	Alan Smith	Bob Willis
Worcestershire	Don Kenyon	Tom Graveney	Glenn Turner (NZ)
Yorkshire	Vic Wilson	Brian Close	Chris Old

In 1962 all seventeen were eligible for selection, with at least six on a short list, compared with twelve in 1981. The less familiar names of Blackledge and Kirby were one-season appointments. Blackledge was between the Test all-rounder Bob Barber and the Lancashire-domiciled Australian Ken Grieves – two outstanding cricketers. Kirby, captain of Cambridge University the previous year, succeeded Willie Watson, and was replaced by Maurice Hallam, a high-scoring batsman, who in another era would surely have been capped for England.

By 1969 there were two overseas captains; by 1981 there were five, including Mike Procter, then qualified by residence for England, who gave up in mid-season to make way for David Graveney. Barry Wood also took over in mid-term from Geoff Miller, which was a disappointment to the selectors as he had been England's vice-captain in the West Indies in the previous winter after the injured Bob Willis returned home. Miller was the type of young player we had hoped would take on county responsibilites, as the tendency was to go for the senior member of the side as

179

captain. In making these observations I acknowledge the contributions made by Mike Procter, Eddie Barlow, Clive Lloyd, Clive Rice and others. But any chairman eyeing the list and seeing his choice restricted is bound to sigh for captains eligible for England.

Changing social patterns have not always been to first-class cricket's advantage. The Oxford and Cambridge entry policy in the sixties put the emphasis on the academic rather than the athletic – thus depriving the counties of many potential players and captains – and some comprehensives, which replaced cricket-playing grammar schools, opted for football all the year round or turned to athletics in the summer. Individual sports have also increased in an age of more leisure for the masses. Television coverage and cash injections from commerce have boosted sports which were never regarded as cricket's competitors, and the long-running Yorkshire saga, damaging enough to the club, did not help, any more than the three-year ban on English players who toured South Africa. What was it said of Yorkshire? A strong Yorkshire is a strong England! As an old pro I find it extraordinary that one player should be the centre of such strife and bitterness – and even more that he allows it to happen. If the players of my day had been the cause of dividing their county, however unwittingly, I think at the first sign of strife they would have been on the first available train to Outer Mongolia! Years ago Dickie Bird, the umpire and a Yorkshireman, predicted, 'Geoff Boycott will finish up with more power in Yorkshire than Lord Hawke.' A fascinating thought, particularly as Lord Hawke founded the old Yorkshire traditions.

If it is old-fashioned to believe in a special relationship of trust between players and administration, in the absolute authority of the captain, and in team work – which I suggest extends in all cooperating to produce the best possible national side – then I am old-fashioned and have learned nothing. All the most successful sides I played in, and against, cemented individual flair with team effort. One is not possible without the other. A century ago Lord Hawke declared his team to be a cooperative body and not a collection of individuals, a simple philosophy as true today as it was all those years ago.

12

Run-ups that Run down Cricket

Strange to relate in the story of a professional bowler who took 1924 first-class wickets in a war-interrupted career – and many with late in-swing – I did not bowl with a new cricket ball until I was sixteen and a half years old. Until then I had used an old-fashioned composition ball which obviously did not swing. When, for the first time, I was handed the genuine article with its glossy surface and hand-stitched seam which I could hold, I was surprised and gratified to find that it not only swung in like a boomerang but moved very late in its flight. In due course I realized the swing came from a natural body action based on a sideways-on delivery, wrist action and literally putting my back into it at the end of a controlled and not over-fast approach to the wicket. Rhythm and coordination have always been the basic requirements of bowling.

My height of 6 feet 3 inches was a distinct advantage. A medium-fast bowler of my type needs to be tall and make full use of his height to hit the ball hard into the pitch to achieve bounce at a fuller length than is necessary for an out-and-out fast bowler. And to get bounce from a full length the ball has to be delivered with the arm high, in the 12 o'clock position, otherwise it tends to skid through and gives the better batsmen the opportunity to drive, especially on the average Test pitch. Bowling on the Australian shirtfronts of 1946–47 I found it necessary to bang the ball in with all the strength I could muster to prevent being driven. If I could not get the ball past the bat I tried to hit the blade as near the splice as possible. I had had it drummed into me from the start of my apprentice days at The Oval that the cardinal rules of bowling are line and length. To the end of my playing career, and since, I have never had cause to doubt those early teachings passed on to me by time-wise players.

181

Hard work though it was in Australia, the experience of trying to dismiss the best batsman on the best of pitches was invaluable. The more I bowled to Bradman, who avidly punished the smallest of errors (as did other Australians), the more I learned, and, if I had done nothing else than to get him out in five consecutive Test innings, I would have regarded my playing career as more than worthwhile. My ego, however, was somewhat deflated when I was asked in all seriousness by an England player, then following the television series 'Bodyline', whether I had ever bowled against Bradman. I was tempted to quote Sir Pelham Warner, who insisted that all cricketers should be familiar with the history of the game. Then it crossed my mind that I would have to explain who Sir Pelham was.

Long before my Surrey and England days there were two important incidents which affected my future bowling methods. During a net practice in my first week as a pro one of the senior players took me aside and told me I would never make it in county cricket unless I bowled the out-swinger. He had the very best of intentions and began to give me a demonstration. Allan Peach, the Surrey coach, was in another net, spotted what was happening and quietly advised me to ignore what I was being told, to carry on as I was going and to work things out for myself. I never had better advice, and the more cricket I played at every level the more I understood that a non-thinking bowler is unlikely to get far or, should he by chance get to the top, his prospects of staying there are slender. The best of coaches can only take a young player so far. He cannot, in the end, accompany him to the middle: only the player himself knows what he can do and how far he can stretch himself. A player should keep his eyes and ears open and seek as much advice as he can, but he should work out his own techniques. It is also up to him to profit from his mistakes. Above all I believe in developing one's natural ability, not stifling it.

My second lesson was to discover, while bowling in the nets at The Oval, that I could bowl just as well off ten paces as I could from eighteen. From that day I cut my run down to ten paces. In fact, I could make the ball move more with my new run because at the point of delivery I had to put in more body effort in order to maintain my pace. The saving on physical wear and tear was enormous. Starting with eighteen first-class overs in 1939, I had completed 15,346.4 overs, including eight-ball overs abroad, by the time of my retirement in 1960. Assuming each pace to be a yard, I saved myself in excess of 400 miles by reducing the length of my run.

Too many modern bowlers run too far and harm not only themselves but the game, for there is nothing more tedious than a lengthy gap between the delivery of each ball, especially by a medium pacer. The odd bowler may find it impossible to adjust to a shorter run, but there are many who would surely benefit and be better bowlers by having a sensible length of run. Absurdly long run-ups have become the bane of cricket, and I am forced to the conclusion that the only solution lies in a restricted run limited to, say, 22 yards, the length of the pitch. Bowlers, I am convinced, would not be unfairly handicapped by such a measure. Their art lies in a subtle alliance of skill and strength, of rhythm and the right action, plus effort, and it is sadly all too evident that the sheer physical strain of getting to the wicket by some bowlers makes the achievement of those essential qualities all the less likely. Harold Larwood and Ray Lindwall are prime examples of great fast bowlers who did not need anything like the same run as we now see by bowlers of nowhere near their speed. We have become accustomed to watching what are, after all, medium pace bowlers lumbering up from a point towards the boundary. The late Jack Fingleton, Test batsman and brilliant writer, had this to say in the 1966 *Wisden* (note the year):

I have been hammering for years that fast bowlers and particularly alleged fast bowlers should be restricted in their run-up to, say, sixteen yards. Keith Miller, fast enough to displease any batsman, ran ten yards and sometimes twelve. A run-up, surely, is to enable a bowler to get up momentum. Those who know the science of athletics can say how long it takes a one-hundred-yards sprinter to reach top speed after his take-off. It would not, I guess, be very far and yet I constantly see in first-class and Test cricket a bowler travelling forty yards who is running as fast after ten yards as he is after thirty-five yards. Indeed, I have seen some worthies even lose pace in their run as they came near to delivering the ball.

At the time of writing, Charlie Griffith and Wes Hall are in trouble with some Australian umpires for taking too long to bowl an over. Griffith, timed at seven minutes for an eight-ball over, was advised in Melbourne to take a taxi, so long was he in getting back to his far-distant mark. This long run, with its official sanction, is the most nauseating absurdity of all cricketing time. How we put up with it, year after year, is beyond comprehension. Next time, I invite you, when you see one of those dreary runners in action in a first-class game, to look at the faces around you and see how bored they are. The poor batsman, who stands there in frustration, awaiting a ball a minute – and that often delivered pretty wide of the mark – generally incurs the wrath of the critic and the slow hand-clap of the spectators when these condemnations rightfully should be directed at some innocuous bowler whose only attribute is that he clamps down the scoring rate. He does that by holding up play and not delivering smartly. I see no genius in that.

I once saw a bowler at Kennington Oval who trudged into the distance and then put foot after foot in a dull manner for forty yards to deliver a ball about as fast as a London bus going up Fleet Street.

It was a piece of fulsome, unexciting running. I would not mind so much if a bowler turned a catherine-wheel for variety in the middle of his run. It would not, I am sure, affect the speed of the delivered article; it hurt more than ever when someone said the same bowler, on a Sunday, had cut his run by half in a time-limit game. I broached this pet hate of mine to an important member of Surrey and he floored my by saying the tactics in a long run were to catch the batsman in between taps of his mark! I think he was pulling my leg. But while I continue in this berating mood let me call down a murrain on all fast bowlers, seamers and alleged fast bowlers who walk back into eternity and take an eternity to emerge from it.

No doubt attempts to cut down the run-up would provoke an outcry; the death of genuine fast bowling would be predicted with the same certainty as there was when the front-foot law was introduced to defeat excessive drag. In 1958–59 I was following Peter May's well-considered side in Australia as a journalist and broadcaster for the Australian Broadcasting Commission. The job proved to be more satisfying than the cricket, which was blighted by bitter controversies over throwing, bowler's drag and umpiring decisions. England were generally expected to do well, but by the end of the series they were broken and demoralized, defeated 4–0. Suspicious action by some Australian bowlers made a telling contribution to the outcome of the series, and Gordon Rorke's drag was so pronounced that Peter May, who was no coward and would stand up to bouncers without flinching, admitted that he was physically frightened for the first time in his career. Rorke released the ball well over the batting crease. Once at Sydney it was measured at 7 feet 2 inches. The effect was dramatic and his action too was among those England questioned. England had draggers in Frank Tyson, Freddie Trueman and Peter Loader, but Rorke's drag was the most pronounced of all. The most vexing aspect of the problem was that it had been allowed to creep into the game without action being taken. Much the same could be said about throwing.

Eventually the law was changed to stipulate that any part of the front foot has to land 'whether grounded or raised' on or behind the popping crease. Inevitably opponents of the alteration, including many eminent old cricketers, forecast the demise of genuine fast bowling. They reckoned, however, without a new generation growing up and adopting styles to meet the law. Now the complaint might well be that there is precious little else but fast bowling.

While I agree bowlers should deliver the ball from a legitimate area I have never been a convert to the front-foot law, as bowlers have to look where their front foot is landing instead of concentrating on the spot where they aim to pitch the ball. Umpires are also at a disadvantage as they have to watch the popping crease at the moment of delivery, and immediately pick up the flight of the ball, which could be travelling at speed from 60 to 90 miles an hour. To judge on the fairness of a delivery *and* look for leg before and thin-edged snicks in a matter of a few fleeting seconds is asking a lot, and particularly in these days of all-pace attacks. However, it is fair to say that the present law has prevented bowlers from stealing yards and gaining an unfair advantage.

Throwing or jerking seems to visit cricket with the regularity of the plague in the Middle Ages. From the earliest times there have been controversies over the fairness of a bowler's action, partly because it is almost impossible to put into words what the eye of the experienced player and watcher knows by instinct to be wrong. Again, it is a question of inaction and buck-passing – no umpire enjoys no-balling for throwing, particularly in the early stages of a bowler's career. There have been some umpires who adopt the convenient line that if a bowler has not been no-balled his action must be acceptable. Some umpires also hide behind the contention that a bowler would not have been chosen if he threw . . . and so a vicious circle begins.

Throwing problems do not spring up overnight. In South Africa in 1948–49 many of the touring England team had misgivings about Cuan McCarthy's action. In 1951 he came to England and the debate began again. Umpire Frank Chester was among those not satisfied, and some years later he told me that during a lunch interval in the First Test at Trent Bridge he spoke to two of the leading officials of the time. He told them of his concern and he asked the question which an umpire should never have to ask: would he have official backing if he no-balled McCarthy for throwing? The reply was: 'If you do, it will be the last time you umpire in a Test match.' At least it can be said cricket has progressed beyond that type of thinking.

Behind the official reasoning was the principle that on no account must England's guests be put to embarrassment. Indeed, it was not until 1960 that a visiting cricketer was called for throwing – and South Africa's Geoffrey Griffin offended no less than seven first-class umpires twenty-eight times apart from the incident in the exhibition which followed the early ending of the Second Test at Lord's. In the Test Frank Lee had called Griffin eleven times in England's only innings, and in the exhibition which followed Sid Buller, who had not had an opportunity to pass judgement during the Test, no-balled him four times and the over was finished under-arm. All the players felt sorry for the bowler and perturbed that the South Africans, who cannot have been ignorant of the doubts, should have taken a chance which ended in the humiliation of one of their players. Even in the pre-tour nets Gubby Allen had predicted it would end in tears.

Slow bowlers too have had suspect actions. Probably the most publicized in recent years was that of Tony Lock of Surrey. When Tony came to The Oval as a young man of nineteen he bowled in the classical slow left-hander style. He had a wonderful flight even at that age and collected 100 wickets with this type of bowling. After a winter in an indoor school he arrived for practice at The Oval in 1952 with a completely changed action. He played for Surrey and England for some years with this action, which some people suspected. Eventually Tony saw a film of himself and immediately decided to go back to his old action with magnificent results, as his career with Leicestershire and Western Australia showed. Tony was able to change because he went back to what was his natural action. Others have tried to eliminate the throw or jerk in their action but have been unable to do so simply because the suspect delivery was part of their natural way of bowling; Tony's was the reverse.

Ask any old player what he most dislikes about the game today and he will invariably complain of slow over rates and intimidatory bowling. Together they have become the curse of the age.

Over rates have been the concern of selectors and legislators for far too long. Clearly, ridiculously long run-ups are an important cause of the decline, and captains have cynically used the situation to slow down the tempo of an opponent's innings and to break a batsman's concentration. Of course, older bowlers knew how and when to take their time, but the essential difference is that slowly bowled overs were not a common occurrence and were only used as a tactical ploy in Test matches. In the late fifties Gubby Allen, then chairman of selectors, wrote in the *Daily Mail:* 'Some bowlers take too long over their business. I have examined the figures from every angle. The drop in the rate at which overs are bowled is alarming. Compared with prewar the public is being denied forty-five minutes to an hour's cricket in every day's play. It is one of things which irritate spectators.'

Despite the high-level displeasure, we have grudgingly come to accept the rate Gubby Allen complained about all those years ago. In the course of time I was to hear my predecessors, Walter Robins and Doug Insole, both of whom were very hot on the subject, add their protests. I followed in the same vein. The players answered my exhortations with the same excuse: 'We do not consciously slow down the tempo of the game, and we can't understand how an average of some twenty overs an hour was managed before the war.' The Test and County Cricket Board, it must be said, have done their level best to face up to the problem and have met with some success by imposing fines for not reaching an arbitrary number of overs both in the County Championship and, in 1985, in limited-over competitions. But overseas countries are apt to jib at controls of this nature and their players will not submit to a system of fines. They are equally opposed to suggestions, which

187

many think are imperative for the future of cricket, to curb the number of bouncers.

I feel I am entitled to speak as one who practised what he now preaches on the question of over rates. Back in 1959, when I was hardly in the first flush of youth, E. M. Wellings had this to say in the old *Evening News*. Under the heading 'Bedser Lesson for Those Strolling Players', he wrote: 'One pace bowler sets a splendid example. Late in his fortieth year Alec Bedser shames most of his younger rivals by the slick manner in which he delivers an over. Umpires should regard him as a pattern for all.'

Wellings also pointed out that in the days before over rates slumped fielders wasted no time crossing between overs. It was second nature for me and my contemporaries to walk briskly back to the bowling mark as soon as the ball was delivered. After the ball had been bowled there was seldom an inquest with the bowler standing in the middle of the pitch. Indeed, had there been signs of demonstrations with the hands-on-hips glare down the pitch at the batsman, he would soon have been told to cut it out either by his captain or an umpire. Unfortunately the bad habits of cricket often appear to be subtly infectious, and once it became the trademark of Freddie Trueman to indulge in a few histrionics – largely for the benefit of the crowd – others felt impelled to get in on the act. Every bowler should get on with his job, and if he did so without fuss the over rate would improve to the benefit of the game and the enjoyment of spectators.

For all the official cajoling and threats, there has not, to my knowledge, been a bowler disciplined for time-wasting. Yet Ken Barrington in 1966 and Geoff Boycott a year later were dropped by England for slow scoring, and Brian Close lost his Test captaincy after Yorkshire, under his leadership, exploited delaying tactics during a close finish in a match against Warwickshire at Edgbaston. England cannot be fairly accused of not trying to overcome the problem of slow over rates by legislation but no doubt figures could be produced to prove their recommendations are not always followed on the field of play. And it is in the middle where the problem has to be solved in the end. Poor over rates are a threat to the five-day Test match. In the Adelaide Test of the 1984–85 series, Australia and the West Indies averaged twelve overs and four balls an hour for the four innings. In the West Indies' first innings the average was eleven overs and five balls an hour.

Many years ago E. H. D. Sewell, a noted Essex amateur batsman and writer on the game for the old *Daily Sketch*, condemned bodyline in his book *Cricket Under Fire** with words which are still appropriate in today's arguments over the barrage of short-pitched bowling. Sewell wrote:

The irrefutable charge against bodyline is that, when accurately bowled, it cuts the off-side out of the game. For such a crime no censure is severe enough. Bodyline inserted ugliness into a beautiful game. For that alone cricket lovers could never condone it. Cricket's two chief claims to beauty are the off-side stroke of an accomplished batsman and the run-up and fluent delivery of a physically well-built bowler. To cut the off-side out of cricket would be a wicked operation, certain not to prolong its happy life, but to kill it – stone dead.

Go through your list of the Greatest Batsmen. You will find that without exception all those who were, or are, justly famed for beauty, style and grace of action were first and almost last strong off-side players. Now write down the strong on-siders and try to name one – only one – beautiful bat. You cannot do it. . . . Is first class cricket in such a flourishing condition that you can deliberately excise from the game its main, almost its only beautiful and attractive feature?

Moderns might immediately point to Viv Richards as principally an on-side player, and few have ever come better than Richards. Sewell might have answered that Richards is superbly functional rather than aesthetic – as indeed he said in so many words of Bradman, whom he put no. 3 to Victor Trumper and Charlie Macartney. Richards, of course, has to deal with bowling as it is and not as it was. It is a sad and sobering thought that if short-pitched bowling with its aim of preventing the batsman attacking on the front foot had been permitted at the time there would have been no so-called Golden Age of batting, Victor Trumper's charm may never have emerged, and my generation would have been largely deprived of the majesty of the cover driving of Wally Hammond, Len Hutton and Peter May. As Ken Barrington signific-antly pointed out after a century against the West Indies at Port-of-Spain in the 1959–60 series, when he was said not to have

*Stanley Paul, 1941.

scored many in front of the wicket, 'There were only three balls pitched up all day.'

Bodyline, as such, with its concentration of fielders on the leg side supporting short-pitched deliveries fired fast at the leg-stump area, was swiftly outlawed once the theory was properly understood and partisan emotions had cooled. While a barrage of short-pitchers is not bodyline without the special field placings, surely it is a blood relation. Just as bodyline was recognized as a threat to the future of cricket so is persistent short-pitched bowling. The answer is to ensure that the law is obeyed. Apart from the obvious physical dangers, short-pitched bowling is dull to watch, often creates bad feeling and has contributed to the dearth of high-quality spin bowling which was one of the game's delights.

The easiest way to bowl a maiden over and limit the scoring opportunities of the opposition is to get each delivery to rise to chest or head height by pitching short; and when the ball is bowled at the speed of greased lightning the batsman has an awesome task defending his person. His choice lies in evasive action or taking a chance with a scoring shot knowing that the odds of completing it successfully are against him. As one newspaper proclaimed after one bout of unchecked bumpers, the happy term of 'cricket, lovely cricket' had become 'cricket, ugly cricket'.

Most serious cricket writers have not minced words and John Woodcock in successive editions of *Wisden* has written that 'the viciousness of much of today's fast bowling is changing the very nature of the game' and of a 'chilling new dimension to the game.' Denis Compton, who was as brave as he was brilliant, has written of 'bumper madness' and Tony Lewis, the former England and Glamorgan captain, has declared that it is no longer the object to bowl at the wickets in order to knock them over. *Wisden* also refers to the 'thuggery of the bouncer' and New Zealand's Geoff Howarth declared after a Test match at Kingston, 'I have been a professional for sixteen years but what happened out there has nothing to do with my ideas about cricket. The bowling was aimed at the body.' Jeremy Coney, whose left arm was broken in the same match, said that in the twenty minutes for which he batted only two balls were pitched up. 'I didn't say anything,' he added. 'I still believe it has to be left to the umpires to legislate, but I think batsmen should be given the right to talk to the umpire and point out that perhaps it's gone too far. Batsmen can appeal against the light, why not against short-pitched bowling?'

Why not, indeed, but in today's climate an appeal to an umpire would probably be a futile gesture. If an umpire needs to have it pointed out to him that a bowler is breaking the law it is hard to believe he would be strong enough to implement it. However, it is an interesting suggestion which ought not to be necessary.

Even it it were possible, no one seeks the outright ban of the bouncer. Provided it is used sparingly it is a fast bowler's fair and legitimate weapon. He has the right to try to unsettle a batsman, to test his nerve and skill, and to display his own aggression. The spectator, too, would be deprived of a sudden drama – a contrasting emotion to being dulled to desperation by a nonstop barrage of bumpers when it becomes an offence to the eye and the game. No one with a knowledge of or feeling for the game would dispute the comment in *Wisden* of 1985 that it should be a real concern to the administrators that 'the batsman has become as much a target for the fast bowlers as the wicket he defends.' The fighting John Woodcock continued in his 'Notes by the Editor':

It was hard to watch the West Indian, Marshall, bowling at Pocock in last season's fifth Test match at The Oval without recoiling. Pocock was the night-watchman from the previous day. As such, he could expect few favours. However, the Laws of Cricket make it abundantly clear that the 'relative skill of the striker' must be taken into consideration by an umpire when deciding whether the bowling of a fast-pitched ball amounts to 'intimidation' and is therefore unfair. That Marshall, a superb bowler, should have kept bouncing the ball at so inept a batsman was unwarrantable; that Lloyd should have condoned his doing so was disconcerting; that Constant, the umpire at Marshall's end, should have stood passively by was unaccountable. It was a woeful piece of cricket, entirely lacking in chivalry. Miller and Lindwall, who played the game hard enough, would never have thought of bowling in the same way to Bedser when he acted as night-watchman at Headingley in 1948; nor, I feel sure, would Gregory or McDonald, or the 'Demon' Spofforth. Perhaps, when the International Cricket Conference do no more than pay lip service, it is not surprising that umpires are so compliant.

To be strictly accurate, Miller and Lindwall did bowl some bouncers at me, not only at Headingley where the pitch was too slow for them to be dangerous, but in the previous Test at Old Trafford, and at Melbourne in 1946–47. Indeed, a bouncer at Melbourne flicked the side of my head, but they were rare and not unfair. I would also lay claim to have been a useful tailend batsman at the time and, with my height, I was able to fend off the ball or, if need be, move aside and let it pass. In the two home Tests I shared century partnerships with Denis Compton and Bill Edrich, and the occasional bouncer only arrived after I had been batting for some time. I had no complaints. I cannot recall either Lindwall or Miller deliberately bouncing at tailenders ill-equipped to defend themselves. It is to be much regretted that the customs of the game have slipped to a state when no holds are barred. We had no personal animosity and, in fact, the harder the game the better friends we became. On my birthday, 4 July 1985, the phone rang at my office and a voice said: 'Can't stop as I'm dashing to catch a train. But just rang to wish you a happy birthday.' The caller: Keith Miller.

Woodcock's reference to the failure of the International Cricket Conference to deal with intimidation hits the nail squarely on the head. While it can be fairly argued that a succession of captains must bear some of the blame, the final responsibility rests on the various Boards of Control and the International Cricket Conference. I have been told that criticism of intimidation is exaggerated as intimidation expresses the spirit of the times, and that spectators still watch Test matches. The laws of the game, however, have not been changed to suit the age; only the spirit of the laws has been bent. I sometimes wonder, when a batsman ducks and weaves as a ball whistles around his head, how many potential players and parents of potential players have turned away from what appears to be a violent and dangerous game.

Personally I do not accept the suggestion of a line drawn across the pitch to be a practical solution to short-pitched bowling. The idea is that if a ball is pitched behind the line at the bowler's end it should be declared a no-ball. The difficulty would be literally where to draw the line.

Michael Holding, the fastest bowler in the world in his peak and one of the West Indies fearsome quartet for many years, made an interesting contribution to the continuing debate in an interview in *The Cricketer International*.

I can understand why it arouses such passions. . . . I do not agree with

192

excessive use of the bouncer, but it would be naive and misleading of me to claim that I never bowl bouncers without trying to intimidate the batsman. On the contrary I want him to be aware that if he gets on to the front foot against me he might find himself in trouble – in other words he might get hurt. But that is quite a different thing from actually wanting or intending to hurt him.

I have no desire to hurt anyone. But I do want to get batsmen out, as quickly as possible, and if that means pitching a few deliveries in my half of the wicket in order to keep him on the back foot I – like any fast bowler – will do what the law and umpires allow. The flatter and slower the wicket, the more important it is for the fast bowler to let the batsman know that he mustn't feel safe on the front foot.

I freely admit there may have been times in recent seasons when the West Indies fast bowlers have overdone the short-pitched fast bowling, although in my case the only occasion I can remember being warned by an umpire is at Old Trafford in 1976. But that was on a poor wicket when many balls were lifting nastily from only just short of a length and Brian Close was trying to play off the front foot. Perhaps in circumstances like these the umpires need to enforce the law more strongly – or perhaps the law itself is not strong enough.

Holding went on to say that the real villains were not the fast bowlers but the pitches, and that batsmen were getting hurt more because of an unpredictable bounce. The problem, however, is not so much *one* fast bowler bowling at a length to stop batsmen from playing off the front foot but *four* in the same attack.

I have often been asked if, as a selector, I would support the choice of four fast bowlers were that number available to England. As England's ration of genuine speed men over thirty years has been confined to Freddie Trueman, Brian Statham, Frank Tyson, John Snow and Bob Willis, the situation is hardly likely to arise. Opportunity would be a fine thing. Once a winning format was to have two authentic fast bowlers hunting as a pair and supported by someone like Bill Johnston, Max Walker or Trevor Bailey. There have been series won with one outstanding fast bowler tipping the scales, as Snow did for Ray Illingworth in Australia in 1970–71. A balance was not considered achieved unless at least one slow bowler was also included. When I now hear spinners dismissed as non-match-winners several names cross my mind like Bill O'Reilly, Clarrie Grimmett, Jim Laker, Tony Lock, Hedley Verity and Derek Underwood.

193

The West Indies of late, however, have turned conventions upside down. They have been able to preserve a balance because Malcolm Marshall, perhaps the fastest bowler in the world by 1984, can bat well, although, admittedly, he did not show any run-getting form in England in the series of that year. Others in the lower order can also swing an effective bat, as Mike Holding and Eldine Baptiste showed at Edgbaston in 1984. When tailenders can flog the bowling in such a cavalier fashion it is devastating to the opposition. Marshall began the series at no. 7 and, accordingly, there was room for off-spinner Roger Harper, who also raised the fielding standards. Clive Lloyd did not have a suspect position in his team, and his task was made all the easier by the fact that he did not have to concern himself with conserving the strength of only two strike bowlers. He had four to share the workload and, it might be added, all with impressive strength. Moreover, no more than seventy to eighty overs a day were expected from them instead of 100–110, which was once considered par for the course in a Test match. If each bowler was required to bowl, say, twenty-five overs a day instead of sixteen there would be a better chance for batsmen to take advantage of a tiring attack from tea onwards, which was expected in the days when over rates were higher.

The West Indies' achievements have been fantastic. My respect for the quality of their players began when I played against John Goddard's side in 1950 – the team of three wonderful Ws and Ramadhin and Valentine which set the pattern for the future by winning in England for the first time. Even before the war older pros waxed lyrical about George Headley, the first of the line of great black batsmen, and predicted their success as an international force when they became more disciplined. The instant qualification of overseas players for county cricket was undoubtedly a turning point, and with so many playing regularly in England they no longer need to acclimatize at the beginning of a tour. For most, England is their second home, and at best they have such exciting flair that cricket might have been specially invented for them. That they are the most powerful of the modern sides is beyond argument and, after a record of eleven successive Test victories over England and Australia between 4 April and 11 December 1984, the question was inevitably raised: are they the best side of all time?

Much as I admire them, my preference is for Bradman's

immediate postwar team. The sheer quality of Australia's batting went deeper – down to no. 9 – and their attack was more balanced. Bowling comparisons are difficult as the new ball was available after fifty-five overs in 1948, an experiment which not surprisingly was hastily discarded. What a contest it would be if the two sides could meet and our theories put to the test! The incredible thing is that the West Indies produce cricketers of world stature from comparatively tiny communities. In the autumn of 1984 I was invited to Bermuda to celebrate the Somers Isles Cricket League's 45th anniversary. A match was played against Antigua, which can boast no less than Viv Richards, the champion batsman of the world, Andy Roberts, Eldine Baptiste, Richie Richardson and George Ferris. Bermuda and Antigua are two tiny dots on the ocean, yet the standard of play there was excellent. Having seen Sri Lanka make 491 runs for 7 wickets in their first Test match in England only weeks previously, I was left to ponder why such small areas, at least in size, can produce a calibre of players which we in England with our population, schools, club and county cricket, not to mention other resources like indoor facilities and coaching, would be pleased to have.

None of the Sri Lankan players had appeared at Lord's before the match in 1984. Yet Sidath Wettimuny, A. R. Silva and L. R. D. Mendis hit centuries, and the skipper Mendis failed by only 6 runs to score his second century of the match. In his first innings his 100 came off only 112 balls, and included three 6s off Ian Botham, who has taken well over 300 Test wickets. It is easy to dismiss England's performance as that of a jaded side after being crushed by the West Indies, but the fact is that Sri Lanka had a first-innings lead of 121 and had the better of a draw. There is immense potential in the natural skill and enthusiasm for cricket in Sri Lanka. The Lord's successes must have given them much encouragement, and was a reminder that cricket power is now well distributed. There are no easy Test matches and the older nations, England and Australia, have to look to their laurels. In the long term it may be that Australia will be facing many of the problems that beset England, one of which is to retain the interest of youngsters beyond their middle teens. At that age, as many coaches in England and Australia will testify, some are lured to other and more sophisticated pursuits.

Don Wilson, once of England and Yorkshire and now MCC head coach, and his staff train thousands of boys. According to him, 'From the ages of twelve to fifteen they are magic. They love coming to Lord's whether during the Easter classes or to the indoor school. The general standard is good, and the enthusiasm heartening, but from around fifteen on it tends to begin to change. A lot of real promise is wasted. It is a mystery to me what happens to many of them, especially if they have to find their own way around. I do my best to find suitable clubs for them, maybe thirty to forty a season, and to put them on the right road. This, however, is an era when success seems to be expected right away and things begin to get a little difficult when I tell them there is no easy way to the top and hard work is necessary.

'It is completely different from the days when I used to go to the nets at Headingley, then under Arthur Mitchell, who was a notoriously hard man when he played for Yorkshire. But he was a marvellous coach. While batting one day, I kept being bowled by Freddie Trueman and others, and Mitchell eventually came up to me and asked, "What's tha trade?" "I'm an apprentice joiner," I replied. "Right," said Mitchell. "Next time tha coomes better bring tha bag of tools and board up tha wicket." The old coaches did not make it comfortable for their young charges but, looking back, you realize how much you owe them. As I say, the kids nowadays are wonderful, a joy to work with, and I only wish the enthusiasm would stay with them.'

Tom Graveney has said it was much the same when he coached in Queensland. Once the boys were old enough to hold a driving licence they were off to the beach and drifted from the game. Perhaps the attractions of a more sophisticated life do not exist in the West Indies islands. At home the National Cricket Association, which is responsible for the grassroots, is in good hands, but it seems peculiar that in the major team games England has gone backwards. In cricket, soccer and rugby union the recent results have been moderate, to say the least. The only areas in which we seem to breed world champions are middle-distance running, snooker, ice skating – and Sandy Lyle won the Open.

There can be no better life than that of a cricketer who is being paid for something he enjoys. The number from university and public schools, who might normally be expected to enter the professions and industry, in the county ranks serves to support my point. If a player makes a success of his game the rewards usually follow; and they can now be high. We hear of players about to become millionaires and we see pages of advertisements in the cricket magazines endorsing equipment and the like. Even in a period of modest standards it is possible to enjoy an income on a scale far beyond the dreams of the old masters. Presumably, so long as South Africa remains on the outside and is prepared to offer huge inducements to players to take part in sponsored private tours there will be no shortage of players and their agents ready and willing to step inside a gold mine. Contracts of £100,000 were said to be offered to Australians in 1985 and, as a result, there had to be three changes in the selected side to tour England. The ironic twist was that Kerry Packer, having thrown the international game in turmoil and enticed the world's leading players to his World Series Cricket, is said to have taken an active role by offering cash inducements to players to remain loyal to the official game. Clearly, the temptation to ensure a financial future with a relatively short tour is very great. One of the members of the Australian side spoke of being able to set up his dream of a farm in Queensland in one swoop. Yet the Australian captain, Allan Border, insisted there was no money in the world that would entice him to play in South Africa. The extraordinary part about it all is that so many ordinary cricketers pick up large sums; some of those who have profited so considerably are hardly of international class. The teams that cost South Africa's sponsors so much are nowhere near representative. Presumably the South Africans believe the money well spent if they can attract a few top players in each of the teams.

On the playing side I hear much talk of reverting to the old lbw law, changed in 1935, which is said to have induced too much in-swing bowling to the detriment of out-swing and leg-break bowling and off-side strokeplay. The old law went out before my time in first-class ranks so I am unable to make personal comparisons, but before another crucial change of law is contemplated I would prefer to see pitches uncovered, at least for domestic cricket in England. I am sure the game would be all the better for uncovered pitches. I am not in favour of four-day County Championship matches, much as I want to see the serious side of cricket preserved. The Championship is an absolute must as a training ground for Test cricket. Rather than a fourth day, I would aim for more balls to be delivered per day. If the old rate of 120 overs in a full day could be reached there would be no need for a fourth day. Three days at 120 overs a day mean 360 overs – four days at 90 overs a day also mean 360 overs. A fourth day would merely serve as an encouragement to stay at the present over rates or go even slower. It is also necessary to avoid the rush of experiments which overwhelmed the game in the fifties and sixties, and, above all, to avoid gimmicks introduced in the hope of attracting a new type of spectator. In all sports mass support for bread-and-butter events has disappeared with changing social patterns and the advent of television coverage of big events.

The Championship should stay as it is, played hard but fairly and always with serious intent. Contrivances thought up to gain a result are undesirable, and I much applaud the honesty of Lancashire's Steve O'Shaughnessy, who scored a century in thirty-five minutes on the last day of the 1983 season and equalled the record set by the late Percy Fender for Surrey at Northampton in 1920. 'I would rather have had to work hard for a fifty,' Steve said afterwards. Long hops and full tosses were served up to him in an effort to get a declaration and, accordingly the proceedings degenerated to pure farce. That kind of enterprise cannot be good for the name of the Championship, which must be a priority to win for any county captain.

Like all major sports, cricket has to live with television and, happily, there is invariably amicable cooperation. There are those who believe the BBC ought to pay more for its contracts but, so long as the other channels do not compete, cricket's bargaining power is restricted. Television must never be cricket's master. The same has to be said for sponsorship, but again cricket has been singularly fortunate. While it may be true that sponsorship is a form of cut-price advertising and some firms do very well commercially out of it, there are other backers who support less publicized parts of the game and get virtually no national publicity.

Generally first-class cricket has been both realistic and imaginative in adapting to changing times and modern needs; indeed it has often been in the vanguard of change. A study of any county club balance sheet demonstrates how successful promotional activities have become. And, it might be added, how essential they are to survival. Clubs have seldom, if ever, been able to manage on revenue from the actual county game, and although there has been many a crisis none of the seventeen counties have gone out of business. But the old pillars of security – gate receipts, members' subscriptions and share-out from the Test match pool – are not enough as costs rise. Surrey's accounts for 1984 are an example. Gate receipts were a mere £37,064, subscriptions were £162,555 and the Test and County Cricket Board distribution £184,091. There were two other items of income amounting to £11,367 and £107,836, but the key amount was £645,221 from promotional activities. Income was £1,148,134 – a figure which in pre-inflation days would have taken the breath away – and expenditure was £1,049,769. Outlays included £392,648 on cricket, £252,833 on marketing and £404,288 on finance and marketing. I recommend playing staffs to look at their club's figures and consider how they can help to make their product more attractive to the paying customer. By raising the over rate, for example.

Cricket has avoided some of the modern developments which have caused administrators to believe top-level sport has become part of showbiz, with the cult of the individual, the rise of the impresario, more money and less sportsmanship. Those of us who care for the game must not let standards go, for once they are gone they are gone for ever. Take, for example, wild, orchestrated appealing designed to stampede umpires into making mistakes. It has been said that the only solution is to eliminate appeals completely, but it is part of the game: cricket would not be quite the same without it. Fair appealing is the aim and, once more, we return to strong captaincy and team discipline.

As chairman of selectors I was involved in an unprecedented incident when Arthur Fagg threatened to walk out of a Test match at Edgbaston in 1973. Umpire Fagg, once an opening batsman for England and Kent, was upset by dissension shown by the West Indies captain Rohan Kanhai after an appeal against Geoff Boycott had been turned down. Fagg did not appear for the first over on the third morning, being engaged in a discussion at the time with Esmond Kentish, the West Indies manager, and myself. His place was taken by Warwickshire coach and former Test player Alan Oakman, who fortunately had been a first-class umpire. No doubt Alan would have continued to everyone's satisfaction, but it was

199

a very tricky situation, not made any easier by the fact that Fagg had held forth to some reporters in a carpark at the close of play on the previous evening and his intentions not to continue were spread over the back page.

Fagg was, in turn, criticized for overreaction. He could have ruined his future as a Test umpire, but there was no disguising his indignation that his decision over Boycott had been questioned and that the fieldsmen did not let the matter rest. *Wisden's* comment was that Kanhai openly showed his annoyance for the next two hours. Fagg demanded an apology, and it took a lot of persuasion on the part of the touring manager and myself to get him to carry on. He was somewhat mollified by the manager's assurance that the West Indies team were fully satisfied with his umpiring. The affair ended with handshakes all round. I have since wondered if Fagg had stuck to his guns whether he would have struck a blow for umpires everywhere. Umpires like Frank Chester, Syd Buller and Harold Bird shared strength of character and stood no nonsense from the most belligerent of players. Surely one of the classic umpiring performances of all time came from Bird and Tom Spencer in the Prudential Cup final at Lord's in 1975 between the West Indies and Australia. The match lasted from 11 a.m. to 8.43 p.m. and, although there were five run-outs in Australia's innings and a 26,000 crowd was on edge from start to finish, the pair did not make a mistake. A wonderful example of sustained concentration and devotion to the game. How many among that excited crowd gave a second thought to two men who had played such a notable part on an unforgettable occasion?

A second trip for me in the winter of 1984–85 was to be transported to Australia on the magic carpet provided by Qantas for the Benson and Hedges World Series Cup tournament, which was surprisingly won by India, who had been comfortably beaten at home by England in single-innings games only months before. Such are the vagaries of form in this type of competition. I felt considerable sympathy for David Gower and his players, who had emerged from the serious mission of their winter tour programme with such distinction. They made no impression in the World Series tournament which, in the public's eyes, took some of the gilt off the gingerbread. But the paramount fact was that on a tour of India of unique difficulties, starting with the assassination of Prime

Minister Mrs Indira Gandhi, England's team spirit, composure and emerging skills gave hope and promise for the future. The results in Australia did not alter that earlier accomplishment.

After his triumph both as batsman and captain in winning the Ashes in 1985, I have high hopes that Gower's already distinguished career will continue to flourish. Also the emergence of Mike Gatting as a free-scoring Test batsman gave the selectors immense satisfaction in the happy summer of 1985, particularly as there were doubts that he justified his selection for India. How well he answered those misgivings.

In Australia it was impossible not to be aware of the conflict of interests between the players and the marketing representatives over single-innings matches. On one side was Lynton Taylor, the managing director of PBL Marketing, the company which promotes and markets cricket officially for the Australian Cricket Board, and on the other Allan Border, captain of Australia and a batsman who has emerged as one of the best in the world. Mr Taylor, who will be remembered for his part in the Packer saga, was reported as saying that he did not think twenty-seven one-day internationals in a normal season were excessive; and he did not see why there should not be additional one-day games if necessary.

Mr Taylor is obviously entitled to express his opinion, but I hope attention is paid to comments by Allan Border in *The Age*.

For the last two months I have been playing nothing but one-day cricket, which means I've been stepping away to leg, slashing at everything outside off and for ever trying to lift the ball over the field to make more impetus on the scoreboard. In other words, playing all kind of shots I would never dare to play in a Test match . . . These one-day strokes obviously creep into your technique and there is a danger it may have harmful effects. Certainly there are problems for some players in making that change back.

Fortunately the transition had no adverse effect on his later performances in England, but the authorities, while cashing in literally on the popularity of the restricted game, have a clear duty first to consider their prime assets – the players. Let us have our single-innings cricket by all means, but let us all strive for the proper balance which is one of the key issues of modern times.

13

Last Over

Sir Donald Bradman once declared selectorship to be fascinating despite its many complexities. He also calculated that, during his term of office, which, excluding the years 1952 and 1953, stretched from 1936 to 1971, he spent about eight years away from home. Since there is more first-class cricket in England and more players to watch than in Australia, it is possible, for once, that I have out-scored the mighty Don. Selection certainly is fascinating, but if I have learned one lesson as selector, it is to exercise patience, and particularly not to expect too much too soon of a young player. There can be no greater satisfaction for a selector to see a player he spotted as a rough diamond develop into an international of standing, but in an age when instant success is demanded, it is a tall order for a young player to live up to some of the extravagant praise prematurely showered upon him. It needs almost two seasons to gain as much experience in the middle – the only place that really counts – as it did in a single season before the game was divided between the County Championship, the two knockout competitions and the John Player Special League.

It is strange how fortunes ebb and flow. A few years ago the main need was batsmen of class. As I write, there is no scarcity of batting. Mike Gatting has justified our faith in him, and Tim Robinson, whom I have watched since he was nineteen (a fact which might surprise some Nottinghamshire supporters) was drafted in at the right moment. Like others, it took time for him to mature, but the selectors were always aware of his potential.

An eminent critic wrote an article in the seventies naming twelve players for the future. Only one really made the grade, which emphasizes the dangers of prediction. Nevertheless, Peter May and his team have been much encouraged by the number and the

202

quality of several young batsmen, even bearing in mind that this is not a vintage bowling era. The names of Kim Barnett, Paul Prichard, Robin Smith, Mark Benson, Simon Hinks, Neil Fairbrother, Ian Butcher, John Whitaker, Robert Bailey, Worcestershire's David Smith – an excellent player of fast bowling – and Martyn Moxon immediately spring to mind. A double century by Wilf Slack for Middlesex against Allan Border's Australians did not pass unnoticed, and my list is far from complete. Almost every county can nominate a promising batsman.

However, many modern batsmen make a half movement forward before the ball is bowled, which restricts back play and the full use of the crease when playing back. It also makes it harder to execute the pull shot so that the ball is hit on the ground, and if a study were to be made of dismissals from the hook and the pull it would probably be found that the batsman's foot had not moved ouside the line of the ball. There is an increased use of a deep square-leg fieldsman, and many batsmen are caught in that position. I do not like the method of standing upright with the bat in the air, which, if memory serves me right, was first used by Tony Greig and Mike Brearley. The truly great batsman has a comfortable, relaxed stance, enabling him to keep his head perfectly still and to move forward or backward without loss of balance and with the minimum of movement. All the famous batsmen from Bradman downward to whom I have spoken have one common criticism to make – that the flow of the bat must be uninhibited or rhythm is sacrificed. Holding the bat high in the air must present a tempting sight of all three stumps to a bowler, especially if he is capable of slipping in a swinging yorker.

Bowling standards have declined in England. Indeed, apart from the West Indies, all countries are looking for genuine pace. If it is not there, selectors look for the fast-medium to medium bowler able to move the ball. I rarely see a ball swing late, which is a ball to get the best batsman out. Richard Ellison gave an illustration of the art in the Edgbaston Test with Australia in 1985. Too many fall into the error of bowling too short. The ball must be given time to swing. Like the majority who have known lusher times for spinners, I am sad to see the decline of slow bowling. As he strives to spin and master control of length and direction the young spinner can be expensive, and captains understandably argue that he is a luxury a side cannot afford in limited-over cricket. His chances are therefore restricted. More's the pity, for a good spinner is still a matchwinner, and specialist batsmen with an ability to spin – Kim Barnett is a notable example – should not give it away. Chatting to Barnett, an impressive young captain and opening batsman of Derbyshire, I suggested to him that he should try to bowl ten overs a day – if necessary in the nets. If there is competition for batting places it is obvious that the vote will go to the player with an extra contribution to make to the side.

I am a confirmed believer in allowing natural talent to be given free expression. It is a crime to stifle it by overcoaching and, at youth level, by inexperienced teachers. Guidance and encouragement are something different, and I have always felt that better use could be made of the retired professional cricketer. I have had a vision of a select few given a free rein to explore the country for young talent, and, having found them, to help them on their way by remaining in contact. Here could be a chance for a sponsor with an ambition to help cricket and it would not interfere with existing schemes or the work of the individual counties. It is a matter of regret that so many of the leading players fade out of the scene on retirement. Some are lured to television and journalism. The days have long passed since there was a drift to the major schools. George Hirst coached at Eton, Wilfred Rhodes and Patsy Hendren at Harrow, and George Geary at Charterhouse – they are examples of a tradition now largely forgotten. Social conditions have changed, and understandably today's top-liners have higher economic goals, but it is a pity that their influence is lost. Some, of course, work tirelessly behind the scenes on county committees, but there is so much accumulated wisdom to be passed on that it concerns me if only a proportion drifts away. Those who served their time in the middle, especially at Test level, have a special knowledge and contribution to make which would be of inestimable value in the times to come.

Cricket has been swept along with the rest of life's changes. Old records tumble with the increasing number of Test matches played. It is not all that long ago that the selectors announced that Roy Marshall, the brilliant West Indies batsman who was playing for Hampshire and domiciled in this country, would not be considered for England because he had learned his cricket abroad and had played for the country of his birth. Now we think nothing of selecting players born in the West Indies or South Africa. A county secretary would never have considered appealing for crowd decorum before a match, as happened in 1985. And perhaps only Ian Botham could take guard at 5.35 p.m. and reach his century by 6.25 p.m., as Sir Don Bradman did against Middlesex at Lord's. Yet, for all the difficulties, including those caused by outside sources over which cricket has no control, I am hugely optimistic about the future of the greatest of all games, provided there is sober direction and players and public alike respect and maintain the traditions in all parts of the world.

Little did I think in my callow days as a fledgling professional that in the distant future I should be honoured with the Presidency of Surrey. In the spring of 1986 I was invited to become President-elect which means my succession to the office in 1987, the proviso being, as chairman Derek Newton said with a smile, 'that I was not caught with my hand in the till in the meantime.'

My appointment to an office I cherish did, however, leave me with a dilemma as it would not be possible to do my job properly as President and remain a Test selector. Having spent twenty-three continuous years as a selector including thirteen as chairman, I therefore opted to accept the privilege of becoming President of Surrey.

Obviously I was sad to tell the Test and County Cricket Board that I was no longer available to be considered for the Test Selection Committee. All good things must come to an end, but I shall very much miss not being involved in the selection of England's teams both home and abroad. Cricket has been my life-long love affair, and I look forward to the future as much as I have enjoyed the past.

Career Record

All First-Class Matches

	Overs	Maidens	Runs	Wickets	Average
1939	18	2	59	0	–
1946	1033·1	202	2577	128	20·13
1946–47 (Australia)	392·3	57	1359	28	48·53
1946–47 (New Zealand)	140·3	30	310	19	16·31
1947	1220·4	267	3175	130	24·42
1948	1139	283	2632	115	22·88
1948–49 (South Africa)	475.1	97	1273	45	28·28
1949	1005·2	251	2344	110	21·30
1950	1243·4	341	2797	122	22·92
1950–51 (Australia)	350·6	58	1010	51	19·80
1950–51 (New Zealand)	71	17	138	2	69·00
1951	1100	338	2024	130	15·56
1952	1185·4	296	2530	154	16·42
1953	1253	340	2702	162	16·67
1954	957·4	299	1828	121	15·10
1954–55 (Australia)	206·7	33	659	24	27·45
1955	1146·3	296	2752	144	19·11
1956	900·5	250	1950	96	20·31
1956–57 (India)	49	10	119	2	59·50
1957	1031·4	272	2170	131	16·56
1958	457	169	816	48	17·00
1959	963	256	2208	91	24·26
1959 (Rhodesia)	54·2	13	120	4	30·00
1960	786·4	229	1729	67	25·80
	15346·4	4406	39281	1924	20·41

and 1424.6 in Australia and South Africa

In Australia (all tours) and South Africa (1948–49) eight balls were bowled to the over.

County Championship Matches

	Overs	Maidens	Runs	Wickets	Average
1946	741·5	140	1910	83	23·01
1947	878·3	189	2364	97	24·37
1948	643·2	162	1411	72	19·59
1949	696·1	180	1535	81	18·95
1950	832·5	238	1873	90	20·81
1951	583·3	182	1025	63	16·26
1952	739·1	173	1583	102	15·51
1953	721·5	215	1427	84	16·98
1954	649·3	202	1184	89	13·30
1955	882	247	1980	117	16·92
1956	711·5	192	1562	83	18·81
1957	823·1	217	1698	109	15·57
1958	405	145	750	40	18·75
1959	831·2	213	1945	78	24·93
1960	674·2	193	1506	53	28·41
	10814·2	2888	23753	1241	19·14

Test Matches

	Overs	Maidens	Runs	Wickets	Average
1946 (v. India)	147·2	33	298	24	12·41
1946–47 (v. Australia)	246·3	34	876	16	54·75
1946–47 (v. New Zealand)	39	4	95	4	23·75
1947 (v. South Africa)	112	24	233	4	58·25
1948 (v. Australia)	274·3	75	688	18	38·22
1948–49 (v. South Africa)	206·5	37	554	16	34·62
1949 (v. New Zealand)	85	19	215	7	30·71
1950 (v. West Indies)	181	49	377	11	34·27
1950–51 (v. Australia)	195	34	482	30	16·06
1950–51 (v. New Zealand)	71	17	138	2	69·00
1951 (v. South Africa)	275·5	84	517	30	17·23
1952 (v. India)	163·5	57	279	20	13·95
1953 (v. Australia)	265·1	58	682	39	17·48
1954 (v. Pakistan)	74·5	28	158	10	15·80
1954–55 (v. Australia)	37	4	131	1	131·00
1955 (v. South Africa)	41	3	153	4	38·25
	1730·3	560	5876	236	24·89

and 685 in Australia and South Africa
My 236 wickets was a Test record.

Fourteen Wickets in a Match

| 14 for 99 | England v. Australia, at Trent Bridge | 1953 |
| 14 for 69 | Surrey v. Glamorgan, at Cardiff | 1956 |

Thirteen Wickets in a Match

13 for 46	Surrey *v*. Nottinghamshire, at The Oval	1952

Twelve Wickets in a Match

12 for 35	Surrey *v*. Warwickshire, at The Oval	1953
12 for 96	Surrey *v*. Leicestershire, at The Oval	1950

Eleven Wickets in a Match

11 for 145	England *v*. India, at Lord's	1946
11 for 93	England *v*. India, at Manchester	1946
11 for 89	Surrey *v*. Lancashire, at Manchester	1946
11 for 102	Surrey *v*. Derbyshire, at The Oval	1947
11 for 91	Surrey *v*. Derbyshire, at Chesterfield	1948

Eight Wickets in an Innings

8 for 42	Surrey *v*. Middlesex, at Lord's	1949
8 for 53	Surrey *v*. Leicestershire, at The Oval	1950
8 for 18	Surrey *v*. Nottinghamshire, at The Oval	1952
8 for 18	Surrey *v*. Warwickshire, at The Oval	1953

39 wickets for 682 runs in five Tests against Australia 1953

Batting (First-Class Matches)

Innings	Not-Outs	Runs	Highest-Score	Average
576	179	5735	126	14·94

My one and only century was made for Surrey *v*. Somerset, at Taunton in 1947.

Index

Wilson, Don, 196
Wilson, Hugh, 163
Wilson, Vic, 179
Wisden Cricketers' Almanack, 39,
   50, 59, 66, 76, 78, 93, 111,
   116, 126, 129, 151, 155,
   183–184, 190–191, 200
Woking, 13, 15–16, 21, 29, 46,
   79, 88
Woking Cricket Club, 34
Wood, Barry, 179
Woodcock, John, 78, 107,
   190–192

Wooldridge, Ian, 113
Woolley, F. E., 16, 29
Woolmer, Bob, 172
Worrell, Sir Frank, 40, 77, 194
Worsley, Sir W., 87
Wright, Doug, 30–31, 41, 144
Wyatt, R. E. S., 164

Yallop, Graham, 132
Yardley, Norman, 32, 48, 77,
   143–144
Young, Jack, 131